GOLD

Its beauty, power and allure

Detail of 7th-century Byzantine jewelled cross inset with 4th-century portrait group on gilt glass

GOLD

Its beauty, power and allure

C. H. V. SUTHERLAND

69 plates

15 in full colour

11 drawings and maps

THAMES AND HUDSON LONDON

CONTENTS

LIST OF ILLUSTRATIONS

PREFACE

THE NUMBER OF SINGLE SUBSTANCES which have held the attention of man in every age, recorded or remembered, is not large. Most of them have been the simplest and most basic necessities of life: flour to eat, clay for bricks with which to build houses, wool for warm clothing, copper and iron for implements, and timber for a thousand constructional purposes. Gold does not come into the category of simple and basic necessities.

None the less it has always been prominent in human thought. Few other things have succeeded as well as gold in tingeing metaphor, providing material for proverb, and creating legend. One of the rarest of metals, it has gained a peculiar and indeed unique place in human experience. Taste and style will change, decade by decade and century by century; but there are few in any age who are not immediately affected by the colour and lustre of gold. This reaction may, to some extent, be a matter of instinct: nearly six thousand years have passed during which it has been remarkably constant, and it would be very surprising if the love for gold had not at most times drawn strength from earlier convention or tradition. But there is more to gold than colour and lustre, for it remains —as it has always been—a substance which is also very precious because it is very rare. As a measure of value and a store of wealth, therefore, its importance for Western civilization (and it is with Western civilization that this book is concerned) is altogether exceptional.

It is not easy, however, to survey its place in history. As a metal, gold should call for the geologist and the metallurgist. As a substance which has a long and superbly distinguished record in the applied arts it should have treatment at the hands of those who claim expert and intimate knowledge of jewellery and plate. As a medium of value not less old or honoured than any in the world it should claim analysis no less from the professed economist than from the anthropologist. I myself cannot pretend to play any of these special parts. My interest in gold arises mainly and, as it seems to me, naturally from the fact that in my own professional occupation I have handled it almost daily, year in and year out, as a substance applied with particular care and particular beauty to the purposes of coinage. To handle it thus is to appreciate, without difficulty, its unbroken appeal from remote antiquity, its constant and natural loveliness, and its very consistent record of rarity. In attempting to outline the history of gold down to the present day I have therefore tried to keep clear of specialism. This is not a book for the learned geologist, metallurgist, connoisseur or economist if they desire to expand their particular fields of detailed knowledge. My object is, rather, to observe the human reaction to gold in the general terms which a span of six thousand years not only encourages but also necessitates. The history of gold is a very long one, but it possesses a curiously strong unity; and it is this unity which the following pages attempt to describe.

The use of technical terms has been kept to a minimum, for gold, embraced as it has been by the studies of mining engineers as well as metallurgists and economists and connoisseurs, has in places accumulated a specialist vocabulary of its own, and this can sometimes be burdensome. A particular problem had to be faced in regard to the terminology of weight. Apart from such ancient measures of weight as the Greek talent and mina and the Roman pound and scruple one meets (among very many others) with the ton, the English pound, the kilogram, and—the measure universally adopted by modern gold-producers and financial economists—the troy ounce (= 20 pennyweights = 480 grains). Whenever possible, weights have been given in terms of the English pound (lb.) of 7000 grains, for it seemed to me that the concept of a pound avoirdupois is likely to be much more generally familiar, simply as a weight-unit, than the troy ounce of 480 grains (see Table on p. 187). I am aware that the quotation of gold-weights by the English pound may appear unorthodox, but it does possess the undoubted advantage of uniformity (important, above all, for the immense periods covered by the ancient cultures), as well as the convenience of avoiding the much higher figures which are called for by the use of a far lighter unit of quotation. It should be added that, where weights are quoted, these are generally in round figures, as exactitude to the last digit seemed likely to bring less benefit than boredom.

Plate 2

The writing of such a book as this would almost certainly have been much less easy if it had not been possible for me to feed both eye and mind on the massive yield of South African gold in current production and on the mines from which it is extracted. For the opportunity of seeing these things for myself, and of learning a little at least of an industry the golden fruit of which still helps to keep world economies in a balance secured by nothing else, I am most deeply indebted to the generosity of the Transvaal and Orange Free State Chamber of Mines, which, through the kindness of Dr W. J. Busschau, invited me to visit Johannesburg and has, especially through Mr Angus Collie, helped me in many other ways since. And finally I must express gratitude to my wife, whose help, whether in passive endurance or active and stimulating criticism, has been more valuable than gold itself.

C.H.V.S.

Cumnor, Oxford

Chapter I

THE HUMAN ZEST FOR GOLD

I T HAS BEEN ESTIMATED that the total amount of gold won from the earth's surface in the last five centuries is about 110,000,000 lb. That weight of gold, over 50,000 tons—for its specific gravity is very high at ±19—could be contained in a cube measuring 15 yards in each direction.

This estimate can be no more than approximate, for although output began to be recorded much more carefully from the fifteenth century of the Christian era, when gold was playing so important a part in the competitive economy of European powers and came under the keenest State scrutiny, it is beyond question that much was produced in small quantities, at all times, that escaped official vigilance. Moreover, the quantity of gold found in Asiatic Russia at any given time has seldom been capable of clear definition, from the time when the deposits were first worked systematically a little more than a century ago until the present day, when Russian gold output represents so constant and constantly formidable a question-mark in the world's economic calculations. But, with all these reservations, the figure of 110,000,000 lb. may not be far wide of the mark.

How much gold was produced in the previous five thousand years during which it was avidly sought, jealously treasured and lovingly worked no one can say. Of the 110,000,000 lb. extracted from the earth since the fifteenth century, the last century has claimed over four-fifths of the total, and the last half-century well over one-half, as the result, mainly, of applying ever more elaborate and scientific mechanical methods of mining. Production in ancient and medieval times may therefore have reached a figure modest in comparison with post-medieval and modern output. For deep mining, in anything like the modern sense, was unknown: the lack of adequate power to raise heavy loads of ore from great depths or to provide ventilation against heat and fumes or—most important of all—to guard, by pumping, against the deadly danger of flooding from underground watercourses (a danger always urgent until the development of machinery in the eighteenth century) meant that it was impossible to follow a gold-bearing reef much farther than could be reached by a comparatively shallow vertical or sloping shaft or short gallery. Ancient gold-mining was, of course, in essence, surface or near-surface working: the deeper veins branching in the earth were reserved for a mechanical age.

On the other hand, it is quite possible that ancient production during the five thousand years preceding the fifteenth century of our era was considerably greater than has sometimes been allowed. Although deep mining, as the result of modern science and machinery, makes it possible to pursue gold-bearing deposits into and through the very bowels of the earth, to a depth sometimes even exceeding 10,000 feet, where the temperature may be one of well over 100° F., it is a costly process. In order to win some 400 tons of gold today in the course of a year the Rand group of mines in South Africa may have to raise and mill over 60,000,000 tons of ore—many times the mass, let us say, of the pyramid of Cheops—in order to gain a cube of gold of about 9 feet, involving a vast capital outlay on machinery, a huge labour force, and an immense reserve of power. Gold production in ancient centuries was infinitely simpler in method: in addition, circumstances may have made it relatively high in yield, as the following considerations may suggest.

Gold, as one of the metallic elements in the earth's crust, was subjected to all the massive processes of nature when that crust was formed and pressed and re-formed and folded. Most gold veins occur in the near neighbourhood of granite, and auriferous quartz is one of the richest sources of gold, where cracks in the earth's crust have been filled with quartz and gold heat-pressed at great depth. Such veins, together with others of different geological formation and often shallower occurrence, have in many places been extruded by the folding and cracking of the earth's crust. These outcrops have been weathered by millions of years of rain and frost and wind, disintegrating into eluvial deposits on or near the surface of the ground where, because gold is virtually insoluble and proof against Nature's reagents, the metal has collected as 'placer' gold, often of remarkable purity. Because of its great natural weight gold in such circumstances has tended to settle in masses which, after compression by time and also by the fresh deposit of eluvium above them, have formed into solid lumps or nuggets. Sometimes these are very small—mere pellets; but sometimes they are large. Ballarat's 'Welcome Stranger' nugget, found in 1869, weighed nearly 160 lb.; the Peacock nugget from South Africa weighed over 12 lb.; and a recent report credits the Lena River goldfields of Russia with a nugget of nearly 30 lb.

Plate 1

Where eluvial gold has fallen into the path of a stream or river it has been carried to lower levels, and the heavy grains of the metal have settled wherever the water-currents have allowed, again forming near-surface deposits and again, in suitable circumstances, being from time to time compressed into nuggets. Alluvial gold, naturally, may be found spread over a very wide area, according to the area covered by the waters which carry it. The gold grains may sometimes be very small after being ground in the turbulent course of a rocky river; and these small grains may some-times be invisible among the rest of the sand and gravel and fine rock in which they lie. This is the case with the gold which is mined in the Rand area of South Africa today, for the 'reefs' there are thin bands of a pebble conglomerate which, according to one theory at least, represent 'placer' deposit which has in its turn been covered to a great depth, after being sharply tilted, by fresh deposits of rock. The same is true of Alaskan gold found at Nome, where the action of sea waves and currents was responsible, before the great recession of sea-level, for pounding fine deposits of gold into beaches now lying as much as 70 feet above the sea.

When men first became sufficiently aware of gold to desire it actively they therefore had the accumulation of millions of years of eluvial and alluvial action ready to hand. Almost certainly the first discoveries of gold must have revealed it in nugget form, and we can (with Strabo) afford to discount the dramatic story told by Poseidonius, that fierce forest fires smelted precious surface-deposits out of the ground, even though the same unlikely phenomenon was attributed to the Alps and the Pyrenees as lately as the eighteenth century (and though the burning down of a house has been ascribed as the cause of the discovery of Sumatran tin in 1710). The truth is surely much simpler. A tree is uprooted, with small pellets of placer gold shining among its roots—as happened with the silver of Potosi in Peru. An avalanche or landslide strips the surface of the soil. Simplest of all, a man digs a trench or a well and finds placer gold: the great Russian gold discoveries of the early nineteenth century showed many such instances of nuggets, large and small, being found immediately below the surface of the ground in the area of the South Urals, no deeper— in some cases—than could be reached by the normal exertions of a young woman.

The possible picture of the earliest seekers after gold being confronted by deposits of the greatest richness, eluvial or alluvial, formed naturally during the whole vastness of unmeasured time since the earth's crust solidified and settled, is not by any means an idle one. To ancient writers and poets, like Hesiod, the Golden Age was an age of primitive perfection, in which mankind dwelt in mutual harmony without the necessity or desire for restrictive law or crippling warfare. It would, obviously, be foolish to take any such rosy view of early civilization. But it may still remain true to say that man, in his earliest awareness of metals, found gold lying ready to hand in surprisingly large quantities and that, even if he did not immediately take advantage of it—since, being so soft, it was of no use for practical implements—the tradition of this natural largesse was handed down to later ages when it had come to be so highly prized. Estimates (if the word has any relevance at all) have been made of the total stocks of gold in the ancient world; for example, that at the end of the eighth century of our era stocks did not exceed something like 250,000 lb. It is quite certain that ancient stocks were immensely smaller than those today, which owe their origin to highly organized and highly mechanized methods all over the world. Whether they were, however, so small in relation to post-medieval stocks is very doubtful indeed, and it is probably wise to dwell, with a little more than wonder, on the dramatic stories of ancient writers—how, for example, 'in Paeonia they say that, when showers of rain fall continuously and the soil is loosened, gold is found, called "unfired" . . . one man found two lumps and took them to the King, one weighing 3 minae and one five' (a mina weighed just over 1 lb.), or how in Spain 'the gold dust glitters where the rivers flood' and among the dwellers of the north-west 'the soil burgeons with silver, tin and gold-silver alloy'. Even without a Golden Age of universal peace there may still have been an early golden age in which large natural and super-ficial deposits played a part, in relation both to small population figures and negligible commerce, which became memorable enough to pass into legend.

Against this possible prehistoric picture we may set the current picture: a vast programme of intensive exploration, made possible by increasingly scientific methods of survey, and carried out by methods which are as mechanical as they are also deeply selective. An industry which, on the Rand, for example, began nearly three-quarters of a century ago on a basis of ounces of gold per ton, extracted and refined by comparatively simple methods, now finds it possible to show a profit where the yield is as little as 4 pennyweights—less than a quarter of an ounce—and where some £15,000,000 may have to be expended on a mine's development before any gold is recovered at all. In that same area over 60,000,000 tons of ore are annually hoisted to the surface for crushing, from underground shafts and galleries which, if they were put end to end in a straight line, would probably drive a hole almost clean through the centre of the globe. Essentially the picture is the same, whether it is that of the present century or that of the earliest seekers for gold, or that of any intervening age. Men's

tails and high grass conceal sex. By time car stops and hunter gets out, loads rifle and takes aim, fast quarry is 175 yards away.

wonder if an elephant might have made that big track?

Bits of background information I'd picked up before the trip flicked through my mind. Chad admitted to the United Nations in 1960. Formerly part of French Equatorial Africa. Still friendly with France, sends representatives to French parliament. Second year as republic in January, 1963. Almost as big as Alaska. More than half desert, with northern boundary in mid-Sahara located just under Libya.

Proud, friendly people, I thought of the Africans we'd met at the airport. It was a thought I was to have again and again in the Chad. . . .

After the screwball stories I'd heard about Claude Vasselet, it was a relief to meet him at the tiny Oasis Hotel in Abeche and find that the stories must have been hatched in envy. He drives a new [*Continued on page 60*]

Author and Roger Fawcett (right) pose with two big addax. These antelope are among world's most inaccessible game.

43

much survived, including the objects that make up the golden figure at left. The priest's tunic, the most spectacular single piece in the Mujica collection, is covered with 30,000 separate pieces of gold. Goggle-eyed mask was used as a false face for the mummy of a nobleman. Golden gloves, with carefully outlined fingernails,

Ceremonial puma pouch of hammered gold is more than two feet long, 10 inches wide. Pocket in stomach held coca leaves.

Double-spouted 21-carat ceremonial vessel is ornamented with an idol on the bridge, two serpent heads and dogs on its base.

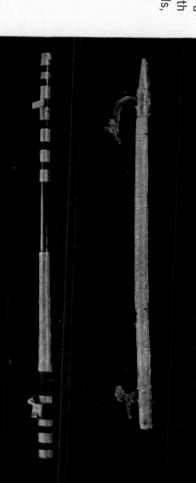

Twelfth-century throwing sticks, about 5½ inches long, were used to throw spears. Top stick is made of wood covered with hammered gold. Its weight, or hook, is a copper bird. Bottom stick is also wood and is banded with gold. It has a crystal bird weight.

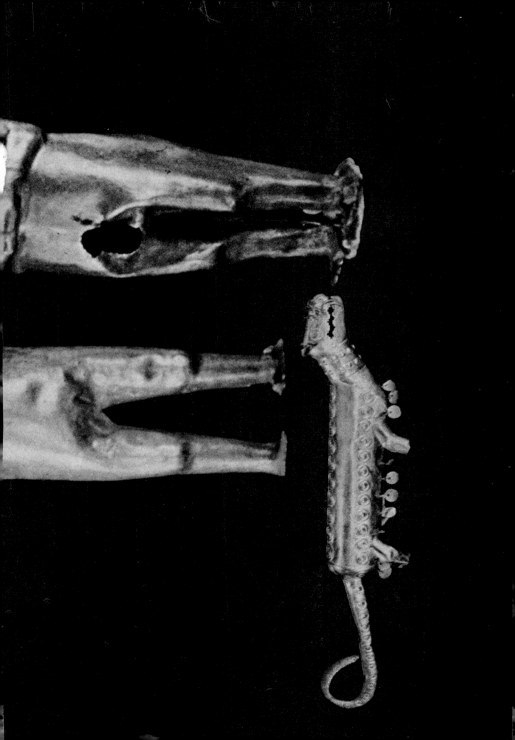

be some bitter protests that the dead owned the best part of the kingdom.

Gold was a symbol of the sun to the Incas, used for prestige and adornment. The gods were not forgotten, however, and many idols were made of gold, including the 18-carat pair, at left. The companion golden lizard, hung with spirals and pendants, is 14 inches long —symbol of golden plenty. ■

Huge earrings of 22-carat gold inlaid with turquoise are hollow cast or they would be too heavy to wear.

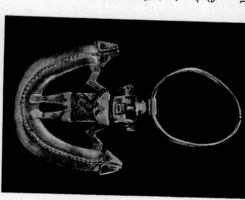

Idol standing on two-headed serpent is actually a golden tweezer, for beard-pulling and adornment.

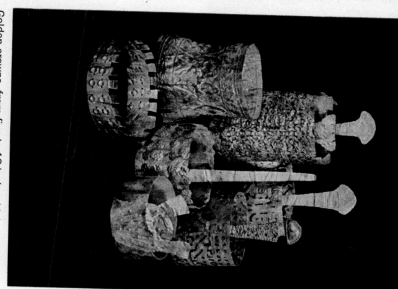

Golden crowns, from five to 18 inches high, show range of color of gold. Most are covered with hammered designs. Some have plumes cut from sheets of gold.

In his mine, Homer would
let suckers see the gold for themselves.

48

Twenty-two carat golden idol holds ear of corn and a drinking vessel. It wears removable golden ceremonial garments and a crown symbolizing the half moon.

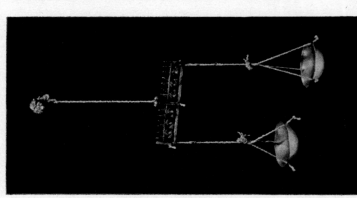

Tiny 2¼-inch high balance of gold and silver is one of many utensils

were also part of the burial dress of an aristocrat.

An opulent life for the Inca—the king—and the aristocracy was provided by the El Dorado of gold, silver, copper and precious gems that washed down from Andean streams. Noblemen wore golden shirts and shoes, ate from golden plates and even trimmed their beards with golden tweezers. In the king's palace, furniture and musical instruments were made of gold and silver. Goldsmiths were always busy because as each Inca died, his palace and all his golden possessions were preserved intact —the new Inca had to build a new palace and order a new batch of golden equipment. In time there came to

PHOTOGRAPHED FOR TRUE BY DAVID B. EISENDRATH, JR.

GOLDEN HOARD OF THE INCAS

■ When the gold-lusting conquistadors with Pizarro saw Cuzco, Peru, they were almost too dazzled to believe it. The capital of the Inca empire was literally a city of gold. The earth in the garden of the great temple was gold nuggets; all of the flowers, trees and insects—even the lizards—were made of gold.

The golden treasure on these pages was photographed for TRUE at the Brooklyn Museum during the first U.S. showing of the private collection of Peruvian industrialist Miguel Mujica Gallo. Worth half a million dollars by weight, the collection of more than 500 pieces is

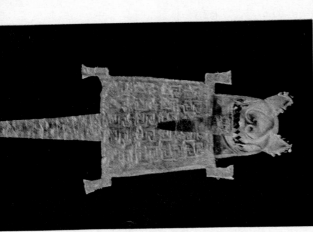

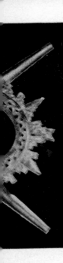

Gold receptacle in form of crowned idol is attached to vase inlaid with turquoise. Temples were filled with goblets, vases, beakers.

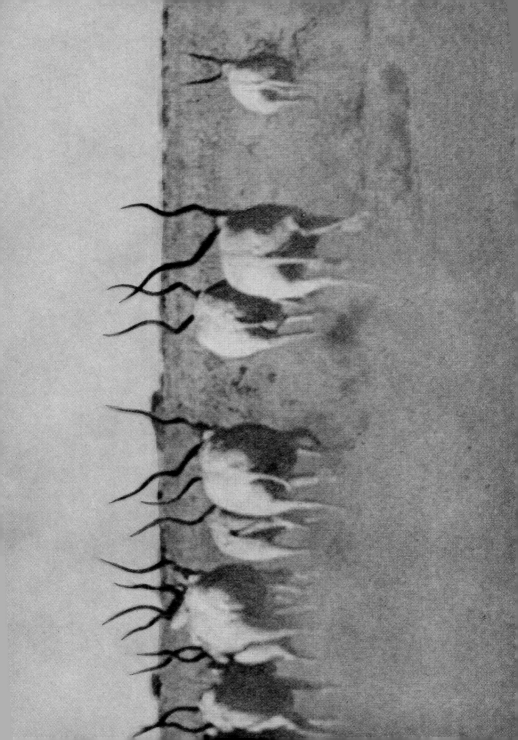

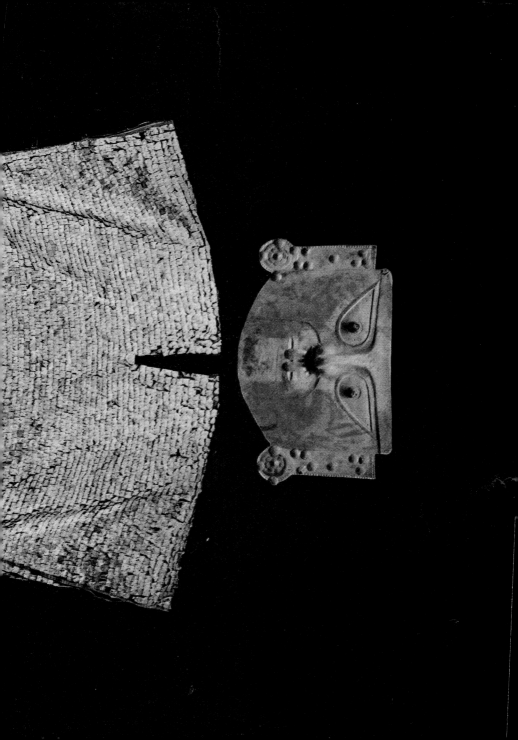

hunger for gold has never ceased: in search of it, as the Elder Pliny wrote with all the sententiousness at his command, they explore every vein in the earth, and dwell upon her hollowed frame; and from the earliest times it has achieved a place in their economic history which (as has been well said) is out of all proportion to the assistance it has given in their struggle against Nature.

What, then, is the force of its appeal? It is possible to list some 150 substances which at various times and in various parts of the world have been invested with some universality of value, almost equally divided between the animal, the vegetable and the mineral. Of the minerals, some (like copper and iron and lead and tin) have always been prized for their practical utility. Silver, too, has always been prized, but for its decorative quality; and it is this same quality which has always in the past made gold the king of metals in nearly all places where knowledge of it has penetrated. For gold is much more scarce than silver, and it is a curious fact that, though it has been always available, the quantity in which it has been produced has always lagged behind the universal demand for it: even today, when output is immeasurably higher than in any previous century, it is still perfectly true to say that the demand is much greater than the supply. Nevertheless, relative scarcity is not the only reason for an age-long hunger which has sometimes amounted to a passion. Scarcity must be combined with positive beauty before it can exert such over-whelming attraction; and it is the positive beauty of gold, allied to the comparative ease with which it can be worked, which in past ages has given it a unique position.

It is right to emphasize the words 'in past ages'. For although the modern world is, to an astonishing degree, dependent upon gold for the mutual and international balance of currencies, it is also a fact that it is less aware of gold, and less familiar with its beauty of appearance, than can be said of many preceding centuries. Many people today have never handled a gold coin, and, not knowing the characteristic differences in either colour or weight, are even liable to confuse gold with brass. This is largely because the ownership of gold has in present economic conditions become increasingly the function, if not the privilege, of States: the opportunity of the individual to enjoy what his ancestors could so often enjoy has been drastically curtailed, partly by the element of State control and partly by the factor of rising price. An age of 'costume jewellery' has largely banished the use of gold for personal adornment, apart from finger-rings; and though Ruskin could say, around 1880, that it was then the ambition of every well-to-do young married couple to acquire and own some small amount of gilt plate, his view now has a truly archaic tone. Gold is still as precious as it has ever been, in spite of its greatly increased production, but its purely decorative quality is something which is forgotten or unsuspected outside museum collections or special displays.

This decorative quality, however, is something of which people were well aware until quite recently and which from very early times was responsible for much of the special position accorded to gold. Human desire for decorative substances seems to be almost as old as humanity itself. That desire was satisfied, in very early times, by the use of naturally ornamental objects which needed no working. Foremost in this class there seem to have come shells, often borne immense distances from their place of origin in order to serve as primitive, ready-made pieces of ornament, suitable for piercing and stringing together. The Palaeolithic Age saw Mediterranean shells carried on the one hand to the mammoth hunters on the Dnieper, and on the other to the reindeer hunters of Central France. In the Middle Stone Age they penetrated farther, into Central Europe; and later they found their way to the north, from which in turn was to come, again a little later, the supply of amber which Mediterranean and Aegean peoples prized so highly. Nor were shells unpopular elsewhere. Cowries from the Indian Ocean and eastward were widely distributed: Layard found them at Nineveh, Marco Polo found them in Asia and China, and they were used by the Indians of California. It seems likely that in the warmer zones clothes, by their very paucity, were not a primary object of decorative desire in early times, and that in the colder zones their sheer necessity may have robbed them of that added glamour. The accessories —shells, then beads, and pins a little later—were much more universally sought after.

Models of shells, especially cowries, made in metal have been found in widely separated parts of the world. In Burma they have been fashioned out of silver and copper. In China they have been made of gold. Gold, again, was the metal of which were made the cowrie 'models' found by Schliemann at Troy, which may themselves have come from Egypt, where
Plate 4   similar objects have been discovered. Much has been written by anthro-pologists about the significance—half magic, half religious—of cowries in ancient civilizations. They have been regarded as a symbol of life, and so in some sense as life-giving amulets. Their shape has been likened to that of the mouth of the womb, or alternatively to that opening of the eye which itself argues life; and from these supposed resemblances the reproduction

The Peacock nugget, weighing over 12 lb., found in the Barberton district, South Africa, in 1912

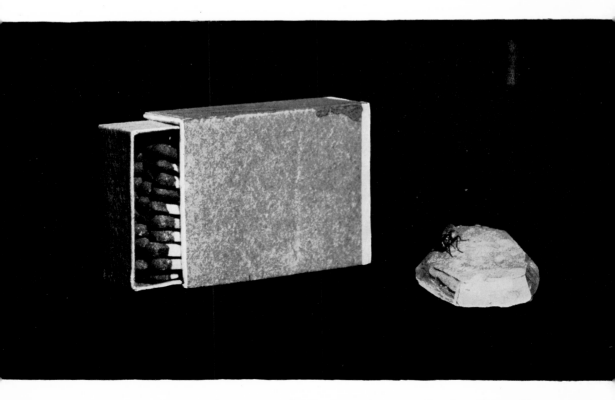

2   A troy ounce of gold compared in size with a fly and a matchbox

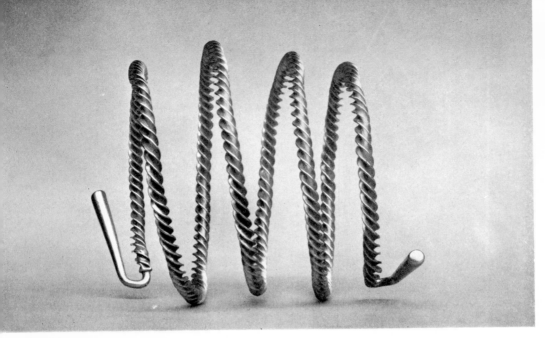

3   British torque found at Stanton, Stafford: *c.* 15th century B.C.

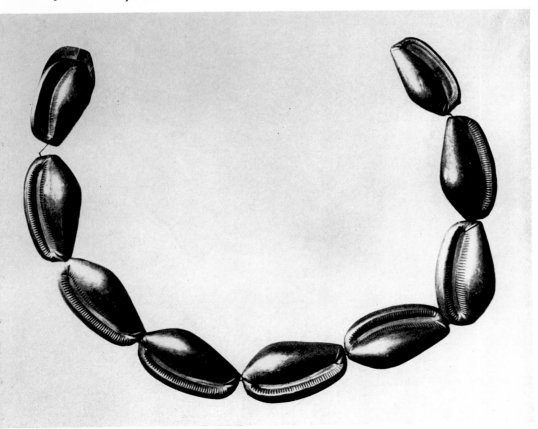

4   Necklace of gold cowries found at Dashur, Egypt: *c.* 1850 B.C.

of cowries in gold—a virtually indestructible metal—has been invested with remarkable magical meaning, as when the golden cowrie is viewed as the emblem of the Egyptian mother-goddess Hathor, 'not only because she was originally the personification of the life-giving shells, but also because she was the guardian deity of the eastern wadis where gold was found and of the Red Sea where cowries were obtained'. To the historian, as distinct from the anthropologist, such views seem difficult to follow. Shells—even cowrie shells—are fragile; and, granted a prehistoric tradition that regarded these naturally curved and subtly irregular shapes as being of the very essence of personal, and especially feminine adornment, it is hard to deny the likelihood that their reproduction in a permanent and durable form would have been desired and achieved as soon as possible. It was possible when gold was found and realized to be at once an extraordinarily durable metal and a very easily worked one. A man wishing to make small gold ornaments for personal adornment could easily do so by the simple expedient of hammering the metal cold; and, if Hathor was the tutelary spirit of an auriferous section of southern Egypt, that fact, though it may and probably should link her psychologically with gold, need have very little to do with cowries. The reproduction of shells in metal was, in other words, the result of a widely spread desire to give permanence, strength, and a new beauty to an immemorially old form of ornament.

Metallurgically, therefore, gold offers the minimum of problems to early craftsmen lacking full skill in the working of metals. It can be hammered cold; and though the hammering of gold constantly hardens it, to the extent that the fashioning of a hollowed gold vessel by this method would have demanded systematic annealing (i.e. re-softening by heating and re-hardening by quenching) to allow the progressively flexible rearrangement of the crystalline structure, no such problems faced the man who undertook such simple tasks as the hammering and chasing of a natural pellet of gold into the shape of a cowrie, or a bead, or a pin. Peruvian finds of a period as relatively late as the ninth century B.C. onwards tell the same tale: the earliest smiths in this richly auriferous area cold-hammered their natural nuggets, making from them a variety of objects, mainly from sheet gold, such as ear-ornaments, pins, plaques, and beads. Wherever we look the connection between the early use of gold and the desire for ornament is strong; and the oft-quoted view that the Egyptian hieroglyph for gold was a collar of beads does no more than remind us that gold beads would have been among the technically simplest and also the most decorative forms of early jewellery.

It must have been true, nevertheless, that the very permanence of gold gave it, from the first, a uniquely high position in the early scale of metallic values. It is proof against all normal decay, for, though it will 'tone', especially if alloyed with copper, it will not rust or laminate or flake or indeed react in any obvious way against the usual attacks of chemical enemies less strong, for instance, than a mixture of nitric and hydrochloric acids. A hoard of copper coins removed from its hiding-place in the soil may show each coin heavily covered by a corrosive crust. A hoard of silver coins may show the silver, not corroded (unless it is markedly impure), but at least stained and tarnished until it is quite black. But a hoard of gold coins will reveal gold as bright as it was on the day it left the mint two hundred or two thousand years ago; and this quality of imperishability has at most times exerted a very strong appeal. In a mystical sense it has been connected, by the queer imaginings of alchemists and others, with immortality: gold, which seemed deathless, was a symbol of eternal life, and the symbol, if controlled and (literally) infused, could itself form an elixir. Potable gold was prescribed for certain cases in antiquity, and the Elder Pliny listed certain conditions—fistulas, piles, ringworm, and ulcers—to which external gold treatment could, with care, be applied. Small wonder that a metal which appeared to defy all dangers of death and decay should encourage, over so many centuries, all the efforts —philosophical, chemical, and purely bogus—to analyse and so reproduce its essential constitution, or that its own imperishability of substance, combined both with its bright yellow lustre and with the fond hopes of making some potent, life-giving elixir, should result in the choice by alchemists of the sign ☉—the sun—for gold.

In another age, and at another stage of scientific inquiry, when alchemy of a kind infinitely more subtle than was ever dreamed of before is a routine matter in centres of physical research, the appeal of gold must lie in different directions. It still remains scarce enough in relation to demand to keep its value very high, and, though something very near one-half of the world's measurable output of gold comes from a single country, there is enough elsewhere to prevent its becoming any single country's entirely narrow monopoly. New finds of great richness are reported from time to time—most recently, for example, to the south of Quebec City; and there is no reason to suppose that supplies will die out. Its durability is an obvious commendation, and so too the fact that, unlike some other very precious substances such as diamonds, it is divisible. In none of these qualities, however, can we find the appeal of gold as it has most often been exerted in the past upon men's minds. It is true that gold has very frequently been the substance out of which kings and States have built up enormous bullion reserves in ingot form, from the time of Darius of Persia down to the United States today, in which more than half of the world-stocks of gold are hoarded away. But in nearly all past ages gold has been regarded as more than a store of worth, and as more than the measure of value which it has also been in coinage form. For it has been in a unique degree the decorative metal, loved by the great and wealthy as a means of ostentation, loved by the lesser man (according to his ability to acquire it) because of its beauty of colour and sheen and texture in addition to its intrinsic value, and loved by the goldsmith because of its splendid working qualities.

These latter are indeed impressive. Gold is extremely soft—nearly as soft as lead; and in reasonably pure state it is extraordinarily malleable. It can (as has already been noted) easily be beaten when cold, and this property was turned to constant advantage in the most ancient times, when gold was hammered into sheet that was thinner and thinner as technique improved. The Elder Pliny recorded that an ounce of gold could be   Plate 1
beaten into more than 750 thin leaves 'measuring four fingers each way'. Today a troy ounce can be beaten out, by methods inherited from medieval goldsmiths and carefully improved, into a thin film which would cover 100 square feet—so thin, in fact, that it could be less than 1/282,000th of an inch, and show light through it: indeed, it has been recorded that a single grain of gold has been beaten to a thinness of 1/360,000th of an inch—over a thousand times thinner than normal paper—so as to cover an area of 75 square inches. Moreover, if during this process (which involves the hammering of the foil, thinner and thinner, for some hours between specially prepared pieces of ox-gut) the metal should crack or break into a hole, the remedy is easy. For gold can be pressure-welded: in other words its malleability is such that the 'flow' of the metal under pressure causes enough internal heat to make loose segments cohere; and, just as a dentist welds gold into a compact mass by hand-pressure when he forces it into the cavity of a tooth, so too the gold-beater will, quite literally, repair a defective piece of gold leaf by hammer-welding a fresh patch on to the cracked or broken area.

As well as being so remarkably malleable, gold is also highly ductile; and here again statistics must be allowed to state their surprising case. One grain of gold may be drawn into a fine wire 600 feet long, and one ounce into a length of no less than 50 miles, while, if 'gold thread' is required for gold lace or gold tissue (from which 'tissue paper', originally designed for placing between folds of gold-woven fabric, gets its name), an ounce of gold very thinly plated, in leaf form, upon a silver or copper wire base will suffice for over 1000 miles. It is not surprising that such ease of behaviour has always endeared gold to the smith and jeweller, since, being so soft, it is also so readily chased and engraved and, once formed into a work of art, is proof against tarnish and decay.

When the modern eye, now relatively unfamiliar with gold, dwells reflectively upon the metal it is difficult not to be aware of the properties which have been touched on above. Whether we look at small pieces of jewellery, or some quite large vessel of solid gold (as distinct from the 'gold plate' which is so often silver heavily gilt), or even at the bars of gold scrupulously refined and formed at a great refinery, the first impression—apart from that of a wonderful colour—is of an unusual softness of texture. The actual forms of the jewellery or the vessel may themselves contain great angularity, as for example in the case of an Iron Age torque — Plate 3 —a thin square rod of gold exquisitely screwed into a regular spiral—or of — Plate 13 a sharply fluted gold vase. But the actual surface of the metal has a liquidity and sheen upon it which no other metal seems to present, and this indeed is perhaps most obvious in a gold bar fresh from the refinery, when the metal, though it has set hard and grown cold, shows a curious smoothness and softness which allows the light to play upon its natural colour in a manner which is entrancing.

It is probably these qualities of a smooth, soft texture, a beauty of colour, and a capacity to shine steadily (and not scintillate), which, quite apart from the metallurgical properties which have always recommended it to smiths and jewellers, have at most periods in the past given gold its supreme appeal. In decorative jewellery the softness of texture has led in all past ages to the creation of small pieces, often of astonishingly fine elaboration, in which curving forms were designed to extract the maximum of light-reflection from a given surface area. In larger objects such as golden vessels, — Plate 37 or the fantastic equipment of Egyptian royal tombs, or the set masterpieces — Plate 14 of Renaissance and later goldsmiths, the metal has generally been used in — Plate 56 such a way as to display both a truly royal area of yellow sheen and also a maximum play of those same softly curving forms. According to the purpose of the object being made, therefore, gold can provide extreme delicacy of effect, through its remarkable working properties, or a strong impact of yellow lustre, or (in the hands of a great artist like Cellini) both at once. It is no more proof against vulgarity of treatment than any other decorative material on which men may work. Worked with taste, however,

5   Miner panning for gold in Alaska

6 Hawk's head found at
Hierakonpolis, Egypt: c. 2300 B.C.

it may be much more beautiful than most other materials; and, if so, this is probably due to the combination of seductive natural colour, lustre, softness of texture, and potential delicacy of workmanship.

It is, of course, for such reasons that the literature of so many ages has applied the adjective 'golden' in a certain way. It has been used only in a secondary sense to imply rarity: its foremost and constant connotation has been that of something which is naturally lovely, naturally desirable, naturally pre-eminent. The operation of this combined and complex appeal can be nicely seen and judged in the action taken by King Charles I, when he ordered that the goldsmiths of London should be concentrated in Cheapside and Lombard Street (traders of other kinds being, if necessary, ejected and transferred elsewhere), so that this area should be 'an ornament . . . and lustre to the City' on a route, leading to its heart, which important (and impressionable) foreign visitors might often traverse. The same appeal is implicit, though in characteristically different terms, in Ruskin's words. After observing that fine goldsmithing has often been the training of those who have afterwards become great painters and sculptors, like Francia, Ghirlandajo, Verrocchio, and Ghiberti, he continued: 'Gold has been given to us, among other things, that we might put beautiful work into its imperishable splendour, and that the artists who have the most wilful fancies may have a material which will drag out, and beat out, as their dreams require, and will hold itself together with fantastic tenacity.'

The winning of gold from the earth has for long been difficult. But the rewards, in value, in beauty and in permanence, are correspondingly great. Diodorus Siculus, in the first century B.C., summarized the matter with all the rhetorical antithesis of ancient writers. 'Nature herself,' he said, 'makes it clear that the production of gold is laborious, the guarding of it difficult, the zest for it very great, and its use balanced between pleasure and pain.'

Chapter II
THE GOLD OF THE PHARAOHS

G OLD HAS ALWAYS BEEN RARE in relation to other metals. Its natural colour and untarnishable lustre have constantly been loved, either (more simply) as a means of decoration or (more amply) as a means of ostentation. And the ease with which it can be worked has endeared it to the smiths and jewellers of all ages.

For these reasons, considered together, gold has always been the ornamental metal *par excellence*, and likewise the royal or aristocratic metal *par excellence*, as the records of both archaeology and history show so convincingly. The wealth of royal gold in Egypt and Sumeria has burst fully upon consciousness only in modern times as the result of the excavator's spade. But for many other periods there is good historical record. Biblical sources give ample evidence, however poetical in tone or even in scale, of the ancient wealth in gold of the Near East, whether in the person of Solomon, with his huge tribute-income in gold and his fantastic programme of temple-decoration and general court luxury, or of David, with his immense contributions of gold for the adornment of the House of the Lord, or in the case of Tyre, which 'heaped up silver as the dust and gold as the mire of the streets'. Poetry this is; but, lest exaggeration be suspected to a point at which all truth vanishes, it is well to remember the numberless instances of wealth in gold which are detailed by historians: Pythius, the subject of Xerxes of Persia, with his famous treasure of some 7000 lb. of gold; the booty of perhaps 500,000 lb. of gold, perhaps more, captured by the Emperor Trajan from the Dacians; the treasure of 320,000 lb. of gold left by the Byzantine Emperor Anastasius at his death in A.D. 518; and the fabulous quantities of gold accumulated by the Inca emperors. And, if it be objected that these are just so many pre-eminent peaks in an otherwise quite ordinary story, it is enough to refer to the gold crowns and circlets of medieval royalty and nobility, who literally wore much of their personal wealth in this safely

Plate 45   ostentatious form.

If, therefore, gold is such a metal as this, so obviously destined to be linked closely with the economics of political power, it is necessary for a moment to glance at its natural distribution over the world's surface. This must be done, so to speak, with hindsight. Gold sources worked during the last thousand years or so are, for the most part, well known:

those worked earlier are in some cases equally well known, especially when they consisted of ore (the working-sites of which are still visible) and not simply alluvium; but in many cases again the very early sources are little more than conjectural. From all the available evidence, however, a clear picture can be built up: the main deposits worked in both ancient and modern times make an intelligible pattern on the map, whatever the number of smaller deposits, now unknown, where gold has been picked up or scratched from the near surface of the ground for briefer periods.

Gold has been found and extracted in all five continents of the world. In the Americas its distribution lies mainly down the west coast, from Alaska in the north down through the great extruded mass of the Rockies into Mexico and the northern half of South America: a secondary gold-producing area can be defined southwards from Quebec to the south-eastern area of the United States. The principal European deposits have extended from the British Isles south-eastward through France and along the line of the Alpine and Balkan mountain ranges, together with north-western, central and southern Iberia. In Asia an immensely extended belt of gold deposits has lain across the heart of Asiatic Russia: in addition, Anatolia, Armenia, Arabia, southern and eastern India and the Hindu-Kush have produced gold, together with Korea, the Chinese littoral and Japan. The pattern of these latter deposits spreads downwards through the eastern archipelago into Australia and New Zealand. Finally the African continent (from which the gold of the Union of South Africa has leapt, in less than seventy-five years, from about 1 per cent of world output to about 50 per cent) has produced gold also in its central and western zones, as well as from the regions of Upper Egypt, Nubia and Ethiopia.

This distribution makes a pattern, as was said above, though it would be wrong to read any great significance into the word. Smaller deposits of gold, eluvial and alluvial, have been found and worked in numberless places which would tend to blur and obscure the main lines of distribution on the map. Nevertheless, if it is the principal deposits that we are seeking to define there is indeed a pattern. Sometimes these principal deposits are due (as is perhaps the case with the South African goldfields) to the discovery of what may be a huge and very deeply buried alluvial mass. Sometimes they consist of ore-bodies, often associated with granite mountain structures, from which both eluvial and alluvial gold has been produced independently by the forces of nature, as in the western American chain. Regarded as groups they are reasonably compact, even if extended

23

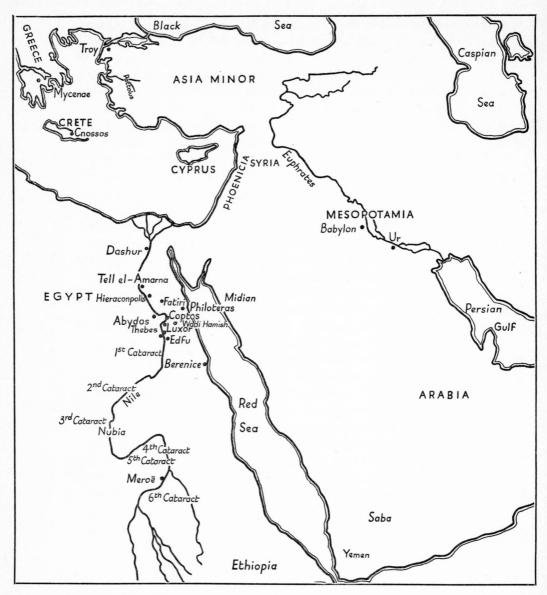

Map 1 Egypt and the Near East

over very great distances, since they tend to follow closely the upthrust over those distances of particular rock-systems, from which in turn weather and water have extracted a proportion of gold from the ores, sometimes carrying it to much lower levels a long way away. The suggestion of the grinding power and carrying power of water becomes unbelievably great when the eye first rests upon gorges like the Grand Canyon or Yosemite and the mind reflects upon the colossal quantity of rock which has been pulverized and borne clean away while those formidable chasms were carved.

This fairly clear-cut pattern of gold distribution is of a kind that might tempt the anthropologist to connect it with a human settlement pattern; and it is indeed true that in recent centuries such a connection has existed. The gold-rushes of California in 1848-9, Ballarat in 1851, and Klondike in 1896, to say nothing of events in South Africa, resulted in sudden 'colonizing' shifts of population which have had far-reaching effects; and Spanish efforts to secure firm possession of American gold—of the extraordinary wealth of which early navigators from Christopher Columbus onwards seem to have been clearly aware—resulted to an amazing degree in Spanish domination in Central and South America. In more ancient times, however, it seems very doubtful if the availability of gold had any direct influence on settlement patterns. At the time when gold first began to be worked in any quantity, around 4000 B.C., there were necessities far greater than that of winning gold. The battle for food was of supreme importance at a period when populations were increasing in conditions which were more and more stabilized. At this juncture the prime necessity was a metal from which could be made implements for use in either agriculture or defence. To the average man in these conditions, whether in the Near East in the fourth millennium B.C. or in Central America somewhat later, the search for copper and iron, on a community basis, would have seemed to be of much more urgency than that of gold. Indeed, until he could make strong metal implements to supersede either wood or horn or flint he could do but little prospecting for gold, and anything like digging a shaft (once he had made the association between alluvial gold and an appropriate and adjacent ore-body) would have been quite impossible.

The most ancient discoveries of gold, therefore, would probably have been chance discoveries. Two of the oldest civilizations known to us in any detail are those of Egypt and Mesopotamia. Each was a valley culture, relying upon a great river-system for the vital and unchanging routine of a seasonal flood to bring down fresh soil, to irrigate and to fertilize in areas where the sun could then be depended on to complete the harvest cycle. One of these civilizations, that of Egypt, embraced rich sources of gold. The other, that of Sumeria, did not. As archaeology has revealed, however, early Mesopotamian culture was rich in gold, even if much less rich than Egypt. This gold had to be gained in other ways than that of exploiting domestic sources, and it could be so gained when political organization and military strength had reached a certain international degree of acquisitiveness and assertiveness. For Egypt gold lay ready to hand from the very first, to be worked as soon as it was found and its genial properties understood; and it is therefore in Egypt that the continuous history of the use of gold begins.

Map 1

Egypt was probably the richest gold-producing area in the ancient world until the systematic Roman exploitation of Spanish gold-deposits started with the beginning of the Christian era. Her wealth was first unearthed at a time in the world's civilization when the potentialities of gold were largely unrecognized and unsought in anything wider than regional commerce within the limits of a single culture, very much as was the case with the earliest gold of South America. But historical and archaeological evidence leaves us in no doubt of the astonishing degree of that wealth, or indeed of the great extent of the goldfields from which it was produced. These lay in two main areas. The first, in Upper Egypt proper, consisted roughly of the plateau, some 60 miles wide, which bordered the Red Sea for about 200 miles from Philoteras, north of the 26th parallel, to a point below Berenice north of the 23rd. This was a quartz plateau, sloping westward down to the Nile, and gold was ex-tracted from it in a great number of places from which it could easily be transported (for example, by a route which traversed the plateau diagonally from Berenice to Coptos) to such centres as Edfu or Thebes. The second main area lay south and west of the first, in what was known in antiquity as Nubia, and consisted of a tract, again of auriferous rock, stretching east and west between the Nile and the Red Sea, immediately north of the 22nd parallel. This tract, like the Coptos-Berenice plateau, was very systematically worked for gold by shallow surface mining, and it may be assumed that large quantities were won: whether the Egyptian 'nub'=gold gave its name to Nubia, or vice versa, the association seems to be plain. But the Nubian mining area was not the only region in which rich supplies of Nubian gold existed. To the south, west and north of it lay cataracts of the Nile, from the fifth to the first; and here, either in the Nile sand itself, as the result of recurrent alluvial action, or in the higher terraces which were the result of much earlier alluvial processes, there were rich deposits of placer gold. Moreover, southwards once more from the fifth cataract, and extending into the Ethiopian plateau, there were further alluvial deposits on a very considerable scale, which were probably to account for the later importance of the ancient Meroë just below the sixth cataract.

Upper Egypt, therefore, and its hinterland contained wide areas of gold-bearing ore-bodies, together with an immense river-system which since the beginning of prehistoric time had, in Nubia and to the south of it, been scouring the gold from the rock. It was, as we may be certain, this alluvial gold that was first systematically collected and worked. Archaeology has shown that Egyptian gold objects made their first appearance at the very beginning of the pre-dynastic period, at the end of the fifth millennium B.C. and the start of the fourth. In this very early period the extraction and processing of copper was itself still a comparatively young art; and, while the working of copper certainly preceded that of gold, it is unlikely that it advanced for some time to a stage at which the technical problems of shaft-mining could have been at all easily solved. Washing for gold, on the other hand, could be undertaken with all the simplicity which at all times and in every land has characterized the process of 'panning'. Prospectors throughout history, whether the most ancient Egyptians of pre-dynastic culture, or the first settlers around the infant nineteenth-century Johannesburg, or even the twentieth-century European scholar of high repute who washed gold from the Rhine for his wife's wedding-ring, have all employed the basic instrument and method. A shallow circular dish is taken, which could be, in any given age, of wood or copper or iron: it is shallow, and perhaps 12 inches or more in diameter, with sloping sides. This is filled about two-thirds full with the 'pay-dirt' to be washed, and is held in a stream or in a hole filled with water. The prospector separates and removes the larger stones by hand, and meantime, by a knack which he learns to master, both rotates and twists the pan so as to keep its contents suspended in the water which covers them. The movement thus given to the water results in the lighter particles being carried away, leaving a residue either of pure gold or heavier gold-bearing ore or both; and by repetition of the process the separation is made more certain and the residue becomes more pure.

The simplicity with which gold can be washed from alluvium, owing to the weight of its particles, coupled with an abundance of gold in the sands and terraces of the Nubian Nile, allow us to understand how the

Plate 5

Fig. 1 Egyptian goldsmiths at work, showing different stages in process and control. Detail from grave-relief at Sakkara, middle of the third millennium B.C.

appearance of gold objects succeeded so quickly in pre-dynastic Egypt to that of copper. For the earliest gold objects found in Egypt are not, metallurgically, highly developed: they are simple ornaments which, as Ridgeway stated so vividly of early gold, are beaten out of gold from the brook. And they were beaten cold: smelting and kindred processes in Egypt were only developed in the course of the fourth millennium B.C., *Figs. 1 and 2* when the use of the blow-pipe was perfected to urge chaff furnaces—a treeless land's substitute for charcoal—to the temperature (just over 1000°F.) at which not wholly pure gold melts. Pre-dynastic goldsmiths at first produced cold-hammered gold beads; but it was not long before they were also beating out gold into thin sheets which, as time went on and technique improved, could be made thinner and thinner, and so more flexible in use. Thin sheet gold of this kind was 'plated' on to stone or wood in pre-dynastic times.

The passage of the fourth millennium B.C., which saw the development of furnaces for smelting, saw also the general improvement in technical skill which, once the connection between alluvial gold and its parent ore had been understood, was to lead to systematic mining. The extent of this mining, whether along the Red Sea littoral or in the Nubian region, must indeed have been impressive. Its precise chronological development cannot be established with certainty: too many generations have scratched and scratched again at the first workings of Egyptian miners. But each area is thickly covered with sites of great antiquity. In the Red Sea area

7, 8   Two diadems found in royal tomb at Dashur, Egypt: *c.* 1995–1792 B.C.

9   Back panel of the throne of Tutankhamen found at Thebes, Egypt: 14th century B.C.

Fig. 2 Egyptian goldsmiths at work, showing blow-pipe and furnace. Detail from Beni Hassan grave-relief, beginning of second millennium B.C.

granite quarries were hewn out for the ore they contained. In Nubia deep shafts were dug, with tunnels up to 70 yards in length leading from their base, while on the surface, over a tract of 100 square miles, the hillsides were cratered with shallower workings of a few feet in depth, interspersed with round stone huts in many of which granite hand-mills for quartz-crushing have been found.

Although the progress of Egyptian mining technique from dynasty to dynasty and millennium to millennium cannot be traced in detail, and although the exploitation pattern of Egyptian goldfields is similarly obscured, it is quite clear from surviving evidence that it was from Egypt that the ancient world as a whole learned the main principles of gold-mining and metallurgy at a very early period. A brilliant glimpse of Egyptian mining-technique can be obtained from a passage in which the historian Diodorus incorporated a description of the Ptolemaic mines at the end of the second century B.C. The interval of time between that late date and the earliest dynasties of Egypt in the fourth millennium is formidably large, but it is likely that, apart from the development of better tools and of better chemical methods in gold refinement over the centuries, the technique of mining itself did not greatly vary throughout the period. Diodorus' passage is long, but it contains a wealth of detail.

On the confines of Egypt . . . and Ethiopia is a place which has many great mines of gold, where the gold is got together with much suffering and expense. . . . The kings of Egypt collect together and consign to the gold-mines those who have been condemned for crime, and who have been made captive in war . . . sometimes only themselves, but sometimes likewise their kindred. . . . Those who have been consigned to the mines, being many in number and all bound with fetters, toil at their tasks continuously both by day and all night long, getting no rest and jealously kept from all escape. . . . The hardest of the earth which contains the gold they burn with a good deal of fire, and make soft, and work it with their hands; but the soft rock and that which can easily yield to stone chisels or iron is broken down by thousands of unfortunate souls. A man who is expert in distinguishing the stone supervises the whole process and gives instructions to the labourers. . . . Those who are specially strong cut the glittering rock with iron pickaxes, not by bringing skill to bear on their tasks but by sheer brute force, and they hew out galleries, not following a straight line but according to the vein of the glittering rock. Living in darkness, because of the bends and twists in the galleries, they carry lamps fitted on their foreheads. They contort their bodies this way and that to match the behaviour of the rock. What they hew out they throw down on the floor—all this without pause, and under the severe lash of an overseer.

The boys who have not yet reached manhood go in through the shafts to the rock galleries, and laboriously pick up what is hewn down, piece by piece, and carry it to the head of the shaft into the light. Men who are more than thirty years old take a fixed weight of the quarried stone and pound it in stone mortars with iron pestles until they reduce it to pieces of the size of a vetch. The women and older men then take these: they have a number of mills in a row and throw the stone on them, standing beside them at the handle in twos or threes, and grinding their fixed weight of stone until it is as fine as wheat flour. . . . There is absolutely no consideration nor relaxation for sick or maimed, for aged man or weak woman; all are forced to labour at their tasks until they die, worn out by misery, amid their toil.

Finally the craftsmen receive the ground-up stone and finish the process. They rub the pulverized quartz on a broad board which is slightly tilted, and pour water on it. The earthy part, dissolved by the action of the liquid, flows down the sloping board, but the part that contains the gold clings to the board because of its weight. They repeat the process frequently, first rubbing gently with their hands: then they press lightly with fine sponges, and so take up the soft, earthy elements until pure gold dust is left.

Diodorus' account of Egyptian mining methods in the late second century B.C. may probably be taken, with slight modifications, as a reasonably true picture of very much earlier times, for it is clear that its essentials are an abundance of forced labour which made it possible to follow quartz veins through quite long underground galleries, followed by hand-milling under strict supervision on the surface; and, from a technical point of view, none of this would have been much more difficult in the fourth millennium B.C. than in the second century B.C. The early workings in the Red Sea littoral are good evidence of the determination with which the industry was pursued. Underground galleries at the modern Fatiri, north-east of Coptos, have been estimated to total between 3 and

4 miles in length; and modern assessment of the ore removed at the Wadi Hamish mines, north-east of the first cataract, stands at the impressive figure of over a million tons. Washing for alluvial gold, through the very simplicity of its methods and circumstances, was probably not subject to any centralized supervision in the period of early Egyptian culture— although a royalty of 10 per cent seems to have been imposed, or at least collected whenever possible, in respect of gold produced in this way. This hint of royal interest in the acquisition of washed gold becomes a certainty of rigidly exclusive royal claim when the mines themselves are considered. It is not possible to say just how early that claim was made and enforced. But the very necessity of slave-labour in large quantity to drive passages through the solid rock in conditions of appalling hardship, in an atmo-sphere made foul by dust and by the smoke of the fires employed to split the hardest rock, leaves little doubt that as soon as the gold-mining industry was developed at all it quickly became a royal preserve.

Archaeology alone, with its long picture of royal accumulations of gold, would suggest as much. But there is other evidence besides. In the third millennium B.C. the son of Phiops I—both men are known to us by sight from their statues, found with a superb gold hawk's head—appointed an Inspector of Gold in Nubia: the existence of such officials is commonly known in later periods. If there had not, indeed, been a strict royal control of gold production it would have been difficult, if not impossible, for the first-dynasty King Menes, at the end of the fourth millennium, to set a prescribed and legal value upon gold in the form of small 14-gramme bars marked with his name. And when the kings of the fourth to sixth dynasties (c. 2720–2270 B.C.) initiated or allowed the production of gold rings, not stamped with their name, but of a weight closely approximating to the bar of Menes and in fact constituting the earliest Egyptian currency in gold, they would have been unable to make or continue such an innovation (linked as it was to a corresponding system of stone weights) unless their control of gold itself had been virtually absolute. It will be seen how eagerly the Egyptian kings of a later period sought out any new gold sources which it was in their power to control. As soon as gold had become a measure of value in addition to its earlier function of prized, decorative ornament it was inevitable that its production should be closely supervised, and that the craftsmen who worked it into objects of jewellery and ornament should become invested, as was clearly the case, with a quasi-hieratic and 'secret' hereditary status.

The problems which these craftsmen had to face were indeed consider-able, and not the least of them was the varying purity of the gold which

Plate 6

31

they had to work. At the beginning of the fourth millennium B.C., under the first dynasty, the fineness of gold varied from about 85 per cent to 80 per cent fine: in the centuries that followed down to the second millennium fineness sometimes rose to about 95 per cent or 96 per cent, though it was often not above 80 per cent. Much of the impurity consisted of an admixture of silver, which is so frequently present in the parent ores from which gold is extracted; and there were of course other metals as well in the margin of impurity. The separation of gold from silver was not practised until the eleventh dynasty, around 2000 B.C., so that until that time the purity of gold depended (quite apart from the presence of base metals) upon its content of silver. Moreover, the gold worked by the early craftsmen of Egypt came from very varied sources. That which was washed from the Nile sands and terraces was probably very pure. That which was mined from the quartz, first along the Red Sea and later from the Nubian area, would have contained the characteristic impurities of ore gold. Then again, as time went on and the royal hunger for gold increased, consign‐ ments were obtained from much more distant sources. From about 2000 B.C. onwards, as we shall see, the kings of Egypt sent widely roving ex‐ peditions in search of it: the trade, not only in gold but also in ebony and slaves, which took place with the district round the mouth of the Zambezi—a district called Punt by the Egyptians—was to become very considerable, and its foundations may well have been laid in the fourth and third millennia. Each of the world's major deposits of gold produces some characteristic variation in the degree of natural alloy, and so of purity; and differences of extraction methods will of course add a variation of their own. Thus, although the early Egyptian goldsmiths doubtless strove for the highest possible purity, as a means of working gold more easily, they must often have had to put up with very varying degrees of fineness, from which resulted something of the wide colour‐range which early Egyptian gold shows.

Their method of refinement must, from the first, have been that of cupellation, and the account given by Diodorus (with the exception of the addition of salt and bran, which were eventually found to separate silver— in the form of silver chloride—from gold) probably represents a process that was used from the moment the blow‐pipe was employed to urge a furnace. Speaking of the gold particles which were, as he described, collected up on the 'draining‐board', Diodorus described how craftsmen 'collect it and weigh it and put it into earthenware pots [i.e. cupels], and in proportion to the amount they put in a piece of lead and lumps of salt

10 Head of ceremonial stick from Tutankhamen's tomb

11 Dagger and sheath from Tutankhamen's tomb

12 Head-dress of
Queen Shub-ad, mounted
on her reconstructed head
and wig, from Ur,
Mesopotamia: *c.* 2700 B.C.

13 Beaker and bowl of Queen Shub-ad

and also a small quantity of tin, adding some barley bran too. Then they make a well-fitted cover, and having laboriously smeared each pot over with mud they bake them in kilns for five days and five nights running. They then let them cool, and find none of the other things in the vessels, getting the gold in a pure state though slightly reduced in mass'—the impurities, of course, having been absorbed into the cupel.

The general picture that emerges between 4000 and 2000 B.C. is therefore that of an Egypt which, apparently before any other civilization, intensively developed the mining and refining of gold, as well as a widely ranging search for it. So far as concerns the grinding of ore and the smelting of gold it is a picture of which there is literal presentation, though in simple form, in the wall-painting from the tomb of Asa, an official of Phiops II, some twenty-four centuries before Christ. In this can be seen men hard at work pounding, and, in a fresh sequence beside them, a team of four more men urging a furnace with their long blow-pipes. So far as concerns the search for goldfields the picture must remain imperfect or conjectural. Whatever was being won from Europe and Asia down to about 2000 B.C.—and it is unlikely that the deposits of Spain and Gaul or Arabia or Bactria were for very long neglected—it can scarcely be doubted that the great bulk of the world's gold was coming then (as, curiously, it now does again, though from other sources) from Africa, and mostly from Egypt itself, along the Red Sea mining strip. Estimates of its quantity are probably impossible, though, on the basis of the number of sites mined and the probable richness of the deposits, attempts have been made to give approximate figures. Such attempts are almost certainly fruitless, as when we read that these Egyptian mines, down to 2000 B.C., may have produced over 1,500,000 lb. of fine gold, together with a further 40,000 lb. from mainly alluvial sites in Nubia. What does emerge with clarity, in the light of archaeology, is that Egyptian familiarity with gold and hunger for it easily antedated similar developments elsewhere; and it may not, perhaps, be far wide of the mark if the earlier dynasties of Egypt are credited with the achievement of absorbing four-fifths of the gold in production from all sources at that time.

What, then, became of this vast, accumulating treasure of gold? For it certainly did accumulate, as is surely evident even from the scanty figures which exist for the ratio-values of gold and silver under the early dynasties. Gold was relatively common in comparison with silver in Egypt—more so, probably, than in any other great civilization. Under Menes, in the thirty-second century B.C., it was two and a half times as valuable as silver.

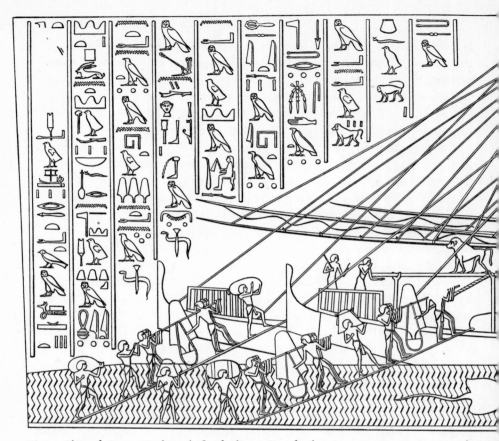

Fig. 3 *Ships of Queen Hatshepsut's fleet loading at Punt for the return voyage to Egypt. From the temp*

A thousand years later the ratio was only 1:2, and the change may well represent the piling up of gold even outside the royal treasuries, for it must be remembered that the alluvial gold of Nubia was not under the strict control which applied to the mines. Nevertheless, by far the greater proportion of Egyptian gold must have passed into royal possession. Some of it, no doubt, took its place in the treasury proper. Much, again, would have been contained in the various temple treasuries of which we hear. And it is certain that an immense quantity was immobilized, from time to time, in royal burials, as the archaeology of the later dynasties has demonstrated so brilliantly. But gold deposited in temples was liable to pillage—of the sort which put Octavian on his feet and paid for all the cost of a long civil war against Antony and Cleopatra. And gold buried in royal tombs was no more safe, though here the danger was that of

l-Bahri, fifteenth century B.C.

organized bands of skilful robbers, who from the earliest times bent all their knowledge towards violating the secrecy that formed the main strength of these cunningly constructed tombs. It has been said that by the beginning of the eighteenth dynasty, *c.* 1800 B.C., hardly a single royal tomb in the 'valley of the tombs of the kings' at Luxor can have remained undisturbed or unrobbed.

For these reasons we should not expect, except by good fortune, to see many gold objects surviving. And they are, indeed, few enough for this early period, which was both long and rich, if we are asking to see the flower of craftsmanship, finer than the simple gold beads and the plain beaten gold strips of pre-dynastic times. But what few there are suffice. The bracelets found in the first-dynasty tomb of King Zer at Abydos—the earliest Egyptian jewellery, it seems, now surviving—are a remarkable

35

achievement for the thirty-fifth century B.C. That they have survived at all is surely the result of a fortunate chance, for Zer's tomb was itself pillaged, and it was on the dismembered and mummified arm of his queen, thrust hurriedly by the robbers into a hole in the wall, that these bracelets were found. In one, gold alternates with turquoise; in two others, with lapis and turquoise; and in the fourth, with amethyst and turquoise. Without showing specially skilled workmanship—and indeed they wear a simple air when compared with what was to come—they are nevertheless of great historical interest and considerable decorative distinction. A thousand years of inherited and massive experience lies between the Abydos bracelets and the Hierakonpolis hawk's head. This is of superb artistry, executed with absolute assurance. The head (which was intended for attachment to a wooden body) is beaten out of gold, and conventionalized gold plumes—the mark of divinity—rise proudly and fantastically above it. In few ancient works of art is a stronger and more direct naturalism to be seen than in the features of the beak, with its cruelly prehensile curve, and the eyes, hard and watchful, inset in polished obsidian.

Another five hundred years pass, and give us, to match the beautifully sculptured gold hawk's head, the personal jewels of the Princess Khnumet, found in her tomb at Dashur, including two diadems of the utmost loveliness. One is made, with the greatest delicacy, of gold wire, to which are attached dozens of little gold florets with red centres and blue petals: the whole frail, almost gauzy structure is reinforced at regular intervals by six larger cruciform ornaments, again red-centred and blue-petalled. This is the diadem of which Flinders Petrie said that it was 'perhaps the most charmingly graceful head-dress ever seen'. Its companion, less delicate and more regal, is no less charming: an arrangement of gold roundels and *uraei*, splendidly inlaid with blue lapis, red carnelian and jasper, and green felspar, and, hovering over it at the back, a vulture in pure gold, sleek and powerful, lightly attached by the very tips of its wings. From these two diadems we can see beyond doubt not only the perfection of taste achieved by the end of the third millennium B.C. but also the high skill of the goldsmiths (like those on the Beni Hassan reliefs) who by this date could beat gold into the most elaborate forms, draw it out into wire for filigree work, inset it with precious and semi-precious stones, and even (as pendants in the same tomb show) decorate a plain gold background with gold granulation—minute gold globules, the art of fixing which was to be practised thereafter for nearly three thousand years before a secret was lost that modern experiment has only recently revealed again. And in

Plate 6

Plate 8

Plate 7

Fig. 2

14 Lid of solid gold sarcophagus of Tutankhamen, found at Thebes, Egypt: 14th century B.C.

15   Goat of gold, silver, lapis lazuli and shell from Ur: *c.* 2700 B.C.

addition, as is known independently, these goldsmiths could by now also separate gold from silver, and so, with far purer gold at their disposal, beat it out into extraordinary thin foil to act as a decorative covering.

From the twentieth century B.C. onwards the methods of refining gold seem to have been systematically improved. Perhaps one reason for this is to be found in the fact that Egyptian appetite for gold, by no means inconsiderable for two thousand years past, now became even keener. The unified control of Upper and Lower Egypt, lately achieved, would plainly tend to centralize still further the administration of Egyptian gold sources: it probably also opened up new trading connections with other countries. There is evidence that old mines were reopened and worked again. The activity of Sesostris III in the nineteenth century B.C., in opening up the trade-routes of the Red Sea and Indian Ocean with his navy, receives an echo from Herodotus, and by this time we may suppose that the kings of Egypt were systematically exploiting all accessible gold sources —the mines along the Red Sea, the alluvium of Nubia and some at least of its mines as well, the gold from 'Punt' in South Africa, and whatever could be won by external aggression. Nor were the Egyptian kings the only people to be on the move. Everywhere there was flux and migration, new conquests and new cultures—in Greece, in Asia Minor, in the Caucasus, in India. Only in Crete would Egyptians have discerned relative stability, as she embarked on her 'Middle Minoan' period of splendour and prosperity.

And now disaster, temporarily at least, struck Egypt herself. The domination of the foreign Hyksos kings in the eighteenth century B.C. was followed by two centuries of cultural standstill or regression. Then, with the eighteenth dynasty, the restoration of Egypt's greatness began, and a further span of two hundred years raised her culture and her wealth to a height never seen before. Now again, hand in hand with her own resumption of foreign conquest, Egypt intensified her search for gold. The recovery of Nubia was achieved, and its gold output presumably fostered: the natural wealth of Ethiopia was now, perhaps, tapped: both Thotmes I and Amenhotep II attacked Syria, gaining booty of gold and many other things; and the reliefs of Queen Hatshepsut's temple at Der *Fig. 3* el-Bahri give their own graphic picture of the departure of her fleet for Punt, urged on by sail and oar, and its return home, with sails now furled and decks crammed high with assorted merchandise. Under Thotmes III the pace was increased, and there is considerable inscriptional evidence for his pursuit of gold, both at home and abroad: in each of two successive years Nubia produced 225 lb. of gold (which, even if it was not merely the 10 per cent royalty on washed gold—as has been conjectured, was still a great deal), and his total gold income per annum has been estimated at the figure of 9000 lb. from all sources. So great, indeed, had Egyptian wealth become that Amenhotep III, in the fourteenth century B.C., was asked by foreign kings such as Burraburias of Babylon for supplies of a metal that they knew he possessed to excess.

The developing splendour of Egypt from the twentieth to the fourteenth century B.C., so admirably displayed by architecture, sculpture and painting, is not at first mirrored by more than a very few finds of gold. These, however, are evidence both of a continuing high taste and also of a growing skill. A beautiful gold pectoral of the nineteenth century Amenemhet I from Dashur shows the use of enamel—a powder of coloured glass fused by heat in a process of great delicacy. By the time of Amasis I in the sixteenth century, in addition to enamel work on gold, smiths had mastered the art of inlaying other metal with gold, as on the bronze blade of the dagger found in his mother's tomb at Thebes. This, too, is a delicate process, involving the channelling-out of a pattern in the bronze, the hammering-in of the gold inlay, and finally a neat and regular hammering-over of an infinitesimally small bronze 'lip' to hold the inlay in place. But all other knowledge of either Egyptian wealth or skill in gold would have amounted to little more than a fragmentary sketch but for the discovery of the fantastic treasure of Tutankhamen's tomb in 1922—the discovery, 'for perhaps the only time, of an almost undisturbed Egyptian royal burial in all its magnificence'.

'Almost undisturbed', because in fact this royal tomb, decked out with all the objects which Egyptian failure to conceive of total and actual death made necessary, had been violated by robbers. Finding the secretly unobtrusive entrance to the tomb, they had penetrated along a passage to the antechamber and its annexe. These they found crammed—and left jumbled—with royal possessions of every kind: chariots, couches, chests, cups, bed, fans, gloves, weapons, gaming-boards and writing equipment, together with a throne of the utmost splendour. But, because of haste or some other reason, they failed to discover the sealed and secret entrance to the burial chamber itself and its adjacent treasury; and it was in these two sections of the tomb that the richest finds were made by Howard Carter and his team. No summary can do justice to the beauty of these finds, for they are of a variety, a profusion, and a technical perfection which, allied to their natural grace and taste, demands long and thoughtful appreciation.

The quantity of gold which it was intended to immobilize in the burial of a young king of perhaps twenty years of age, who had ruled for less than a decade, was immense. A great many of the objects in the tomb were thickly coated with sheet gold, in some cases pressed upon a modelled wooden base and then chased. Such was the first or outermost coffin, though its anthropoid form allowed the head and hands to be made of solid gold. The third and innermost coffin was wholly of solid beaten gold, 2½ to 3 millimetres thick; and upon the mummy itself within this there were a portrait mask and hands of beaten gold. But it would be wrong to emphasize the profusion of gold in the tomb at the expense of other things. The craftsmanship was superb, and the taste was of wonderful refinement. Three examples, all less obviously magnificent than the coffins, may be taken: the back-panel of the golden throne, a ceremonial walking-stick, and a dagger and its sheath.

Plate 14

In the dagger and its sheath we may pick up the tradition of the finest work in gold jewellery as we have met it earlier. The dagger itself is a little over a foot in length. Its 8-inch blade, devoid of decoration save for a little lightly incised pattern below the handle, is of solid gold of a reddish tinge calculated to contrast with the yellow gold of the handle. And in the handle the splendid and the practical are well combined, for a firm grip is assured by the alternating bands of cloisonné work, in various patterns, and fine granulation in chevrons and diamond patterns. The sheath, of solid gold, again presents the maximum of variety within the limits of a single object. On one side it bears elaborate cloisonné work: the other is embossed with a fluid sequence of animal scenes—an ibex attacked by a lion; a calf with a hound upon its back; an ibex attacked by both cheetah and lion; a bull attacked by a hound—subtly connected by plant-forms and terminated by a handsome floral device. In all this there may be seen and admired an essential magnificence which, in deference to the very nature of the object itself, has been controlled by fine taste and executed with great delicacy.

Plate 11

As a further example of sheer magnificence there is the back-panel of the golden throne. The whole of the throne, indeed, is a marvel of elaboration; but its back is surely of outstanding quality. It is about 20 inches square, and is made of sheet gold, upon which was contrived a charming scene of the young king, seated unconventionally and at ease, with one elbow resting on the back of his cushioned chair, being anointed from a jar of unguent by his queen. The flesh of both figures is worked in red glass: their ceremonial wigs are of brilliant blue faience; and their robes are of

Plate 9

39

silver, while the details of their towering head-dresses, their collars, and all the decorative ornament which frames the whole panel are inlaid with a profusion of coloured glass, faience and calcite. In this lovely work of art there was an admirable planning of the use of colour—silver, red, blue and white—against the whole glowing mass of the gold, now subordinated to the status of a background on which the light could most brightly play, not un-like the conception employed in paintings nearly thirty centuries later.

Plate 57
Plate 10

Thirdly, the ceremonial stick—one of two found in the antechamber. Its shaft, of lightly incised wood, terminates in a crook formed in the shape of a negroid captive with his arms bound behind him at the elbows. The body of the figure is built up of gesso modelled on to the wood and over-laid with gold, while the head, arms and feet are of ebony. The carving of the negroid features, complete with thick, straight hair and heavy ear-rings, is of fine quality in itself; but the quality that lends this little work such distinction, and makes it worth singling out, is the success with which a fancy—the translation of human form into a crook for a stick—has been carried out, great economy of line being combined with simple decorative emphasis in the joint use of gold, plainly treated, with ebony. The gold possesses its own splendour and colour, as it always does; but here again, as with the throne-back, it is given a decorative function which gains by its being severely limited in treatment.

If considerable space has been given here, or indeed in other books, to the treasures of Tutankhamen's tomb it is, quite simply, because they reveal in full beauty what could otherwise have been only guessed at. They show, most obviously, the profusion of gold in Egypt in the fourteenth century B.C.—gold chiefly from Egypt itself, but by now increasingly from external sources too. They show the extent to which the possession of gold was a royal privilege—a privilege so strongly claimed that the age-long profession of tomb-robbery can be considered its natural corollary. They show, finally, that the mere possession of gold was not all: it was well refined, and skilfully worked into a multitude of objects in which the arts of goldsmith and jeweller were most nobly combined.

There is no reason to suppose that Tutankhamen's successors were any less magnificently supplied, or that their energy in the collection of gold fell below the record of the previous centuries. Sethos I, at the end of the fourteenth century B.C., was prospecting for new sources of gold, as is

Fig. 4

evidenced by the Turin papyrus—remarkable in the detail of its primitive map. The immediate successors of Sethos did not hesitate to look for external gold wherever they could lay hands on it, from Libya, Cyprus

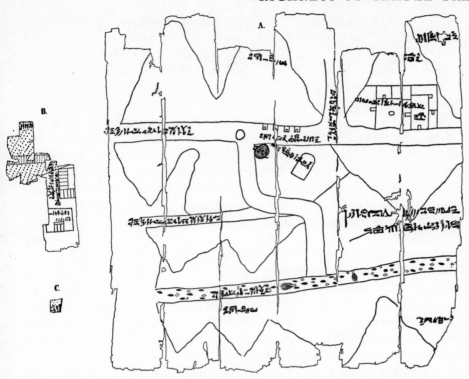

Fig. 4 The Turin papyrus, interpreted as an Egyptian gold-mining map of the late second millennium B.C.

and even Asia, while urging the constant exploitation of all internal sources, including those of Nubia, the output of which at this time has been estimated at something like 1600 lb. annually. The temple treasuries continued to be stocked regularly: under Rameses III, at the beginning of the twelfth century B.C., the temple at Thebes was receiving over 100 lb. of gold a year. It was this immense store of accumulated gold—from time to time diminished by immobilization in royal tombs, and liberated again by tomb-robbery—that awaited the opening up of the Mediterranean, by trade and conquest from new peoples, in the first millennium B.C. And it was not surprising that, with such wealth in gold, the Egypt of Greek times should hunger so fiercely after the silver which the Greeks controlled and Egypt herself lacked, to bridge her age-old gap between gold and copper values, or that, when Ptolemaic Egypt ultimately passed from the control of Cleopatra to Octavian, Rome could congratulate herself on one of the wealthiest prizes ever won in warfare.

Chapter III

FROM UR TO IRELAND:
THE EARLIEST GOLD OF THE
MIDDLE EAST AND MEDITERRANEAN

THERE COULD BE NO MISTAKE greater than that of attempting to view the broad stream of history in terms of a single factor like gold. In the whole recorded span of human development and progress the most important elements have been, probably, those which affected food supply on the one hand and power output on the other. Over-population in one area, leading to shortage of food, has in numberless instances led to an overspill, by conquest or organized migration or simple infiltration, into another, setting off many a long and often involved train of subsequent historical causation. The capacity of one people, or one State, to build more ships, manufacture more arms, or plough more deeply than another has inevitably led, for a time at least, to its greater power or greater prosperity—whether power was supplied by a huge corps of organized slave-labour or by the advent of machinery. Sooner or later, however, there will often come a time when power and prosperity are measurable in concrete terms of actual wealth; and it is in this respect that gold is important—a highly significant thread woven in and out of the complex fabric of history, to which a thousand other threads have also, in varying degrees, contributed.

It is pardonable to sound this note of caution in a survey of gold, since Egypt—the scene of the first great climax in the long rhythm of civilizations —was itself so rich in gold, both from internal sources and from others closely adjacent, and can be said to have taught the Mediterranean world most of what it afterwards came to learn not only of the technique of mining but also of the working of refined gold into objects of different kinds. And no doubt there was a close connection between the natural wealth of Egypt and the great power and continuity of Egyptian culture. A large store of wealth, in the form of an imperishable metal which was especially prized for its ornamental value and easy working properties, inevitably opened up the markets of neighbouring peoples, so that the Egyptian sphere of influence ultimately came to embrace Syria and Crete. But it is clear that the significance of gold as an index of power in ancient civilizations is not restricted simply to those which were fortunate in controlling a rich domestic supply of it. Indeed, one can say that in a civilization which lacked its own supply of gold special efforts were, from the first, made to acquire it from elsewhere as soon as the factors either of trade or of conquest made it possible to do so.

The strong and simple contrast to Egypt is supplied by Mesopotamia, where, in the excavations at Ur, gold was found in circumstances of the greatest interest. Southern Mesopotamia—southern Iraq of the present day—is a wide expanse of marshy land above which flows the great Euphrates, high-banked and fringed by a narrow, fertile strip which terminates abruptly in arid desert. Originally that marshy delta was not delta at all, but a shallow sea-lagoon which centuries of silt, carried down from Anatolia, made shallower still and finally enclosed with a sea-bar. Some parts lay higher, some lower: drainage, by canals and cuts, could make the higher levels habitable, and these were very fertile, since they consisted of river silt enriched by a timeless cycle of decaying vegetation. It was on these little eminences that some of the earliest civilizations of the Near East were born—primitive agricultural communities of the Late Stone Age.

Map 1

Archaeology has uncovered a number of these small communities, and has given to their characteristic cultures—all generically Sumerian—names derived from the sites which have revealed them. Al Ubaid was a small settlement, using stone tools, and then copper, 4 miles north of Ur, and remarkable for its very early painted pottery. Next in order of time comes what the Babylonian texts called Uruk, and the Bible Erech—a little settlement (now Warka) 40 miles north of Ur: the special interest of the Uruk culture is the introduction of the potter's wheel. Then followed the culture of Jemdet Nasr, associated with a little mound east of the later Babylon: in this period the art of writing was being developed, if not introduced, and not content with pottery the people were using steatite and calcite and shells from the Persian Gulf to make bowls and cups and ornaments. These cultures were all quite small in extent, centred originally on some low eminence of ground from which they spread up and down the river valley. Signs of violence or conquest are few. The chief violence that these early peoples had to fear was that of the great river itself, and the excavator's spade has uncovered the vivid evidence of the Biblical Flood —a clean bed of pure water-borne silt nearly 12 feet in depth, lying between the Al Ubaid and Uruk cultural periods. The flood-crest must have been of great height to deposit so much silt: thousands must have died, and thousands been made destitute, and the simple prosperity of the valley people would have taken a long time to reach its previous level.

To these quietly developing periods of early Mesopotamian civilization there succeeded another, in due course, about 2700 B.C.; and it was this period that was to be so brilliantly displayed by Sir Leonard Woolley's excavations at Ur some 4600 years later. The Ur culture, as it now stands amply revealed, was like its predecessors in that it appears to have consisted, up and down the Lower Euphrates valley, of comparatively small 'city-states'. City-states, indeed, may be too grandiose a description of the fairly small though densely populated towns which stood here and there on the higher ground bordering the great river, as high above the terrible and terribly remembered flood-level as could be achieved. But perhaps the term is true enough. For they seem to have co-existed in something like mutual independence. Their not inconsiderable populations must have gained their food from the intensive cultivation of a carefully irrigated area around them. And, as the discoveries at Ur have proved so splendidly, the individual headship of a community or district had by now matured into a truly royal institution. The Sumerian dynasts who are typified by the royal remains at Ur may have been, in effect, little more than regional. But of their possible wealth and power those remains leave no room for doubt.

A little outside the temple precinct of Ur there was a space which, from the earliest period of settlement, was used as a cemetery, and used thereafter so constantly and so long that, like many a village churchyard today, its soil had been turned and turned again as one generation of interments succeeded and displaced another. The majority of the graves which were excavated—over a thousand in all—were those of ordinary citizens, simply buried at the foot of a shaft with the essential things needed in an after-life. But a few graves of the early period were obviously different, being distinguished both by their special structure (a long ramp sloping down into a deep pit containing a tomb of stone or brick) and also by the richness of their contents. Such a tomb was that of Queen Shub-ad. It had been dug in the shaft of a slightly earlier tomb (perhaps that of her husband), which seems to have been violated while the queen's tomb was being made; but the queen's tomb remained inviolate until the modern excavators came upon the whole astonishing assemblage. It was the custom, apparently, that royalty should not be buried without their personal court attendants, all of whom (it must be thought) took some potent narcotic before being either immured or buried beneath the masses of soil thrown back into the open ramp and pit. For here they were: the queen's intimates crouching beside her bier; outside this inner chamber,

16　Helmet of Mes-kalam-dug from Ur: *c.* 2700 B.C.

17   Cup found at Rillaton, Cornwall: *c.* 15th century B.C.

grooms with a chariot drawn by two asses and a group of musicians, one with her harp—all according to the general pattern of the other royal tombs as well. The retinue buried with the king whose adjacent grave was robbed was even more impressive: soldiers, an ox-drawn chariot, musicians and courtiers—sixty-three persons in all. Yet another royal tomb contained seventy-four.

The splendour and beauty of the civilization of Ur at this period can be judged by many of the objects found in these royal tombs. But whereas, in Egypt, the absolute dryness of the air in a sealed rock-tomb could preserve virtually the whole of Tutankhamen's death-furniture, the dampness of soil (and its immense pressure exerted at depth) resulted in the decay of much at Ur that was not made of stone or shell or gold. Apart from damage by crushing, the gold objects were recovered in a superb condition that dazzles the eye and mind with the realization of the difference between the earlier Sumerian cultures and that of Ur. For they are remarkable in many ways. Not only is their quantity arresting, after a series of cultures in which gold, if it was worked at all, was of the greatest rarity, but in form and technique alike they show that the Ur culture, wherever its artistic impulses came from, reached a very high peak of achievement in a comparatively short time.

Among the most beautiful of the gold objects found in these royal tombs are the queen's head-dress, goblet, beaker and bowl; a dagger and its sheath; the figure of a ceremonial goat; and—coming from a tomb which was probably lordly rather than royal—a magnificent helmet. The head-dress was of fantastic elaboration, consisting of an arrangement of three complex wreaths designed to be worn upon what was evidently a very wide and thickly padded ceremonial wig. Low over her forehead came a diadem of plain gold ring-pendants: above this, and overlapping it, a row of thin gold beech-leaves, exquisitely wrought and veined; and above this, and again overlapping it, a third tier formed out of long gold willow-leaves interspersed with golden flowers inlaid with blue lapis and white calcite. All three wreaths were strung on bead-chains of blue lapis and red carnelian; and the whole was surmounted, behind, by a towering arrangement of upright golden flowers with lapis centres.

Against the varied splendour of this head-dress may be set the austere— and probably much superior—beauty of the queen's goblet, of perfectly plain gold, and of her fluted and delicately incised beaker (over 6 inches tall) and oval bowl (5 inches long). The golden dagger, 14½ inches long, is again a contrast: its hilt is a single piece of lapis studded with gold, and

Plate 12

Plate 13

Plate 15

Plate 16

its gold blade is encased in a sheath of gold, its back almost plain, its front decorated in an openwork pattern of what is almost filigree. The goat is a highly elaborate example of polychrome statuary: a wooden core, with the face and legs covered with thin gold foil bound with bitumen, the fleece constructed out of individual pieces of engraved white shell, the shoulders and beard and horns of blue lapis, and the belly of silver. This brilliantly decorative figure, 19½ inches high, was placed rampant against a golden tree which sprouted golden flowers, to which its forelegs were chained by silver chains. And finally, the golden helmet, found in a grave which was princely if not royal, belonging—as some of its contents stated —to Mes-kalam-dug. From every point of view this is perhaps the most outstanding single gold object found at Ur. It is in the form of a wig bound round with a diadem. Below this diadem the longer locks of hair fall in formally curving divisions; above it longer strands of hair lie plaited around the head into a knot at the back; and above this plaited band the crown of the head is covered by hair combed close and flat.

This helmet was beaten out of a single piece of 15-carat gold: the main locks of hair were hammered up in repoussé, and the individual hair lines incised. From a purely technical point of view it is a masterpiece of goldsmith's work; and it illustrates with superb assurance what is illustrated hardly less well by the queen's beaker and bowl, namely, that the craftsmen of Ur had quickly mastered and developed the difficult art of beating gold into the form of hollow-ware. This process calls for constant annealing, for hammering hardens gold, and if gold is to be thinned, and stretched this way and that, and shaped into circular or hollow shape, with all the stresses that are involved, its elasticity must be renewed all the time by fresh heating and quenching. But, apart from the golden helmet, the discoveries at Ur show that the working of gold was understood in many other aspects. The queen's head-dress displays inlay and the most delicate working of thin sheet gold. The dagger is well on the way to filigree. A little toilet container found with it was of cast gold. Granulated gold-work has been found on other objects. And in all cases the craftsmen were able to assess with astonishingly sure instinct the decorative value of gold itself, whether left nearly plain (as in the beaker and bowl and helmet) or slightly decorated (as for an ornamental weapon like a dagger) or highly decorated (as for a queen's head-dress or a religious emblem— which the goat must surely have been).

Without Woolley's long seasons of excavation at Ur modern knowledge of early Mesopotamian civilizations would have been immeasurably less than it now is. But those excavations, while they have painted a most vivid picture, have also posed some difficult questions. There was no gold in Mesopotamia, and all the gold at Ur, while far less than that which would have normally graced any one royal tomb in Egypt, nevertheless amounted to a very considerable quantity. Whence did it come, therefore, and how? It must be remembered that the 'city-states' typified by Ur were, so far as can be established, small regional communities engaged in agriculture: they were neither military nor commercial in the predominant sense—as, for example, the Phoenicians were later to be commercial, or the Spartans military. Their nearest gold sources were not very near, even if it were known for certain that all these sources were being exploited at so early a date. Southern India contained rich deposits in and around the area of Kolar (west of Madras), where gold is still mined systematically and profitably today. In the Hindu-Kush area between Peshawar and Tashkent, at the head of the Oxus valley, gold was to be found in rich supply, together with lapis—itself, like gold, non-existent in Mesopotamia. Farther north again the Ural-Altai area of Central Asia held immense quantities of gold, which were certainly destined in the course of time to have an impact on the gold economy of the Near East. But all these sources were very distant, and, even if it is true that some occasional trickles of gold came from them to Mesopotamia, their competition with other and nearer sources seems to be most improbable.

These other sources must surely be those of Arabia and Egypt. Central Arabia, west of Bahrein, and no very long distance south-west of the Euphrates, contained gold; and along the Red Sea coast of Arabia there were two other auriferous areas: the district of Midian in the north, just below the gulf of Akaba, and the Upper Yemen region above Aden. This last area was associated with Saba—the Biblical Sheba—and although modern estimates of Arabian wealth in gold at the period in question are not high (a small fraction, for instance, of that of Egypt itself) there can be no doubt that Arabia, from a very early date, was recognized as a well-known gold source. The royal tombs at Ur contained, among all their other furniture, small models of ships. These argue, primarily and naturally, the use of the Euphrates itself as a means of travelling up and down the great valley; but, considered together with the large quantity of shells brought inland from the Persian Gulf for decorative purposes, and with the fact that a coast-hugging voyage around the coast of Arabia would have been in mainly calm water, they provoke the speculation that a coast-wise trade might even now have existed between Arabian gold sources on the Red Sea and the Lower Euphrates valley. Indeed, if such a trade existed it would help to explain the frequency with which lapis lazuli and white calcite came to be used in the Ur culture, for these minerals were, of course, strongly characteristic of Egypt and were in abundant use in Egypt; and a maritime route which reached to the Arabian Red Sea coast could scarcely fail to tap some at least of the natural products of Egypt—even if not Egyptian gold. Alternatively it is not impossible that a trans-Arabian land-route was followed.

The general picture which in any case emerges from the excavations at Ur is that, quite early in the third millennium B.C., royal and noble persons keeping state in goldless areas contrived to acquire so much of the prized and precious metal that they could afford to immobilize a quantity of it in ceremonial interments, which (owing to tomb-robbery) we should have been quite unable to guess at without Woolley's finds. It is impossible to reconstruct with anything like chronological probability the detailed steps by which the use of gold spread in the eastern Mediterranean and Near East at this time. The process would have been relatively quicker in areas where gold was to be found, and slower where it was absent: it would, obviously, have been affected also by the willingness with which gold-producing areas parted with their gold in the course of trade with those who lacked it. Nevertheless there are certain firm pointers which may suggest, in general terms, the outlines of that process. The resultant sketch is that of a world in which individual civilizations and economies absorbed gold, or were injected with it, gaining or losing their wealth by increasing conquest or trade, or by sudden subjection, while all the time the total quantity of refined gold in existence mounted steadily and massively.

Crete was in all probability the first main focus of gold usage in the eastern Mediterranean outside Egypt itself. The years which Sir Arthur Evans devoted to the excavation of Cnossus revealed a civilization long in time, great in power and wealth, and connected at many points and in a most interesting way with the cultures of surrounding States or peoples, which became accessible as a result of the very formidable sea-power which the empire of Cnossus built up. That sea-power was a direct result of the geographical situation of Crete, standing as it did at the very cross-roads of maritime traffic in the Aegean Sea; and there is abundant evidence of the close links which existed between Crete and Egypt, Crete and Asia Minor, Crete and mainland Greece, and even (it may be thought) Crete and the western Mediterranean. Considered, therefore, against this geographical factor the knowledge that Crete herself contained almost negligible sources of gold in her own soil and nevertheless emerged as a rich gold-using power involves the clear corollary that she obtained the metal from overseas sources.

Cretan absorption of gold began in the Early Minoan period during the third millennium B.C., when the objects made were at first of comparatively simple form, requiring no technical skill beyond that necessary to beat gold into fairly thin sheet, form it into chain-links for personal ornament, and hammer it into relatively uncomplicated shapes. By the end of that millennium, when the late Early Minoan period was about to give way to the first Middle Minoan stage, the techniques were being elaborated: gold was being beaten into thin and delicate reproductions of flowers and leaves; it was the subject of repoussé work; it was being inlaid with crystal and semi-precious stone. Further advances were clear in the Middle Minoan period (c. 2100–1550 B.C.), for now, in addition to the earlier techniques, repoussé work was of a high quality, granulation was understood, and thin gold foil (evidently much admired for a wide variety of decorative purposes) was used not only as an appliqué ornament for carved steatite vases but also as an overlay for objects of bronze—the technical problem of binding gold to bronze had been mastered. Artistry in gold in the Late Minoan period, which ended, effectively, with the sacking of Cnossus c. 1375 B.C., can be most clearly estimated from that of Mycenaean Greece, to which not only Cretan technique but also objects had been exported. Among the best and most deservedly known of these are the two gold cups found at Vaphio in Laconia: these consist of an Plates 18a, 18b, outer repoussé shell, with a beautiful and very boldly worked up theme of 19 bulls and foliage, fastened to a plain gold inner liner. Even more remarkable, for their beauty and their technical mastery alike, are the bronze daggers from Mycenae. In these the main bronze blades have been inset with a Plate 21 smaller bronze panel; and these panels are themselves most splendidly inlaid with exquisitely delicate animal and foliage designs in gold, both 'red' and pale (i.e. gold-silver alloy of 'electrum') for effect, as well as silver and black niello (powdered silver, lead, sulphur and copper). Moreover, Mycenaean goldsmiths excelled in purely geometric design. Plate 20

Such was the familiarity with gold, and the splendour and assurance with which it was turned to decorative purposes, in the period of Cretan supremacy and influence. Crete was indeed the home, in later Greek tradition, of those little dactyls, wizard 'finger-men', whose skill in metal-working was legendary. The picture is one which can be illustrated from a source which, though later, is accurate in its essentials—Homer's account of how Hephaestus, the lame smith-god, made new armour for Achilles.

> He went unto his bellows and turned the fire upon them and bade them work. And the bellows, twenty in all, blew on the crucibles, sending deft blasts on every side. . . . And he threw into the fire bronze that wearyeth not, and tin and precious gold and silver, and next he set on an anvil-stand a great anvil, and took in his hand a strong hammer, and in his other hand the tongs.

Into the shield, wrote Homer, he set, among many different motifs,

> a vineyard teeming plenteously with clusters, well wrought in gold; black were the grapes, but the vines hung all on silver poles. Around it he ran a ditch of blue cyanus, and round that a fence of tin. . . . Also he wrought a herd of kine, fashioned of gold and tin. . . . And herdsmen of gold were following with the kine, four of them, and nine swift dogs came after. But two terrible lions . . . had seized a loud-roaring bull that bellowed loudly as they seized him . . . rending the great bull's hide and devouring his vitals and his dark blood.

Here, then, as so often at all other periods of history, the use of gold in conjunction with other metals to secure the beauty of polychrome effect bespeaks both an abundance of gold and an abundant familiarity with the problems of its working.

Crete may have obtained gold from a number of sources. Of these Egypt would certainly have been one. Connection between Crete and Egypt seems to have been fairly close over long ages, and when, for example, sculpture in stone began in Crete in the seventh century B.C. much of the idiom employed was derived from Egyptian influence. Tradition had it that the legendary figure of Minos himself had emigrated from Egypt; and we may imagine that a steady maritime relationship between the two powers was built up from the third millennium B.C., when Egyptian output of gold was fast increasing and commercial export of it (together with the relevant techniques) would have been a strong possibility. But if Cretan sea-power could be instrumental in getting Egyptian gold it could get it from other sources as well. Cyprus contained a little gold, especially at Akamas, where it was still being worked in Venetian times. Siphnos was a much richer island source, equally renowned in Greek days for its abundance of silver; and Siphnos lay but a little way north of Crete. Farther north still there was a rich complex of gold sources, stretching up from the island of Thasos and the Pangaean district of Thraco-Macedonia through the Balkan highlands and across the Danube eastwards into the Carpathian mountains and westward to the Adriatic extremity of the Alpine chain.

The hypothesis has been advanced that it was from these areas of south-west Europe that a large proportion of Cretan gold was obtained. Evidence is claimed from the numberless shallow surface workings which have been found—all clearly of great antiquity—over most of these areas, and from the fact that the very numerous miners' picks that these sites have yielded are of copper, and therefore presumably of the second millennium B.C., a period when gold, if it was being extracted on any systematic scale in south-east Europe, could scarcely have gone elsewhere than to Crete. To what extent Crete may be allowed to claim (what has certainly been claimed for her) an all-out initiative in the steady prospecting of these areas should probably remain doubtful. That these European workings coincided with the great age of Crete is very likely; and it is likely too that much of the gold extracted found its way to Crete. But caution may discourage the view of Cretan entrepreneurs in the mountain fastnesses around the Danube, and it might appear much more probable that a well-known demand for gold repeatedly enunciated by Cretan seamen at the northernmost point of their Aegean voyages (i.e. Thasos and its hinterland) resulted in the steady canalization of gold from Car-pathian and Balkan sources to such collecting-points, where Cretan ships could easily pick it up. For the Cretans were, above all, a maritime people, and together with this it should be remembered that the peoples of central and south-eastern Europe appear, at this epoch, to have been loosely formed into small armed bands, travelling rather than static, using and collecting metals rather than settling to a placid, agricultural community life.

But if the sea-power of Crete was responsible for no more than the regular collection of gold from sources in the North Aegean, it probably contrived to do the same thing in other and far-distant places as well. The evidence for Cretan penetration to the extreme west is obviously most conjectural. Nevertheless it is probable that the production of gold (as also of silver and other metals) in Spain went back at any rate to the period of Cretan sea supremacy; and, even farther away, Britain may have been tapped of her tin by sailors who were not afraid to sail the length and breadth of the Mediterranean and even to venture into the Atlantic, and so through the bay of Biscay to what was then, perhaps, the farthest northern limit. If they did they might well have been able to draw also on supplies of gold from Ireland. These, though not bearing comparison in quantity with those of Egypt or the Balkans, were nevertheless rich—rich enough, indeed, to make it worth while to wash the gold of Ballinvally in County Wicklow until a century ago. Irish gold was probably being produced from the second millennium B.C.; and objects made of this gold—neck-ornaments in particular, together with other objects—were later, as the record of archaeology shows, to be most beautifully made and also widely exported.

Plates 17, 22

It has been said that Crete, during that millennium, was the rival of Egypt in the acquisition of gold. But to say this may be to make a mistake of emphasis. Egypt controlled extremely rich domestic sources which she could, if she wished, swell by external additions. Crete, if she desired to use gold in the steady elaboration of her own long culture, must seek it elsewhere. The indications suggest that she sought it wherever her ships could sail. In doing this, however, it is unlikely that she was acting in open competition with Egypt. It was simply that Egypt had shown a way, in the possession and use of the yellow metal, which any other great power would surely follow and which even much lesser powers, like those of Mesopotamia in the third millennium, were capable of developing themselves. If rivalry was involved at all in respect of something like gold, that was not a staple of livelihood, it is more likely that it existed between Crete and other nascent cultures in the Aegean area. The excavation at Troy of the many towns piled upon each other, age by age, showed that Troy I (just before 2000 B.C.) was poor in gold. But in Troy II (just after 2000 B.C.) Schliemann—who, oddly enough, had set up a bank for dealing in gold in California after the gold-rush of 1848—found a wealth of gold: diadems, ear-rings, bracelets, brooches, together with granulated gold-work and faience beads that surely derived from Crete. It might of course be argued that the gold wealth of Troy II was drawn primarily from the gold-mines twenty-odd miles away at Abydos, of which Strabo wrote later, or even from the gold found much farther away at Colchis (washed down by the River Phasis) or in the distant Caucasus (resulting in the early gold culture of the Kuban), and that it was the Hittite invasion of Asia Minor at the end of the nineteenth century B.C. which broke these supplies. But it seems to be more probable that the lack of gold in Troy III–V (c. 1800–1500 B.C.) is to be related to the coincident climax of Cretan sea-power and that the new prosperity of Troy VI (c. 1500–1200) reflects the decline and fall of that sea-power, leading in turn to the maritime dominance of the Achaeans and a widespread redistribution of the rich stocks of gold accumulated over the centuries by a now semi-derelict Cnossus.

At this same period Egypt was, by contrast, entering upon the age of

18a

19

18b

18a, 18b and 19   Two cups found at Vaphio, Laconia: *c.* 1600 B.C.

20 Geometric discs found at Mycenae: second half of the 16th century B.C.

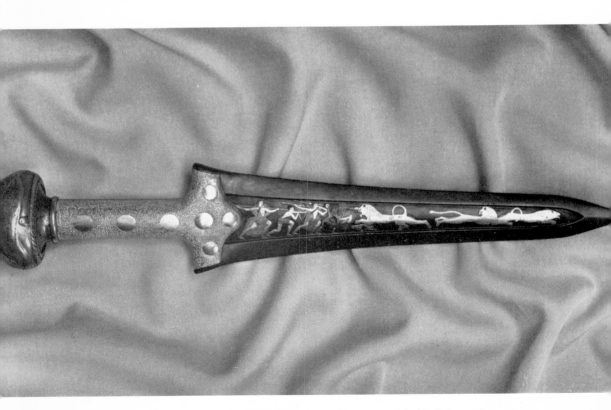

21 Bronze dagger, inlaid with gold, found at Mycenae: second half of the 16th century B.C.

her maximum gold production and, simultaneously, extending her physical power east and north towards the Levant. The effect of Egyptian wealth upon the civilizations of Asia Minor and the Near East during the thousand years that followed the Hittite invasion in the nineteenth century B.C. is most interesting. Doubtless a certain amount of gold entered the area direct from the deposits in Arabia, the Caucasus and the Asia Minor seaboard: when Hammurabi of Babylon, in the eighteenth century, tariffed the value of gold he was dealing with a metal which, as will be remembered, was totally absent in natural form from Mesopotamia. But as time passed and the whole wide region from the Persian Gulf to the Aegean was steadily consolidated, not only did royal houses acquire an increasing appetite for gold—obviously beyond the capability of those peripheral sources to satisfy it—but, with Egyptian eastward expansion a reality, they also came to look upon Egypt as a gold source of superlative richness, where gold 'was as common as dust'. The principal evidence for commercial contacts (of unexpected intensity and urgency) between the Asiatic kingdoms and Egypt lies in the Tell el-Amarna letters of the fourteenth century B.C. and early thirteenth. These show not only the familiarity with which Egyptian influence was recognized as far east as the Euphrates valley, but also the readiness with which the kings of Babylonia and Assyria, together with Egypt's vassals in Syria, requested consignments of Egyptian gold. Thus King Burraburias II of Babylon, in the mid-fourteenth century B.C., complains on one occasion that he has received only 2 minae (about 2 lb.) of gold, and on another occasion, in a letter which implies the accurate degree of Babylonian refinement methods, states that the gold sent to him is of inferior quality—so poor that of the 20 minae put into the furnace only 5 came out.

The extent of Egyptian willingness to export gold at this period, as well as the varying quality of the gold exported, may well suggest the re-export by Egypt of gold acquired from non-Egyptian sources, and of possible sources the legendary Ophir has perhaps attracted most attention and most controversy. In a later age Ophir was to become famous for the wealth which Biblical kings derived from it, as when 'the navy . . . of Hiram . . . brought gold from Ophir' and Jehoshaphat 'made ships of Tarshish to go to Ophir for gold'—ships which, under Solomon, returned from a three-year journey bringing also silver and ivory and apes and peacocks. Modern historians have taken widely different views about the location of Ophir. Some have inclined to place it in Arabia. Some have felt that the name Ophir may conceal a generic term for gold refined into a particular quality which might have come simultaneously from more than one source. Others have felt strongly that the persistence of Ophir in legend and literature as a source of great richness demands that it should be linked with some one known area of production which was in contact, even if at a very distant remove, with the Near East powers towards the end of the second millennium B.C., and the connection has thus been made, not unnaturally, with the East African gold-bearing region lying between the Zambezi and the Limpopo, embracing and centred upon the ancient and enigmatic site of Zimbabwe.

Map 2

Among the principal arguments made in favour of this identification there are many which are strong. The great size of the expedition fitted out by Rameses III (1198–68) to go to 'Punt'—including some thousands of seamen and merchantmen—is held to suggest that the certainly far-distant Punt was by now an area of major exploitation. That it lay south of Egypt is certain from the earlier Egyptian reliefs showing the tropical or semi-tropical products brought back by his predecessors. If it lay in East Africa it would well explain how the return journey for a circumnavigating

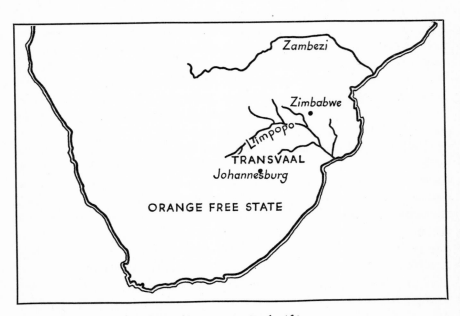

Map 2 Prehistoric and modern gold sources in South Africa

54

Phoenician fleet five centuries later could take three years, by way of Tarshish (Tartessus, near Cadiz in Spain), West Africa and the Cape. The area in question has produced considerable quantities of gold in modern times—over 60,000 lb. in 1916, for instance; and the fact that a soapstone mould for casting metal, found at Zimbabwe, corresponds closely in shape with that of bars shown on Rameses' temple inscription at Medinet Habu may suggest that Zimbabwe was a refining centre for gold worked in the whole surrounding district: a furnace and crucible have also been found.

The main point of controversy lies in the probable antiquity of Zimbabwe and the adjacent workings. Lack of comparative archaeological material makes criticism difficult and indeed hazardous. To those who argue that the famous carved birds of Zimbabwe and its massive cyclopean architecture suggest strong links with the art of Egypt it can be replied that such links could easily post-date the Egypt of Rameses III by a very wide margin, and that it is as dangerous, in an archaeological vacuum, to attempt to date Zimbabwe itself as it is, for instance, to date the compara- tively recent (1933) finds at Mapungubwe in North Transvaal—a gold- plated rhinoceros and other gold objects (some nearly 94 per cent pure). On balance, however, it may be said that, whatever the date of the Zimbabwe culture, the later Phoenician voyages lasting three years and resulting in obviously tropical cargoes together with gold, taken in conjunction with the great Egyptian 'Punt' expeditions, argue strongly for an exploitation of East Africa constant enough to localize it as the site of Ophir—whatever that name may connote.

Towards the end of the second millennium B.C., therefore, increasingly large quantities of gold were being pumped into the circulation of the eastern Mediterranean and the Near East. Egypt herself was a primary producer, and may well have re-exported considerable amounts from elsewhere. Crete, without herself being a producer on anything except a purely local and quite negligible scale, attracted stocks of gold through her maritime strength—from Egypt, from the Aegean islands and the Balkans, and from the far west. In Asia Minor and farther east the acquisition of gold depended partly upon the ease with which Egypt could be persuaded to part with it, partly on the degree to which it filtered east- ward in trade from Crete through Cyprus to the Levant, and partly on the quantity which could be secured from more or less remote overland sources in Armenia and the Caucasus, in Bactria, in Arabia, and possibly also in India. The swift decline of Crete which followed the sack of Cnossus thus left her Mediterranean successors to the enjoyment of presumably much larger stocks than they could call on before: moreover, Egyptian gold was still in full production. By this time, indeed, one must suppose that gold, without being anything but essentially rare even now, was nevertheless available for much more universal use than it had been *c.* 2000 B.C. The Mycenaean culture of Greece, already long introduced to gold by Cretan connections, briefly emerged as a civilization which Homer could afterwards call 'rich in gold', until the Dorian invaders from the north of Greece swept through the peninsula with a new and starkly austere régime: the Achaeans of Mycenae worked post-Cretan gold into post-Cretan art-forms, and their richness in gold is good testimony of what the eastern Mediterranean inherited as a whole when the empire of Cnossus disintegrated.

The same picture, of a world much more amply stocked with gold, emerges from observation of Syria and Palestine and the lands east of them in the period from about 1200 B.C. onwards. The swift extinction of Mycenaean civilization under the impact of the Dorian invasion left the sea-ways of the Mediterranean open to the initiative of the Phoenicians, who now began to play a maritime role, *vis-à-vis* an Egypt which did not compete in Mediterranean waters that had formerly belonged to Crete. Phoenician enterprise can be well enough judged by the boldness with which commercial settlements were established in far-distant lands. Tartessus, lying near the mouth of the Guadalquivir in southern Spain, was colonized about 1200 B.C. as a collection centre for the astounding wealth in gold, silver, copper, tin and lead for which Spain was now to become increasingly famous throughout the ancient world. Gades, the modern Cadiz, at the mouth of the same river, followed about a century later, together with Lixus on the North African coast. Phoenician mariners were evidently ready to sail the length and breadth of the Mediterranean in pursuit of their merchandise, for they were essentially a mercantile people who existed and indeed flourished on the turnover of trade; and the story told by Herodotus, how the sixth-century Egyptian king Necho induced Phoenician ships to circumnavigate Africa, starting from the Red Sea, and reporting 'a thing which I cannot believe, but another man may, namely, that in sailing round Libya [i.e. Africa] they had the sun on their right hand', may well be significant of far earlier enterprise of the same sort. Nor was this all, for there was strong tradition of old Phoenician contacts with the North Aegean too: one Greek legend made the Phoenician Cadmus the inventor of gold-smelting—after the

Dorian invasion much remained to be invented a second time—and the Phoenicians were known to have been active from an early period in the regions around Thasos from which the Cretans may, earlier still, have derived much of their gold.

In the period of Phoenician dominance gold was certainly quite abundant in the countries of the Near East. Egypt may have contributed to the abundance, but Phoenicia must have done so as well, and the voyages to Tarshish have already been mentioned: Arabia, too, was evidently a rich gold source. Biblical references give a constant reminder both of the quantity of gold in the Levant at this time and also of its normal uses: the tapestry of words is woven in rich colours. The spoil taken by Moses and the Israelites from the host of the Midianites included 16,750 shekels of gold (over 300 lb.)—'jewels of gold, ankle-chains and bracelets, signet-rings, ear-rings and armlets'. The Queen of Sheba gave to Solomon 'an hundred and twenty talents of gold'—perhaps about 6500 lb.—'and the weight of gold that came to Solomon in one year was six hundred, three score and six talents, besides that which the chapmen brought and the traffic of the merchants, and of all the kings of the mingled people, and of the governors of the country'. Such a number as 666 obviously possesses a poetical symmetry, but there is no doubt of the great influx of gold, or of the variety of its sources.

Nor is there doubt of its uses. The Book of Exodus describes in detail the lavish adornment of the Tabernacle. The Lord of Hosts received his offering of gold from the Midianite spoil. David devised, both from public and also his own private treasure, adornment of the utmost magnificence for the House of the Lord: 'I have a treasure of mine own of gold and silver . . . even three thousand talents of gold, of the gold of Ophir'. Solomon translated David's plans into fact in building a splendid temple of cedar-wood and gold—much of it from Hiram, King of Tyre: 'the whole house he overlaid with gold, until all the house was finished; also the whole altar . . . he overlaid with gold'. But Solomon's use of gold for his own personal splendour was also remarkable: he made 200 targets of beaten gold, and 300 shields of beaten gold, and a great throne of ivory overlaid with gold; and all his drinking-vessels were of gold—'none were of silver; it was nothing accounted of in the days of Solomon'. And although the Assyrian wars brought Syria and Palestine to a new dependency after that of Egypt, so that tribute was exacted by Salmaneser III and Tiglathpileser III in the eighth century, either that tribute was leniently assessed or old treasure was sedulously concealed: Salmaneser captured only 3 talents of gold in Carchemish, and imposed an annual tribute of only $\frac{1}{2}$ lb. of gold.

Meanwhile there was, in the Central Mediterranean, one more culture which was acquiring a desire for gold and a familiarity with its use. Etruscan origins are a notorious riddle: tradition and language appear to link them with Asia, and it was presumably from Asia that their early skill in the goldsmith's art was derived. The finest products of that art may be reserved for later comment; but it is at least noteworthy that the Etruscans founded the focus of their power and influence in precisely that part of Italy which lay most significantly upon the coastal route to Spain and all the natural treasures of Spain. Even at this early period, from c. 1000 B.C. onwards, their work in gold was becoming notable. Later it was to emerge at its highest quality; and the historical record of another age was to show the tenacity with which they were prepared to maintain their geographical position in relation to the Spanish route.

By about 700 B.C. the use of gold, which the rich deposits and high skill of early Egypt had at first made almost peculiar to the Egyptians, had therefore spread in greater or less degree over the whole area from Mesopotamia westward to the Central Mediterranean. Mesopotamian peoples originally derived it most probably from Arabia and the Red Sea —gold, copper, fine woods and stone and ivory were certainly being imported by sea c. 2000 B.C. Crete sought it wherever her ships could scour the Mediterranean. Troy secured it—patchily—from Crete and also from adjacent workings in her own area. Mycenae succeeded to the scattered Cretan store of gold; and Phoenicia amplified the world's stocks by her own vigour in colonization and exploration. And all the time the flow of gold in Egypt herself, partly from her own mines and partly from Punt (?=Ophir), accumulated massively, to an extent which allowed her to liberate a quantity to her eastern dependents. The relative commonness of gold as compared with silver is not easy to estimate. In Egypt the gold-silver ratio of 1:2 or 1:2$\frac{1}{2}$ of course reflected Egypt's almost total lack of silver combined with her abundant gold. Elsewhere the ratio appears to have varied, place by place and period by period, especially since the fineness of gold could not easily be estimated by sight: the hard, black Lydian jasper which afterwards won world popularity as a touch-stone for immediate if not wholly accurate assay—gold being rubbed upon it and its purity judged by colour—was unknown in Egypt and Babylonia. In general, however, the ratio at most times fell within the limits of 1:10 and 1:6.

Estimates of output, area by area, down to *c.* 700 B.C. can be no more than purely notional. Until *c.* 2000 B.C. Egypt herself must have produced nearly all the gold then in existence. After that date Egyptian output may have decreased, that of Nubia more than making good the deficiency; but Spanish gold would by now have begun to make its own contribution to total world stocks, together with a considerable quantity from south-east and north-west Europe. Production in India, Bactria and the Far East, while it may certainly be postulated, can scarcely be guessed at. All told, it has been conjectured that total output down to *c.* 2000 B.C. was perhaps nearly tripled within the next millennium and that a great increase in European and Asiatic production thereafter resulted in a further great rise in production large enough to offset some diminution in the yield of Egypt and Nubia.

It was this increase in total world stocks that was to bring about a change of immense importance in the general usage of gold. In the earliest times the sources of gold were, whenever possible, jealously controlled by the exercise of royal privilege, and gold extracted from those sources was to a very large extent retained in royal possession. Indication of a substantially increased quantity of gold in general possession and use is to be seen in the production of gold rings, nominally for ornament, but also as a form of currency. When the Song of Solomon declares 'Thy cheeks are comely with rows of jewels, thy neck with chains of gold', it is pointing to portable wealth used also as adornment—a much more convenient form of wealth than a plain gold bar notched into subdivisions. Many countries have shown the existence of such ring currency from extremely early times —as soon, indeed, as the supplies of a metal have made it possible to manufacture them. They occur in the early Irish gold culture; they are represented in Egyptian reliefs and paintings of an early date; Troy and Mycenae were familiar with them. Rebecca at the well saw a stranger 'take a golden ring of half a shekel weight, and two bracelets for her hands of ten shekels weight of gold'; and Job, after his tribulations were ended, received from each of his relations and friends 'a piece of money and a ring of gold'. During the whole period reviewed in the present chapter it is to be supposed that, little by little, the quantity of gold accumulating in non-royal hands was growing all the time. Gold sources may in many cases have remained under strict control, but as soon as sources were opened up in Europe, where exploitation was in the hands of small groups of independent miners, the quantity of gold released on to the world market for general possession, as opposed to monopoly possession by kings and princes, must have been greatly increased. Gold was, in fact, becoming a metal which more and more people could, according to their means, acquire and use as personal treasure and personal ornament; and the ancient world was well on the way to the point at which gold money, in the real sense, could finally be conceived.

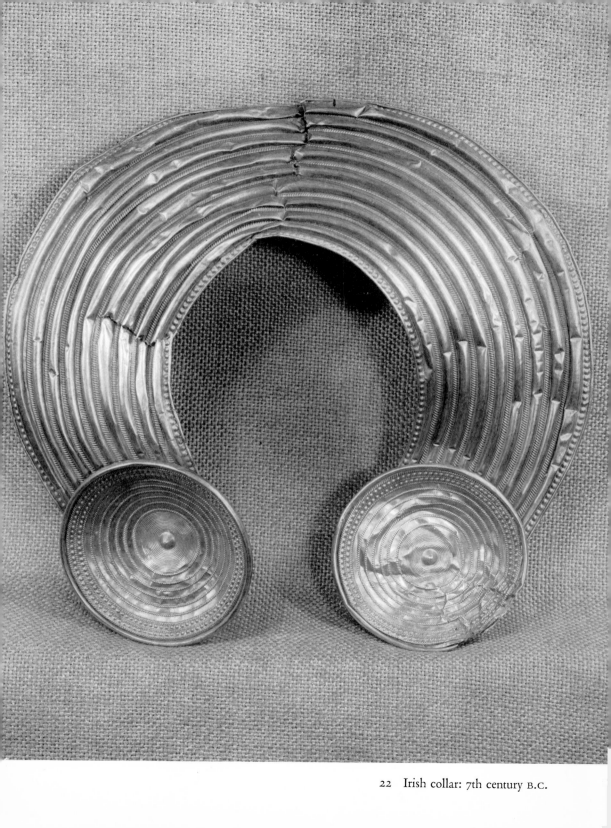

22 Irish collar: 7th century B.C.

23 Coins of the Greek period:
a Lydia, b Persia, c Panticapaeum, d Philip II of Macedon, e Ancient Britain. Scale $\frac{3}{2}$

Chapter IV

PERSIAN WEALTH AND GREEK POVERTY

THE COMMUNAL SPREAD of gold in the form of money was just one factor in the development of Graeco-Roman civilization as we know it today.

In the twelve hundred years that elapsed from 700 B.C. down to the disintegration of the Roman Empire in Western Europe that civilization came to life, and then waxed and waned. As a span of years it was a short one compared, for example, with the immense length of the Egyptian civilization which was, when this period opened, soon to expire, or with that of China, which at this same time was beginning. But length of time is not everything. Much more important is the quality of a culture while it lasts; and in these twelve centuries there was a double flowering.

The Greek flowering was seen in an astonishing versatility in which poetry, history, philosophy, science, politics and the fine arts were developed with great speed and sureness by minds which were empirical at all times rather than dogmatic and by spirits which, though not arrogant, realized without either difficulty or false modesty that the Greek achievement would long outlive its actual creators. The Roman genius ran in quite different channels. Here empirical method always went side by side with system; and if Roman progress was, in its own way, hardly less remarkable than that of Greece it was perhaps because of Roman willingness (surprising in a people so measured and deliberate) to indulge in sudden and usually profitable opportunism. In each culture there was strong emphasis on the interplay of individual rights and political systems. In each, again, there was wide play for self-expression, reflected no less by the rise of public oratory than by the elaboration of a great variety of literary forms. It is, essentially, the transmission of Graeco-Roman literature by the devoted clerks of the darkened Middle Ages that has enabled Western civilization to develop to the point at which we know it today. The long splendour of Egypt and the briefer flashes of Sumeria, Babylon, Assyria, Crete and Mycenae could transmit few permanent ideas beyond what their artefacts suggested; and artefacts are a poor substitute, however magnificent they may be in themselves, for a literature showing the aspirations and achievements of the spirit.

It is for such reasons that a survey of gold takes on, from the Graeco-Roman epoch, a form different from what has gone before. For previously the connecting threads have necessarily been woven out of archaeological material, carefully collected and compared as it has been by the brilliance of many excavators. But from now onwards the chief reliance must be on historical sources proper, for historical composition begins broadly with the beginning of Greek culture, and, with a sharp but not disastrous check in the Middle Ages, continues up to the present day—supported, of course, at innumerable points by archaeology, and often brightly illuminated by the survival of works of art by men whom history makes known to us. So much, indeed, is now taken for granted. But the outcome might easily have been very different. The almost miraculous victory of the Athenians over the Persians at Marathon in 490 B.C. and the double victory of 480 B.C., when larger Greek forces inflicted a second Persian defeat at Salamis and the Syracusans almost simultaneously defeated the Carthaginians at Himera, were the primary means whereby Europe was preserved for the enjoyment of Graeco-Roman civilization. The alternative, as was well realized at the time, was the submergence of Greece beneath the Oriental despotism of Persia—by then the strongest and wealthiest power of Asia Minor and the Near East, and the inheritor of all that earlier powers had accumulated and built up in that area. Viewed in terms of wealth, indeed, the desperately improbable Greek victories over Persia were the victories of relatively poor people, subsisting on silver, over a power which by that time had secured possession of a very high proportion of the world's available gold. As a result of those victories the centre of gravity for gold, which until then had been contained in an area bounded on the south by Egypt, on the west by the coast of Asia Minor, and on the north by the Black Sea, was able to move slowly though steadily into Europe, where it remained until the collapse of the Roman Empire.

The emergence of Persia to a position of unquestioned dominance followed a short period of constant change and confusion. At the end of the eighth century B.C. Assyria, under Sargon, had extended her own power westward to the Syrian coast, and even to Cyprus. North-eastward, however, Assyria lost control of the great Iranian area of Media, which rebelled and herself took possession of Persia, thus encircling Assyria on the east by a large and hostile Aryan realm stretching from the Persian Gulf up to the Caspian Sea. Jointly with Babylonia the Medians turned on Assyria late in the seventh century and carved up her territories. The southern lands fell to Babylon, which now enjoyed a brief renaissance of power and brilliance and even drove the last Egyptian remnants out of Syria: the northern lands, including Assyria herself, fell to Media under

Cyaxares, who at once sought to test the power of the great kingdom of Lydia, stretching from the River Halys to the Aegean. Throughout the first half of the sixth century the final clash was averted; but it came when Cyrus, of the Persian family of the Achaemenids, usurped the Median throne and substituted a Persian for a Median dynasty. The Lydian kingdom collapsed under Croesus with the capture of Sardis in 546 B.C.; and thereafter Persia systematically conquered all territories up to the seaboard of Asia Minor—and indeed beyond, for Cambyses conquered Egypt itself in 525 and Darius (whose proud exploits are set forth in the famous Behistun inscription) began a few years later to extend Persian power across the Hellespont and into Thrace and Macedonia.

By this time the Persian Empire had assumed a stature more formidable than that of any in earlier times. It stretched unbroken from beyond the Persian Gulf to beyond the Hellespont, from the Caspian Sea to the Nile. It was admirably organized and strongly administered. It possessed ample man-power and, from an economic point of view, was favoured by easy access to two great seas. Finally, it was very wealthy, for although Persia had no contact with the precious-metal sources in the western Mediterranean and beyond (which came under close Carthaginian control) she had flung her net over nearly all the richest gold sources in Asia or, at worst, offered a monopoly market for the gold of sources not actually in her own territory.

A warning must be sounded, as before, against any tendency to see the rise and fall of empires predominantly—let alone exclusively—in terms of wealth in gold alone. The factors which have always led to the florescence of particular powers at particular times have generally been multiple, and have operated in a complex pattern. Nevertheless the possession of great wealth, and its wise application, are obviously factors of extreme importance, the pertinence of which is clear, for example, to modern men who keenly scrutinize the policy of the United States of America, where over half of the world's stock of gold now is securely held. The possession of great wealth, and its use, are plainly factors which will be more or less potent, and more or less fruitful, according as national leadership and national organization are strong. In Persia those conditions were satisfied in a marked degree from the late sixth century onwards for a hundred years or more. Her wealth was poured into an expensive administrative system, into the building of great roads and cities, and into the systematic policing of uneasily subject territories.

Persian gold was derived from a great variety of rich sources. Some of *Map 3*

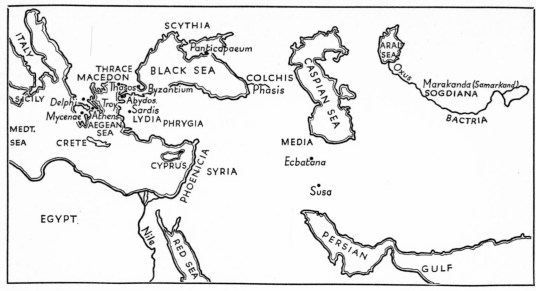

Map 3 *Greece and the Persian Empire*

these were old sources which she now took over. Some were sources upon which the eye of history now falls for the first time, even though their previous existence over long ages may certainly be assumed. The conquest of Egypt assured Persia of the continuation of supplies of gold which, however much they may have fluctuated, were undoubtedly still very great. It has been estimated that over four centuries later, immediately before the Roman conquest of Egypt, Ptolemaic gold output was still running at the rate of about 40,000 lb. a year, even when many of the staple Egyptian and Nubian mining areas were perhaps beginning to show signs of exhaustion. At the moment of the Persian conquest late in the sixth century it would hardly have been less, especially if Cambyses' attention to Ethiopia had, as its stimulus, the desire to exploit the very rich gold deposits which were known to exist there and centred their wealth at Meroë, a large and fertile island in the Upper Nile. Across the Red Sea there were the mines of Arabia, to which reference has already been made. Strabo, writing years later under the Roman emperor Tiberius, described the activity of this area, a land of nomads, where:

> there is a river which carries down gold-dust, though they have not the skill to work it, [and where] gold is dug from their land, not as dust but in nuggets, which do not need much refining . . . they pierce these and thread them on flax, with transparent

24 Armlet from the Oxus Treasure:
5th–4th century B.C.

25 Etruscan fibula from tomb at Vulci: 7th century B.C.

26 Etruscan ear-rings: 6th–5th century B.C.

27 Etruscan bowl found at
Praeneste: late 7th century B.C.

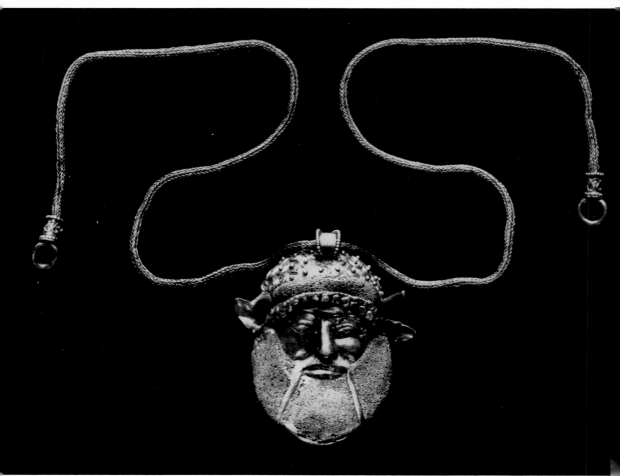

28 Etruscan pendant: 6th–5th century B.C.

stones alternating, and make chains and put them round their necks and wrists . . . and they market their gold cheaply to their neighbours . . . for they lack the skill to work it, and the metals they get in exchange, copper and silver, are rare in their country.

Diodorus, writing earlier, had said much the same of these 'camel-keepers', whose river 'brings down so much shining gold-dust that the alluvial mud at its mouth positively glitters', and who find nuggets in the ground as large as walnuts.

Northward from Arabia there lay the gold-tree tract of Phoenicia and Syria; but, north of this again, Persian expansion incorporated gold-producing areas of notable fame, associated with such names as Croesus and Midas. Midas, indeed, the King of Phrygia, belongs to legend rather than to history. He stands for a post-Hittite dynasty in north-west Asia Minor with immediate access to gold-mines both at Lampsacus and also near Troy and, probably, in contact also with much richer sources rather more distant. Tradition links him in some sense with the northern coastlands of the Aegean where immense supplies of gold were to be fought over and exploited in later periods. He is also to be connected with the most famous gold source in the East Greek world of the Asia Minor coastlands—the River Pactolus, which rolled down great quantities of gold-dust from Mount Tmolus in the Anatolian highlands. The identification of the Pactolus is now uncertain—even by the time of the Roman Empire it had ceased to bring down alluvial gold, presumably because in its upper mountain reaches it had literally cut through and washed away the whole matrix of gold-bearing quartz; but throughout the Persian and Greek periods its riches were proverbial, and, even if their fame was exaggerated by a sense of wonder on the part of Greeks who were, in the main, unfamiliar with gold sources, they must have been great. Upon them was founded the great kingdom of Lydia, associated with the kings Gyges, Alyattes and Croesus, and ultimately centred in the city of Sardis.

It was not unnatural that the wealth of Croesus should make so strong an impression on the Greek consciousness, for he was a Hellenophile who not only controlled with beneficence the various Greek colonies established on the coast of Asia Minor but (perhaps even more important) went out of his way to conciliate Greek feeling as a whole by princely offerings of the utmost splendour to the shrine of Apollo at Delphi—that religious centre in Greece which transcended all others in its natural sense of awe, its wide internationalism and its political acumen. He was not, indeed, the first Lydian king to try the effect of treasures of precious metal on the complaisance of the Delphic Oracle, for Gyges, over a century earlier, had sent thither (as Herodotus recorded) 'silver offerings more in number than those of any other man, and besides the silver a vast quantity of gold, and especially . . . six golden mixing bowls . . . weighing 30 talents', i.e. some 1750 lb. of gold. But the generosity of Croesus went far beyond this: in addition to couches overlaid with gold and silver, and cups of gold, he sent an immense treasure in the form of ingots.

> He melted down a great quantity of gold and fashioned ingots from it, making them six palms [i.e. about 18 inches] in length and three in breadth, and one palm high; and their number was one hundred and seventeen. Four of these were of pure gold, each weighing 2½ talents [i.e. some 550 lb. in all]: the others were of gold alloyed with silver, weighing 2 talents each. And he also had made a lion of pure gold weighing 10 talents . . . and two mixing bowls of great size . . . of which the golden one . . . weighed over 8½ talents. . . . He also sent the golden figure of a woman 3 cubits high . . . and dedicated his wife's necklaces and girdles.

Altogether, if the 113 ingots of alloy contained no less than 50 per cent of gold, Croesus' astonishing benefaction to Delphi must have consisted of not less than 7500 lb. of gold, the impact of which upon a land which not only had no gold, but had to strive competitively even for silver, can well be imagined.

Such was the wealth in gold which the kings of Lydia commanded—wealth of which Croesus could say to Cyrus, when the latter's Persian troops were sacking Sardis, 'I have no longer any property in these things: it is thy wealth that they are taking as spoil.' But Lydian gold had in any case procured a great revolution along the Asia Minor littoral, for it was associated under Croesus with the origin of the world's first true coinage. It had been a habit, as previously noted, from comparatively remote times for the ordinary man, using whatever small quantities of gold that came into private possession, to make it up into the form of rings, alternatively for adornment and currency; and from a quite early period the production of such rings was accompanied by that of small pellets or beads of gold, not marked in any way and not necessarily conforming to any standard of weight. These small pellets, however, tended to become standardized in many parts of the Near East around a unitary weight of 8 grammes; and, for the coast of Asia Minor at least, it is known at what period the production of such little pellets began.

The temple of Artemis at Ephesus which was built towards the end of the seventh century included under its basis—just as many a building has done with coinage in later ages—a selection of these currency pellets. In this case they were of gold-silver alloy, like the majority of the ingots which Croesus was to give to Delphi; and the reason for this lay in the fact that the metallic dust rolled down in the Pactolus consisted of both gold and silver, which, when washed out of the river, formed a natural alloy, varying in its proportions, but accepted at something like a fixed rate against pure gold and called 'white gold' or 'electron'. Electrum currency appears to have become quickly popular along the Lydian coast, and it was not long before various groups of electrum money appeared which were given distinguishing marks—in some cases certainly of cities, in others possibly of merchant bankers. But the fact that the intrinsic gold-silver proportion of this money (for money it now was) could not be accurately assessed in exchange was plainly inconvenient; and in an age when a rapidly expanding commerce could clearly be accelerated by a simple system of internationally acceptable currency this inconvenience was too great to be tolerated. Thus it was that Croesus, a man of wide international vision, took the all-important step. He introduced a pure gold coin and a pure silver coin, both marked with his royal device of the facing heads of a lion and a bull. Denominationally the gold was related to silver in the proportion of 1:10; intrinsically the ratio of value was $1:13\frac{1}{3}$. 'The Lydians', wrote Herodotus, 'were the first men known to us who struck and used coins of gold and silver.' In fact the first bimetallic system of coinage had been devised.

Plate 23a

With the invention of true coinage by Croesus new factors of great importance emerged. It is not known by what means he controlled the washing and mining of gold in his dominions, but some control there must have been: a closely related valuation of gold and silver against each other cannot be maintained unless their prices individually are controlled, and the actual cost of issuing coins can only be met by very slight over-valuation of the coins when put on the market—again an argument of central control. Indeed, from that day to this it has been usual for State authority to wish not only to cover the cost of coinage but even to make a profit on it: the frequent monetary manipulations of medieval and post-medieval Europe were seldom devoid of the motive of profit, which could sometimes be very great. Croesus therefore appears to have advanced well beyond any stage of economic theory reached by earlier kings. He injected a very considerable proportion of the gold wealth of Lydia into the public possession of his subjects and, through them, of the adjacent trading world at large; and in so doing he was bound to work out a careful and accurate system of control to keep his metal prices stable.

Plate 23b

The conquest of Lydia by Persia served only to extend the system which he had introduced. With slight modifications his bimetallic system was taken over after a short time: a gold 'daric' and a silver 'siglos' (= shekel) were instituted, again in a fixed bimetallic relationship, and this Persian coinage at once attained a power which was to last for a long time to come. The immense metallic wealth at their disposal enabled the Persian kings to contemplate with equanimity the accumulation of private fortunes, larger or smaller, by their subjects. Just how large they could be is shown by the story told by Herodotus of Pythius, a Lydian who entertained the armed hosts under Xerxes before his invasion of Greece in 480 B.C. and volunteered financial aid in these words: 'As soon as I heard that thou wast coming down to the Sea of Hellas I wished to give thee money for the war, and I found on calculation that I had of silver 2000 talents and of gold 4 million darics all but seven thousand; and this I give thee.' Xerxes' war-chest benefited, therefore, by about 100,000 lb. of silver and 7000 lb. of gold from the treasury of one who, though he was a magnate ('I have sufficient livelihood from my slaves and my landed estates'), was nevertheless only a private citizen.

The Persian conquests in Egypt and Asia Minor alone would thus have secured immense wealth in gold. But these were only two of a large number of very rich gold-producing areas with which this carefully organized empire was surrounded. Farther north, Persian eyes were quickly directed to Thasos and the Thracian hinterland. Of the islanders of Thasos at that time Herodotus wrote that from the mainland mines they received about 4000 lb. of gold annually, together with an amount from Thasos itself which, though smaller, was still very large. He saw the mines in Thasos himself later in the fifth century—'a great mountain which has been all turned up in the search for metal'. Eastward again from Thrace there was an abundance of gold concentrating upon the Black Sea. The richness of the objects found at Panticapaeum (the modern Kerch) pro-vides ample confirmation of the ancient tradition of the gold wealth of the 'Scythians'—a name loosely applied to the tribes living north and east of the Black Sea. It is again Herodotus, historian and indefatigable world tourist, who sets down the charming combination of historical fact and anthropo-logical legend. He noted that the Scythians possessed and used no silver or bronze or iron, but that in any royal burial of consequence (when, as in other civilizations, the king's body was interred with one of his mistresses, his cup-bearer, his groom, his attendant, his messenger and his horses) all the cups were of gold. As for the source of the gold which the Scythian

tribes enjoyed in such abundance, he quoted the legendary Arimaspians—
a race of one-eyed men dwelling far to the north, where winter lasted for
eight out of the twelve months of the year and the air was full of snow-flakes;
these one-eyed Arimaspians, he said, were reputed to get the gold from
griffins, living beyond them, who securely guarded it, and indeed the
gold coins of Panticapaeum struck in the classical Greek period showed on
one side a menacing griffin holding a (possibly captured) spear in its
mouth.

Plate 23c

From this, perhaps, a clue may be extracted. If the Scythian tribes
living around the northern shores of the Black Sea had established a
fruitful trading connection with tribes farther inland, from whom they
secured large quantities of gold (perhaps, like the Arabian gold described
above, at a discount), they would without doubt have taken care to build
up a fierce and terrifying legend likely to daunt the spirit of any rivals in
their sphere of interest. But this, in itself, does not help to define where
exactly the gold-producing area lay with which they traded, and this
question has been the subject of much modern comment. General
opinion now favours the Ural-Altai region of Central Asiatic Russia—
that region which Imperial Russia was to exploit so richly in the early
nineteenth century of our own era, and in which immensely rich deposits
of alluvial gold, often of great purity and very easily worked, have
been found ever since. The one-eyed Arimaspians have even—and
not wholly improbably—been explained as deep miners, with lamps
on their heads; and, less probably, the griffins have been interpreted
as a remote and vestigial recollection of prehistoric monsters in Central
Asia.

The gold of the Scythians, however, was not the only prize which the
Persian advance to the Black Sea gained, for at the eastern end of that
sea lay Colchis, the legendary goal of Jason and his Argonauts in their
search for the Golden Fleece, at the mouth of the River Phasis, which rose
in the mountains of the Caucasus. It seems that the waters of the Phasis
were no less rich in alluvial gold than those of the Pactolus, for Strabo,
writing under the early Roman Empire, could say of his own day (when
the Pactolus had at last become gold-free) that in the region of an evidently
dirty tribe called the Lice-eaters 'the mountain torrents are said to bring
down gold, and these barbarians catch it in troughs perforated with holes
and in fleecy skins', from which (he added) the legend of the Golden
Fleece arose. If the Lice-eaters in fact suspended sheepskins in the water
they were anticipating a principle to be used very often in later times:

coarse woollen blanket-cloth, corduroy, and other such fabrics have regularly been employed in trapping the heavy particles of water-borne gold.

Between this northern Armenian district and that of Bactria and Sogdiana, north of the Punjab, there were no goldfields of outstanding wealth. But the Bactrian district must have been as rich as any to which Persia had access. Evidence comes from multiple tradition, from actual finds, and from the solid figures of a careful historian. Tradition points, among other places, to the valley of the Oxus—that great river which rises south of Samarkand and is further swelled by a tributary on which lies Samarkand itself before pouring its waters westward towards the Aral and Caspian Seas. The wealth of alluvial gold in the Oxus was a matter of legend in Greek times, and it was credibly reported how the river washed down whole nuggets in its course. It is needless to add that the mountains in which the river rose must have been proportionately rich in gold ore. From this general area (embracing the eastern parts of the modern Bokhara, Afghanistan and Kafiristan, together with Dardistan north of the Himalayas) came a massive tribute in gold which the Persian Empire received in the fifth century B.C.—over 20,000 lb. a year. Probably it was mostly alluvial. Herodotus, in speaking of this tribute from the 'Indians', called it gold-dust, and he described in terms of wonder how it was generally collected. 'Where they live it is desert, on account of the sand; and in this sandy tract of desert are produced ants, smaller than dogs but larger than foxes. . . . These ants dwell under the ground, and turn up the sand; and the sand which is brought up contains gold. . . . The Indians come to the place with bags and fill these with sand, riding away as fast as they can; for the ants, as the Persians say, detect them by smell and begin to chase them . . . so that, unless the Indians got away with a start while the ants are gathering, not one of them would escape.'

Very possibly the terror of these large Indian ants—of which various subtle modern explanations have been given (e.g. a resemblance between gold-workings and ant-hills)—was sedulously put about, like that of the northern griffins, as a deterrent against intruders. But there can be no doubt that this remote corner of the Persian Empire was enormously rich in gold: some further gold may have been dug from India proper to the south, where the ancient workings near the present Kolar mines are up to 100 yards deep, but if this reached Persia at all it could not have compared in amount with that which came from Bactria. Much of the Bactrian gold may have entered Persia in made-up form, as is suggested by the 'Oxus Treasure', found in 1877 on a tributary of the Oxus. This comprised a great variety of gold objects, which may possibly have been the treasure of a lost or unidentified shrine in the neighbourhood. Together with a little gold chariot-group there were armlets, hair ornaments, a sword scabbard and many other smaller objects. Although the effect today is one of magnificence, style and workmanship are in many cases mediocre, and the art is obviously provincial. Perhaps the gold-work of the royal palaces at Susa and Ecbatana, of which reports were told, was altogether more splendid. But even this is not certain. When Alexander the Great, in the course of his wide eastward conquest (on which, incidentally, he was accompanied by an expert mining prospector), seized the royal treasure at Susa he took over 2,000,000 lb. of gold and silver in the form of ingots, and a further 500,000 lb. of gold coin; and Herodotus, who was well aware of the splendid external trappings of the Persian court, knew that the Persian kings melted down precious metal received in tribute and kept the ingots in store after removal from the crucibles.

Plate 24

Such was the wealth of an empire which much smaller and poorer Greek communities thrust back by the great victories at Marathon and Salamis. And yet, although Persia never conquered Greece in war, her wealth came near to doing so by playing upon rival Greek jealousies. The invention of coinage by Lydia was followed by the production of a vast Persian coinage, of world stature, in gold and silver; and with this Persia could always afford to buy off one potential Greek enemy against another, thus greatly weakening the whole system of small autonomous city-states which preceded the Macedonian domination of Greece from Philip II onwards. For even the wealthiest of Greek city-states were poor compared with Persia. Athens, enjoying rich domestic sources of silver in her Laurium mines, fought hard and long to extend her domination over other fields of mineral wealth, whether in the Aegean, as at Siphnos (where rich deposits of gold and silver were worked), or north of the Aegean in those areas adjacent to Thasos to which Persia had at one time stretched out a menacing arm. But, simply because Greece as a whole could not command or systematically control adequate sources of gold, her communities, from the time (c. 600 B.C.) when they themselves adopted the new invention of coinage, chose silver as their currency medium, since their silver sources were by contrast fairly abundant. And the value of silver in relation to gold stood in the ratio of 1:13. Small wonder that after the battle of Plataea in 479 B.C., in which combined Greek forces crushed the final rearguard action of the Persian invasion begun in 480, care was taken to collect all possible gold spoil from the battlefield, and that the search for Persian gold there continued in after-years.

The general scarcity of gold in Greek city-states of the full classical period is plain when their civilization is considered as a whole. Their highest achievement was not seen in gold-work, nor even in silver, which was put to relentless use as their chosen medium of a currency system which extended from Asia Minor to north-eastern Spain. It was in bronze and marble and clay that they excelled—cheaper substances, all of them, and turned to superb advantage in architecture, sculpture, vases and decorative work in terracotta. What gold they possessed would normally be stored in temple treasuries. For example, a tithe of the spoils from the Plataean battlefield was dedicated to the shrine of Apollo at Delphi, where a golden tripod was set up; and official inscriptions of later years catalogue specifically any gold held by temple treasuries as part of civic stocks. Such gold might sometimes be in the form of 'Cyzicenes' or 'Lampsacenes'—electrum coins which, long after Athens had brought a large area of the Aegean under the domination of her own silver currency standard, were produced at Cyzicus and Lampsacus on the coast of Asia Minor in order to furnish a currency acceptable generally on the fringe of the gold-using Persian Empire. For the city-states of Greece proper, however, gold was not used for coinage except in some dire necessity, as when Athens, with her great silver reserves exhausted after twenty-five years of bitter warfare against Sparta, decided in the closing years of the fifth century to melt down some of the golden offer-ings to Athena in the Parthenon and convert them temporarily into coin. Many years were to pass before the debt to Athena could be repaid, but in time the gold was restored, and a later inventory recorded that an additional dedication was made of 'a wooden rack in which are the punch-dies and anvil-dies with which the gold coins were struck'.

In such circumstances we should not expect to find gold in frequent use for privately owned jewellery and articles of luxury; and they must in fact have been rare. Gold, whenever it could be accumulated in any considerable quantity, was held as a communal reserve in temple treasuries; and the history of Pheidias and his two greatest sculptural masterpieces— the Athena Parthenos at Athens and the Zeus at Olympia—illustrates this with special clarity. The Parthenos, constructed during the political and aesthetic ascendancy of Pericles in the fifth century B.C., was made entirely of gold and ivory, and was some 35 feet in height. Its beauty of form can be dimly estimated by various small copies that have survived until today; but its splendour can only be guessed at, since it bore over 2000 lb. weight of pure gold as part of its adornment. This gold was put on in such a way that it could be quickly removed, doubtless in case of financial emergency, and Pheidias himself had reason to be glad of this provision when, suspected of peculation, he was able to show that the whole of this gold plating could be taken off and be weighed (and not found wanting) against the official specification. His Olympian Zeus was, if anything, even more remarkable. It was placed in a shrine which was, every four years, the centre of the most famous religious and athletic festival in Greece, frequented by thousands of visitors and enriched by their tourist spending. Like the Parthenos, it was of gold and ivory, wrought with exquisite elaboration: the god's robe and sandals were of gold, and his great throne was decorated with gold and precious stones; and Quintilian, a good Roman critic, could say in after-ages that 'its beauty seems to have added something to the conception of religion, with grandeur of workmanship matched to a divine subject'.

Towards the end of the fourth century B.C. important changes took place in the hitherto uneven distribution of gold between Persia on the one hand and Greece on the other. Although it would be quite reasonable to suppose that the Greek genius in trade, extending all over the Mediterranean, must have secured some quantity of gold whenever opportunity offered, it still remains true to say that two of the richest gold sources— Persia and the Thraco-Macedonia area—were also so rich in silver that, at a world ratio of 1:13, the terms of trade for Greeks attempting to buy gold would have been very unfavourable. Conceivably they may have derived gold more easily from Egypt, which, even if it was still held by Persia, was at all times very hungry for silver owing to its acute deficiency there. But it is plain that the total influx of gold to Greece was small, and that its price was high; and the gold of Spain, which might have helped, was (as we shall see) closely monopolized by other interests in the west. Thus the intensive exploitation of the Thraco-Macedonian gold-mines by Philip II of Macedon early in the second half of the fourth century, his institution of a very abundant gold coinage which cut the previous Persian-dictated gold-silver ratio of 1:13 to 1:12½, and his success in dominating the hitherto democratic little city-states of Greece, are to be viewed simultaneously as the combined means whereby Greece, for the first time, was infiltrated by considerable quantities of gold.

Further events down to the middle of the third century B.C. helped to make gold still more easy to secure in Greece. Alexander the Great, son of

Plate 23d

Philip, flashed in conquest through the Persian Empire, defeating the Persian king at the battle of Issus in 333. Not only were his spoils (alluded to earlier) immense, whether from Susa or Ecbatana or elsewhere; but, as a result of his decision to press his conquest as far eastwards as possible, he was able to tap those peculiarly rich if remote sources of gold which had for so long been a major element in Persian prosperity. Egypt, too, was now released from Persian domination, and her gold as well could flow more widely. The direct consequence of all this was that Philip's reduced ratio of $1:12\frac{1}{2}$ for gold to silver now fell, even more sharply, to $1:10$. Gold, in fact, was much more plentiful, and in relation to silver its price fell substantially to a point at which, with gold coinage now circulating in Greece as well as the formerly Persian east, ordinary men could secure possession of some, at least, for themselves; and whatever theoretical penalties there may have been for melting down gold coinage into bullion there is no reason to suppose they were any more effective then than they were to be for the next 2000 years.

The liberation of gold into more common use by Philip II and Alexander the Great was probably carried a stage further in the period after Alexander's death. Of the Diadochi—the 'successors', his own generals, among whom his vast empire was carved up—Ptolemy and his descendants, to whom Egypt fell, greatly intensified the production of Egyptian gold. It was to the Ptolemaic period that Diodorus' description of Egyptian mining methods, quoted in an earlier chapter, applied; and, although there is no means of measuring the increased output of gold in Egypt from the third century B.C. onwards, Strabo's later evidence was to the effect that under Ptolemy Auletes (80–51 B.C.), father of Cleopatra, output was running at around 45,000 lb. annually—and this at a time when, although the gold of Ethiopia was being systematically exploited, that of Egypt proper and of Nubia was perhaps beginning to be exhausted. For this additional reason, therefore, the Hellenistic world could enjoy a multiplication of gold stocks, and it is from this period that gold objects were intensively made for private possession in Greek lands. Gold plate appears to have been produced—especially at Alexandria—in large quantities. Gold was everywhere to be found in thin sheets, in wire strips, and in 'leaf' form for use by the goldsmiths who were now, more and more, employed in making it up into jewellery. It was hammered, cast, engraved and embossed: it was applied very skilfully with paste to make decorative motifs for the fine glass-ware which Egypt and Syria were now turning out. As soon, in fact, as the extension of a pure gold coinage took place—

at first under Philip II and Alexander; later, very profusely, under the Ptolemies of Egypt; and, less profusely, under the Seleucids of Syria—every man could become a potential owner of gold. And while some, like Pythius the Lydian, doubtless preferred to keep their gold in the form of coin, very many others obviously regarded it as a treasure which was enhanced in value when it was turned into objects of luxury and permanently decorative appeal.

It was, curiously, at a time when gold had become much more widely available than ever before in the orbit of the Greek world that a strong interest began to show itself in alchemy and in the implied possibility of producing gold by artificial means. For this there were, perhaps, two main reasons. In the first place gold had become a substance possessed by many, instead of being, as formerly in dynastic Egypt and the East at large, something reserved for royal usage and thereby almost sacred. Secondly, there was the swiftly pervading influence of Greek philosophers, and above all of Aristotle, who more than any other man of his age set out to analyse and classify and define the phenomena not only of social communities but also of the physical world. After Aristotle's death in 322 B.C. his systematic philosophy spread with strength and speed, and to no country, perhaps, more strongly than to Egypt, where the famous library accumulated under the Ptolemies in Alexandria even housed Aristotle's personal collection of books.

The Aristotelian system held that the material world consists basically of a primitive matter, the existence of which for man depends for its actuality upon its distinction by one or another of a number of properties; and of these fire, air, earth and water were the most important as formative 'elements', each being possessed of appropriate qualities, i.e. heat, dryness, cold or moisture. Each element, so Aristotle held, possessed two qualities (thus fire is hot and dry), and of these two qualities one is predominant. One element may pass into another by the possession of a common quality; or any two elements may so combine as to make a third. All four elements are present in every substance, and thus any substance can be changed into another if the proportions of its elements are so changed as to agree with the proportions thought to exist in that other substance. 'If lead and gold' (to quote E. J. Holmyard) 'both consist of fire, air, water and earth, why may not the dull and common metal have the proportions of its elements adjusted to those of the shining, precious one?'

This was a technological question asked in a non-technological age lacking even a microscope for the detailed surface-examination of the differing crystallography of the different metals. In the absence of scientific apparatus learned men applied abstract theory, helped out whenever possible by the factual results of such metallurgical and chemical experi- ments as could be achieved in their day. The *Physics* of Bolus Democritus, written in Egypt about 200 B.C., treated of the making of gold, silver, gems and purple. The last item was significant: the invention of dyes is simple compared with the mutation of metals, and an early school of thought appears to have supposed that the chemical colouring of one substance to make it match the appearance of another was a long step towards true mutation. Other theories were to teach that the likeliest agent in transformation was heat, and that a furnace of surpassing heat would, if it could be achieved, produce astounding results, or that sulphur, itself a 'hot' substance, would if properly employed secure mutation. It was, how- ever, all too evident at all times that true transformation was impossible. Imitation was one thing: to turn lead into gold was another. And so the early champions of alchemy diverged more and more along a path of high-flown mystical speculation, in which virtues and metals were incontinently mingled in a veritable hotch-potch of philosophy, magic, astrology and simple chemistry; and the Golden Fleece itself could in time be regarded as a precious alchemical treatise written on parchment.

Meanwhile, in a somewhat remote corner of the western Greek world, there was one further manifestation of a civilization rich in gold. This was in Etruria, the origins of which have been viewed as an enigmatic difficulty in the controversies of modern scholars. For some, the Etruscans are to be regarded as indigenous. Others point to the explicit testimony of Herodotus included in his history of the Lydians.

> In the reign of Atys, son of Manes, there was a great famine over all Lydia. The Lydians endured this for a time, but sought remedies when it did not cease. There- fore the king divided the whole Lydian people into two parts, and by lot he appointed one part to remain and the other to go away from Lydia: he appointed himself to be over the section allotted to stay, and his son, named Tyrsenus, to be over the section that went away. The section which drew the lot to leave Lydia went down to the sea at Smyrna and built ships in which they put all their movable goods: then they sailed away to seek a livelihood and a land to live in, and passed by many nations until at last they came to the land of the Ombricians. They founded cities there and live there up to the present day. Their name they changed from Lydians to Tyrsenians, taking the name from the king's son who led them out from home.

Quite apart from the fact that Herodotus, as a historian, possessed wide knowledge and great acumen, his account is supported by a number of

historical and archaeological factors. For although Dionysius of Halicar-
nassus, writing in the first century B.C., rejected Herodotus' version on the
ground that a fifth-century Lydian historian knew nothing of it, other
ancient historians in general accepted it. In addition there was, as there
can be no doubt, a sudden change in burial customs in Etruria about the
middle of the eighth century, chiefly to be noticed in areas most adjacent
to the sea; and the subsequent inhumations were associated with tombs
very similar to those of Lydia itself. The Etruscan language itself has
affinities with Asia Minor; and inscriptional evidence from the island of
Lemnos, off the coast of northern Asia Minor, shows there the use of what
is generally agreed to be an Etruscan dialect. Finally the archaeological
tone of Etruscan finds as a whole offers very strong resemblances to the
styles current in Asia Minor, both in the motifs used and in their treatment.

If a party of Lydians, about the eighth century, did in fact decide to leave
their homeland, as the result of overcrowding and famine arising out of
westward incursions into Asia Minor at that time, there would be nothing
surprising in such a migration. For in the sixth century the people of
Phocaea, on the same coast, also made a mass-migration to the west in
order to escape from the new Persian domination, and set themselves up
at Alalia, in northern Corsica. Indeed the destinies of the Phocaeans at
Alalia were to be linked very closely with the Etruscans across the water on
the Italian mainland, for in 535 B.C.—a mere five years after they had
settled there—the Phocaeans were subjected to double assault by the
Etruscans to the north and the Carthaginians to the south; and although
they won a famous sea-fight they were totally exhausted in the process. The
promptness with which the new Phocaean settlement at Alalia was
extinguished by joint Etruscan and Carthaginian action was startling, and
perhaps suggests not only the Phocaeans' own reason for choosing Alalia
for settlement but also the policy of those earlier Lydians who colonized
Etruscan territory.

The upper reaches of the tributaries of the Po, where they flow from the
western Alps, were known to be rich in alluvial gold from early times,
and for these the Etruscan settlers, with their long inherited tradition of the
alluvial gold of Lydia, were well placed. Moreover, Central France was,
similarly, the source of great supplies of alluvial gold, the exploitation of
which may certainly be assumed during the Etruscan period. This would
tend to be collected for ultimate disposal at the mouth of the Rhône by
the merchant ships which, as innumerable pieces of evidence prove,
hugged the coast whenever possible on the long voyages that were now

constantly being made from end to end of the Mediterranean. Such voyages, however, had often—as is well known—an even more distant objective, namely, southern Spain.

Iberian mineral wealth was of an order which made it legendary and fabulous from the time when the first Greek ships began to penetrate to the Tartessus which earlier Phoenician navigators had known as Tarshish. Tartessus was the great trading mart down to which the vast resources of southern Spain flowed along the valley of the Guadalquivir—gold, silver, copper, tin, iron, lead and quicksilver. To this area Phoenician attention, as already noted, had been attracted long before. Gades, the modern Cadiz, was traditionally founded about 1100 B.C.; and when, from the sixth century onward, Phoenician influence in the Mediterranean came to be extended westward from Tyre and Sidon to the new foundation of Carthage in North Africa the Phoenician monopoly of the Spanish metal trade must have been intensified. It is worth noting that the first treaty between a strong Carthage and an infant Rome, in 508 B.C., specifically debarred Rome and her allies from sailing the western Mediterranean beyond a fixed point on the north-east coast of Spain. Etruria had never yet been anything but a bitter enemy of Rome, and it seems not unlikely, in view of joint Etrusco-Punic action against the Phocaeans in 535, that a working arrangement may have existed whereby Etruria, as a wealthy customer, was able to share in the gold brought by the Carthaginians from Spain. And not only from Spain, for Herodotus made it quite clear that, in the fifth century at any rate, the Carthaginians were getting placer gold from North Africa and even sailing beyond the Straits of Gibraltar to get it from what must be West Africa.

> There are men dwelling outside the pillars of Hercules, and they come to these and take the merchandise from their ships and arrange it along the beach. Then they embark, and send up a column of smoke; the natives, seeing the smoke, come down to the sea and lay down gold to the value of the merchandise and retire to a distance. The Carthaginians disembark and examine it, and if they think the gold sufficiently valuable in exchange for their goods they take it up and go on their way.

Factual evidence for the wealth of Carthage is to be sought not in golden jewels and a whole façade of luxury. It lies in her closure of the western Mediterranean, her later electrum coinage, and her ability to withstand the growing strength of Rome through a series of ruinously costly wars. It is likely, to say the least, that Etruria was able to claim a share of Carthaginian gold in return for her policy of exclusion against

Greek colonization in the west, and that this gold, added to what was so easily available in the western Alps near by and (a little farther off) in France, assisted her to build up her own peculiar position of great prosperity and power in northern Italy. Her power is to be measured in the early history of Rome, to which the Etruscans were such a grim menace. Her prosperity is to be seen not in any coinage of gold—it came too early for that—but in the conspicuous taste and luxury of her material civilization as archaeology has revealed it, and not least in the abundance and superb quality of her work in gold.

It is a quality implicit both in style and in technical mastery. Etruscan goldsmiths appear to have developed their art to a degree of fine elaboration which, in its sense of combined assurance and delicacy, had never before been excelled and very seldom matched. They could beat out a drinking cup of perfectly plain gold relieved only by decorated handles, like the sixth-century piece from Palestrina. They could work in the lightest filigree, as on the slightly earlier Vetulonia bracelet. They could make golden jewels, glittering lightly with golden flower-buds spangled over a network of finely wrought gold wire. They could inset gold with enamel. Most remarkable of all was their skill in applying gold granulation, with globules of gold so small and so thickly set that, to the unwary eye, gold encrusted with these appears to possess a slight 'bloom' until closer inspection reveals the minute granules—anything from 160 to 180 to the linear inch. The secret of this art of infinitely fine granulation, which had of course been discovered much earlier, continued down to Roman times, and was then lost until 1933. In that year H. A. P. Littledale rediscovered it by accident. His fish-glue boiled dry in a copper pot, which became coated with copper oxide: re-heated, the glue absorbed the copper oxide. In antiquity, then, the tiny granules were glued in place, one by one, in a copper-salt mixture from which, when heated, the glue carbonized, combined with oxygen, and then disappeared, leaving a strong metallic copper joint, of microscopic size but great strength, between each gold granule and its gold base.

Plate 25

Two outstanding examples of the wonderful Etruscan mastery in this technique deserve to be quoted. One is the gold bowl from Praeneste in the Victoria and Albert Museum, made about 600 B.C. The casual glance, as it falls on this, reveals a vessel of comparatively pure and simple form, geometrically decorated with a design which does not so much shine with reflected light as catch it, and momentarily hold it, before throwing it back. In fact the vessel is encrusted with thousands of gold globules, tiny in size,

Plate 27

Plate 28

so dense and even in arrangement and proportion that they impart to the underlying gold base what is like nothing so much as the delicate bloom on the golden skin of a peach. The second example is the golden necklace-pendant in the Louvre, made in the form of a bearded human head, and dating a little later than the Praeneste bowl. Here the artist has used his skill in granulation to gain a strong contrasting effect. The face itself, with its long, pendant moustaches, is of beaten gold with incised detail. Over the whole crown of the head gold wire, in the form of triple S-curves, vividly suggests thick and roughly tumbled locks of hair. But a band of hair above the forehead, and the whole of a luxuriant and spade-shaped beard, are rendered in minute, dense and even granulation which furnishes a splendidly decorative emphasis.

Plate 26

It has been said of Etruscan gold jewellery, and perhaps with justification, that 'though the workmanship is often fine, there is a tendency to over-load'. In a sense this is true, and especially of the jewellery made in the fifth and fourth centuries B.C. when, as ear-rings show particularly, the goldsmiths lavished upon their work every possible skill in order to achieve the maximum of decoration in a very confined space. But this was also true of much contemporary jewellery elsewhere—notably among the Greeks of the Asia Minor coast in general, from a part of which the Etruscan culture had sprung. It was also to be true to a very surprising degree of a great deal of Roman and medieval gold jewellery, until the art of gem-cutting allowed goldsmiths to substitute for an almost infinite elaboration of filigree and wire the ampler, broader and calmer aspect of flat-cut gems bordered delicately by gold settings. The comparison of an Etruscan necklace or brooch or ear-ring, intricately worked in pure gold, with the magnificent productions of jewellers in the eighteenth and nineteenth centuries of our era is instructive. In the former the effect is gained by sheer complexity, however small the scale of the work. In the latter it is gained by the contrast between flat, faceted surfaces of translucent colour and the luminous fretting of the gold which contains them. But the art of cutting gems flat and polishing their surfaces to mirror-smoothness was yet to come. Etruscan goldsmiths were, above all, jewellery-makers; they made their jewels of gold, which was used in the most complex and decorative manner possible; and it was in this that their paramount excellence was to be seen.

Similarly complex gold jewellery was subsequently made in many parts of the Greek world proper from the fourth century B.C. onwards, once the liberation and diffusion of gold had taken place on the lines

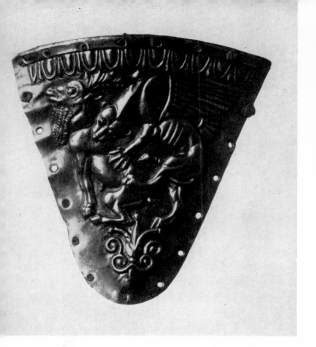

30 Plaques found in the Kuban: 5th century B.C.

31 Necklace from Kerch, Crimea: Greek, 4th century B.C.

32 Comb from Solokha tumulus,
South Russia: 4th century B.C.

described above. Often this was of fine style: not infrequently it was fussy; and, naturally, in the hands of inferior workmen it became coarse and tasteless. The variation which could exist can be judged best by the work in gold which was produced, far from Etruria, at the opposite extremity of the civilized orbit in South Russia and east of the Black Sea. Here was an area in which, as we have seen, abundant supplies of gold existed. It was also an area in which, owing both to the intensity of Greek colonization from a very early period and also to the northward extension of influences from the Persian Empire, a strong cross-fertilization of art-forms and technique took place. In jewellery the style of work produced in the Crimean district seems to have been intimately affected by that of the Greek coast of Asia Minor: indeed it is not improbable that Greek artists were employed in order to fashion the complex and often heavily elaborated ear-rings and necklaces which graced the wealthier Crimean aristocracy— objects like the Kerch necklace at Oxford, with its lightly worked chain of gold crescents and rosettes used as the means of suspending a row of gleaming gold acorns alternating with smaller gold beads, or the ear- rings from Theodosia at Leningrad, fantastically decorated with every trick known to the goldsmith's art. But this north-eastern area, probably because of the sheer profusion of gold supplies, was able to concentrate on other things than mere jewellery, and it furnished more large objects of a strongly decorative character than we have probably met with since the more ancient days of Egyptian and Sumerian prosperity. The difference is, perhaps, one of scale primarily; but when a goldsmith decides to make, not an intricate filigree ear-ring or necklace or bracelet, but a cup or vase or dish, or wide-spreading plaques to be applied to a wooden base, or even a comb for the hair, it is more than just a matter of scale. For objects like this are not simply pieces of personal ornament: they are either (as in the case of a utensil or a hair-comb) objects of everyday necessity trans- lated into special splendour by the use of gold, or (as in the case of plaques, with beaten or repoussé decoration) a specially rich substitute—of a character familiar in Egypt—for less bright and glowing material such as wood or ivory or stone. Moreover, they are of a size to give scope for more than the minute and delicate skill of a jeweller: they call also for that fuller range of the goldsmith's art which includes the plastic sensibility of the sculptor.

North of the Crimea, on the lower reaches of the Dnieper, finds of great magnificence have been made which show these characteristics vividly. The Solokha tumulus contained a golden comb of the utmost

Plate 31

Plate 32

beauty: the long, fine teeth depend from a plainly moulded gold band along which are set five crouching lions that carry on their backs a second band, lightly decorated, above which is a superb group in gold open-work sculpture—a battle scene with a mounted soldier, a fallen horse and two foot-soldiers. A strong love of human and animal forms is seen in general. The gold dish also found in the Solokha tumulus is covered all over in an intense rhythm of animal design. The electrum vase from the Kul-Oba tumulus near Kerch, beautifully formed and with its lower section elegantly chased, bears a broad central band consisting of a frieze of Scythian warriors. Eastward from the Black Sea, at the mouth of the River Kuban, the art of the goldsmiths in this same fifth–fourth-century period excelled in the making of gold plaques and appliqué ornaments, of which those from the 'Seven Brothers' site are admirable examples. They combine Greek with strongly orientalizing influences in studies of birds attacking animals, animals attacking each other, and dragonesque forms, with bands of Greek 'architectural' ornament and Greek palmettes to give the compositions balance and stability. Worked in high relief, and with full assurance, they testify to an age and an area when gold could be used—and to the utmost—to secure an effect of magnificence impossible with any other material.

Plate 33

Plates 29, 30

The relatively short period from 700 B.C. down to Hellenistic times thus saw an intense revolution in the use and distribution of gold. At first most of the richest sources were falling, one by one, under the control of Persia. Persia in turn, by adopting the Lydian invention of coinage, began to pump out her gold into general circulation; and the systematic exploitation of northern Greek gold by Philip II, followed by Alexander's Persian conquests, enormously increased the amount of gold in general circulation, especially since Egyptian output was still running high. In the west, Alpine and Gaulish gold fed Etruria, which perhaps also derived supplies from Carthage, for Carthage exerted the principal control over the vast gold wealth of Spain, now just beginning to be a major factor, together with sources in North and West Africa. The most obvious result of all these developments lies in the multiplication of goldsmiths' products everywhere, chiefly in the field of personal jewellery but also—where gold was abundant enough—in the manufacture of larger objects of pure luxury and ostentation, as in the extreme north-east (where burial has preserved them) and also in Alexandria, where the subsequent destiny of Egypt probably resulted in their being taken, in time, as Roman spoil for the melting-pot.

Chapter V

GOLD IN THE
GROWTH AND LUXURY OF ROME

Few infant states could seem less likely to beckon to a golden future of wealth and power than early Rome.

She first appeared on the historical horizon as a small, poor, rigidly organized community, with a tradition going back to the eighth century B.C. By the beginning of the Christian era this inconspicuous little city, state had constructed a mighty empire which stretched from Spain in the west to the confines of a new Persia (Parthia) in the east. All opponents had been subjugated one by one, including Carthage, the most dangerous of all; and as the result of her ingenious political institutions Rome had not only incorporated vast areas of conquest smoothly but had infused them with a spirit more nearly approaching unity than had been apparent in any comparable empire hitherto. Although the economic strain of many centuries of development—nearly five of them spent in unremitting warfare—was intense, and sometimes nearly ruinous, she emerged in the first century B.C. as a world, power of invincible strength and immense wealth.

The traditional foundation of Rome took place over 3000 years after the earliest quest for gold had made its mark in Egypt. Her development in a real sense, after 500 B.C., coincided with the progressive shifting of gravity for gold supplies from Persia to the Central Mediterranean. Her adolescence, in other words, fell at a time when the world stocks of gold from all sources were mounting to a very great volume and gold itself was being widely disseminated. And yet it was a long time before she attracted anything more than very small supplies to strengthen her limited economy. Conquest of the Etruscans doubtless allowed Rome to secure some at least of the gold which they had formerly absorbed from the head, waters of the Po in the western Alps, and probably some gold booty as well. And it is to be assumed that from the abundance of the world's stocks in general circulation some trickle reached Rome. But gold in the possession of early Rome, from whatever sources, can have totalled only a very small quantity. Indeed, it was not perhaps her primary need. From the end of the sixth century onwards she was growing up on the fringe of a Greek world in which silver, rather than gold, was the key that unlocked the paths of commerce. Italy as a whole possessed little silver, and Latium none; and until the first Roman conquests outside Italy gave her possession of stable sources of silver Rome had to rely, for normal purposes of internal currency, upon bronze. Her standard unit, in its earliest form, was either an ingot or a large cast disc of bronze weighing a Roman pound. Silver coinage was not introduced until nearly half-way through the third century B.C.—and then only for trade with the Greek south: the famous silver denarius, precursor of the medieval European 'denier' and English silver penny, was an even later creation at the start of the second century.

It would therefore have been surprising to find emphasis laid in early Rome upon gold as anything but the precious metal *par excellence*—something more appropriate to legend and poetry than to the hard world of practical fact and possibility. Indeed, it was probably so scarce that its intrinsic value, in relation to an economy based for a long time on the value of bronze, would have been most inconveniently high. The Elder Pliny bore witness to the very small quantity of gold in Roman possession during the early growth of the Republic: in 390 B.C., 'when peace was being bought from the Gauls after the capture of Rome, no more than 1000 pounds' weight could be produced', and the Roman pound, at 5040 grains, was considerably lighter than the standard English pound of 7000 grains. Thus, even after a century of steady development the Roman treasury contained less than one-half of the gold used by Pheidias fifty years earlier for his chryselephantine statue of Athena Parthenos, and less than one-seventh of what Croesus had lavished, 150 years before, upon Apollo's shrine at Delphi. As a reserve it was, no doubt, proportionately precious; but it would not go far in a crisis, and there was urgent need to increase it.

But the immediate sources of increase are hard to distinguish. Roman power in northern Italy became much more effective soon after 300 B.C., and it is possible that Alpine gold was more systematically sought, for the output of the Val d'Aosta and southern Piedmont (which was later to reach large proportions and involve the canalizing of the waters of the Dora Baltea) may even now have been considerable. The conquest of southern Italy, coupled with the defeat of King Pyrrhus of Epirus, must almost certainly have increased Roman gold stocks, for the Greek colonies of the south had for long been commercially prosperous and physically rich, and Pyrrhus' defeat now first invited Rome to extend her influence, however cautiously, beyond the Adriatic and to gain a foothold in the Balkans which had produced and were now producing abundant gold. Then, again, pressure upon Carthage by Agathocles, tyrant of Syracuse,

33 Electrum vase found at
Kul-Oba tumulus near Kerch:
4th–3rd century B.C.

34 Coins of the Roman and Byzantine periods:
a Augustus, b Galba, c Postumus, d Constantius II, e Justinian II. Scale $\frac{3}{2}$

temporarily weakened the Punic stranglehold in the middle Mediterranean and may have made it less difficult for Egyptian gold to reach Italy, and so Rome. Whatever the reasons, singly or in combination, Rome was able in 264 to pit herself against the mighty Carthage in the first of the three Punic wars and, after a quarter-century of fluctuating fortune, to win it and, with it, Sicily—the first of the Roman provinces overseas.

This astonishing victory, gained by an essentially military power over an essentially naval one, brought its own rewards and its own penalties. Rome was by now committed to the existence of a standing army instead of citizen levies willing to leave their farms to fight a seasonal campaign. Standing armies implied military budgets and expensive schemes of land settlement for time-expired veterans: and thus each forward move of conquest necessitated another in order to balance—or help to balance—a dangerously strained economy. It is a fact that for something like 200 years after the first Punic war Rome was ceaselessly expanding her areas of conquest, from west to east. This was not because she wished to conquer for the sake of conquering: it was simply that the liabilities of one conquest, expressed in terms of army pay and resettlement and diminished home production, must be offset by the assets of the next. In Roman theory conquered territory fell to the ownership of the Roman people. Subjected inhabitants became tenants instead of owners, and paid a carefully assessed tribute for the privilege of continued occupation. Such tribute could be assessed in the form of corn or services, or—where a newly conquered territory was rich in mineral wealth—in bullion or coin. Besides these sources of new wealth there were, of course, war indemnities as well. A power like Rome, which proceeded inexorably from war to war, could not afford to overlook the details of a finance system that was based on a perpetually war-time footing.

The second trial of strength between Rome and Carthage began in 218 B.C. It is reasonable to suppose that Roman reserves of gold had increased substantially in the half-century since the first Punic war. For although the gold-silver ratio about 218 B.C. may have been in the neighbourhood of 1:15—half as high again, that is to say, as the ratio which Alexander's eastern conquests had made possible in Greece a century earlier—there are good grounds for thinking that, quite apart from the fruits of the second Punic war itself, the Roman treasury was by now a good deal richer in gold. Livy wrote that its gold stood at 4000 Roman pounds when the war began: the sum was not large, but it was at least a fourfold increase compared with the year 390 B.C. The war itself brought in much more—from the royal treasure of Hiero of Syracuse in 212, from Capua (2070 Roman pounds) in 211, from Spanish New Carthage (over 270 Roman pounds) in 210, and perhaps 5000 Roman pounds from Tarentum in 209. Moreover, a levy of privately owned gold in Rome itself was instituted in 210. From all these sources not less than 10,000 lb. of gold must have flowed into Rome, and this total must have been greatly swelled by the booty which Flamininus brought home after his Greek conquests in 194 B.C.: 'of gold there were 3174 pounds, and one shield wholly of gold; and of the gold "Philippus" coins 14,514 [i.e. another 360 lb.] . . . and golden crowns to the number of 114.' The spoil of Flamininus alone, quite apart from the silver, must have amounted to between 4000 and 5000 lb. of gold.

Nevertheless it was the final outcome of the second Punic war itself that brought Rome her principal harvest of gold, for this war, which began in Spain in 218 and ended with Carthaginian defeat in Africa in 201, transferred from Carthage to Rome the almost incalculable wealth of Spain, as fabulous in fact as it was in legend. It is probably not too much to say that the control which Rome now began to exert upon the output of Spanish gold and silver was one of the greatest economic landmarks in her long history, and one from which derived not only much of her power in the Republican period but also much of her prosperity and luxury under the emperors. The degree to which Spanish gold enriched the Roman treasury is well known from the Roman historians themselves. Pliny, for example, stated that at the outbreak of the third war with a now desperate Carthage in 150 B.C. there were nearly 17,500 Roman pounds of gold in the reserve. This, perhaps, may not seem a very large quantity in view of the large amounts secured during the second war. But between 200 and 150 B.C. Rome was engaged in ceaseless wars; and these wars not only necessitated the payment of vast sums in silver coinage, the metal for which had to be bought if silver reserves were inadequate, but also involved a huge expenditure on military and naval equipment, much of which would call for payment in gold. To put it in another way, the gold stock in 150 B.C. was four times as large as that of 218 B.C. in spite of virtually incessant warfare in the interval; and there can be no doubt that Spain was the principal source of this new wealth.

Livy, in compiling the annals of Republican history, recorded the amounts of gold brought home from Spain by retiring governors and generals. His lists are not complete, nor always very clear; and there are cases when his figures may be questioned as the possible result of later textual alteration. But even so the evidence is striking enough. Between about 210 and 168 B.C. the weight of this tribute-gold amounted, according to the interpretation put upon Livy, to a total of from 8000 to 12,000 Roman pounds. Compared with the quantities of gold which had been from time to time accumulated in eastern lands in earlier periods this may not appear to be very remarkable. It must, however, be set against a wider picture, for the gold of Spain was accompanied by huge quantities of tribute—silver during the same years—amounting in all, perhaps, to nearly 500,000 lb. The Roman need for silver, as a means of providing the denarii which were now beginning to play the part of a world coinage, was paramount; and this silver she acquired in abundance. As a result the gold could play the part for which the economic theory of Republican Rome always designed it, namely, that of a reserve; and it can be assumed that during the period in question it was so steadily accumulated for this purpose that the seventeen-fold increase in gold stocks between 390 and 150 B.C. was a direct and natural consequence.

The truth probably is that, because of the needs of a great silver coinage, Rome was at least as much interested in silver as in gold during this time, and that (provided she had a reasonable and steadily growing stock of gold) her general policy did not make her hunger greatly for much larger supplies. Pliny found this hard to understand. 'I am surprised', he wrote, 'that the Roman people has always imposed a tribute of silver on subjected nations, and not of gold.' Although he had perhaps forgotten the Spanish gold tribute recorded by Livy he was correct in attributing a great importance to silver. But living as he did under the Empire, in a temporal context of great gold luxury, he made no allowances for Republican difference. There was no gold coinage issued by Rome in the second century B.C., and the amount of gold in private possession for articles of luxury was almost certainly very small. Republican Rome, in fact, hoarded a prudently growing reserve of gold but did not use it in the general life of the State, which, even now, after a most imposing record of foreign conquest, remained comparatively austere and unadorned.

That, indeed, is probably why, with Spanish gold now flowing in and gold booty from Greece and Syria reaching very high totals, Rome during the second century could decline war indemnities in gold and insist instead on silver, or accept gold—when she did accept it—at the low Greek ratio of 1:10. Her gold had become, in a very short period, sufficient for her needs. It now seemed, perhaps, to be coming suddenly and simultaneously from a great number of sources apart from the tribute of Spain and the booty of Syria and Greece. The Macedonian gold-mines were reopened towards 150 B.C. Soon afterwards a gold-rush took place in the Italian peninsula itself, the account of which Strabo took from Polybius.

> Near Aquileia, among the Taurisci of Noricum, a gold mine was found of such natural convenience that, on scraping away two feet of surface soil, gold was revealed that could at once be dug. It was never necessary to dig more than 15 feet. Some of the gold was pure from the start (being in pieces of the size of a bean or lupin) when only an eighth part was refined away. Some needed more smelting, but it was very profitable, and two months after the Italians joined them in the work the price of gold suddenly dropped by a third throughout Italy. When the Taurisci realized this they got rid of their Italian helpers and ran the work by themselves.

Nor was this all, for in north-west Italy near the western Alps gold-mining was now actively pursued in the region of Victumulae and Vercellae, apparently with the curious State proviso that the lessees should not employ more than 5000 miners. The number seems large, and may be exaggerated; but any limitation suggests that Rome had one eye on the possible dangers of over-production and falling prices in view of her own need for comparatively modest reserves. For it must not be forgotten that the yield of gold from Spain, once begun, was to continue in a steady and massive increase.

The early Roman conquest of Spain at first included little more than the coastal strips of the east and the south. By the middle of the second century the Roman armies had driven into Central Spain and held everything west of Pampluna, Calahorra, Toledo and Seville, including that area in the valley and head-waters of the Guadalquivir in which gold was then most abundantly found. Strabo's account, written 150 years later, gives what is probably a perfectly accurate picture of the earlier period for 'these everlasting storehouses of nature'.

> The gold is not merely got by mining, but is also washed down. Rivers and torrents carry down the golden sand: it is also to be found in waterless districts, though there it is invisible, but where the water flows over the sand the gold-dust shines out. They lead water to the arid spots and so make the gold-dust glitter. They also get the gold out by digging pits and by other methods of washing the sand. . . . Nuggets of up to half a pound in weight are said to be found sometimes in the gold-dust, and these need little refining: they say, too, that when stones are split little nuggets like nipples are found. . . . In the river-beds the sand is carried along in the stream and then washed in troughs by the river.

Strabo's whole wonder and emphasis are directed towards the rich rewards of alluvial production in southern Spain as opposed to mining proper. Plainly the alluvial yield was so great as to make the more costly alternative of shaft-sinking and ore-crushing and refining unattractive or even un-necessary. Shaft-mining, moreover, called for State control. There is good evidence that from a quite early period Rome regarded the working of gold- and silver-mines as a State monopoly, delegated to licensees. But the washing of alluvial gold, as in all previous civilizations, must have been differently conducted. In areas of maximum richness, perhaps, there may have been some measures of State control, like the imposition of the royalty payment upon Nubian gold-washers by the kings of Egypt. But in a country so rich in gold as Spain, where a humble peasant could probably wash gold, privately and free from supervision, in any small stream, no such system could have worked very effectively: the women who 'scrape it up with hoes and wash it in sieves into a box' were hardly likely to come under any very vigilant State control.

No figures are available for the influx of Spanish gold to Rome from about 150 B.C. down to the establishment of the Empire in 31 B.C. But it must have been great, for during the first century B.C. Republican Rome made the transition from a relatively plain to a luxurious standard of living. It is true that the gold reserves may sometimes have fluctuated uncomfortably: in 63 B.C., for example, the export of gold from Italy was temporarily stopped. On the other hand new supplies of gold were also being tapped, as when Caesar's conquest of Gaul brought so much on to the market, and so suddenly, that the price fell very abruptly by about 18 per cent. In general, the last century of the Republic seems to have witnessed, at last, the dissemination of gold as a luxury possession among the richer citizens especially of Rome and Italy. It was now widely used in personal adornment and for table plate of various kinds. An age had dawned of which Pliny was later to write in his most censorious vein: 'How innocent, how blessed, how luxurious life would even be if we did not crave anything deeper than the surface of the earth—in brief, if we were satisfied by what is around us. . . . Gold is grubbed up. . . . Man has learned to challenge nature. . . . Would that it could be wholly banished from our lives.' But it had come to stay, and Caesar himself encouraged the final step whereby (as with Croesus in Lydia, and Philip II and Alexander in Greece) gold could easily become the private property of any man of moderate substance. Until his day Rome had issued gold coinage only in times of great necessity: from now onwards it was a staple factor in the currency, and every man could own it, so that a little later Petronius, the eminent Neronian wit, could write in his famous *Dinner with Trimalchio* of the brilliantly vulgar freedman who used for his back-gammon-board, not the normal black and white pieces, but gold and silver coins.

Production of a fairly diffuse gold coinage under the Roman Empire and the growth of luxury naturally went hand in hand, and the one tended to encourage the other. From the first century A.D. onwards the world was scoured for jewels, spices, unguents, silks, and fabrics of gold tissue. These luxuries, as it happened, came mostly from the East; and, as it happened again, gold from the East appears to have shown from now onwards some signs of diminution. In northern Greece the mines of Macedon seem no longer to have been productive. In Asia Minor the Pactolus had apparently ceased to roll down gold-dust in its great stream. Farther east, the gold wealth of Bactria was insulated from Rome by the great Parthian Empire. Egypt herself had been well drained of her natural gold unless expeditions were to be made, at great length and cost, right up the Nile into Ethiopia. Jewels had to be sought, above all, from India; and India required payment in gold. So much is evident from archaeology, for although gold was certainly being washed from the waters of such rivers as the Ganges and Indus and even perhaps mined in the south, near the modern Kolar, the formidable accumulation of Roman gold coins of the early Empire in India, along the west and east coasts and to the south, tells its own tale. For silks Rome had to look ever farther, to China, where at this same period the Han dynasty was certainly in commercial contact (however indirect) with Rome. The swift drain of gold to the East was deplored and lamented by many writers of the age. 'We drink from a cluster of jewels and wreathe our cups in emeralds. It is our pleasure to go to India to help our drunkenness, and gold is now just a setting.' Such was the complaint of Pliny, who also made a calculation of currency payments sent annually to the East which, if expressed in terms of gold, would have amounted to over 5000 Roman pounds. Gold, under the Empire, was valuable either because it could buy luxuries of still greater value or because it was a superb means of ostentation in itself. To a people which liked its money's worth the intrinsic beauty of the yellow metal was a lesser attraction than its purchasing power or its prestige value.

Two stories illustrate the characteristic attitude, one no doubt apocryphal and the other purely fictional, but both eloquent. The golden statue of a Persian goddess had been carried off as spoil during Mark Antony's

Parthian campaign, and one of the veteran soldiers, while entertaining the Emperor Augustus to dinner some years later, was asked privily by another guest whether the particular despoiler of that statue had died, blind and paralysed, after this act of sacrilege. He answered: 'Augustus is dining off the goddess' leg at this moment. I am the man in question. And that act of plunder set me up for good.' The second story comes from Petronius' *Dinner with Trimalchio*. This dinner had reached a stage of bawdy ribaldry.

> Trimalchio wiped his hands on a kerchief which he wore in his neck and made his way to a couch where Scintilla was reclining. He kissed her as she clapped her hands, and said, 'May I have the pleasure of your company?' At that moment Fortunata was stripping her own immense arms of their bracelets, to show them to the admiring eyes of Scintilla, and even got to the point of undoing her anklets and hairnet, which, she kept repeating, were of purest gold. Trimalchio at once saw this, and ordered them to be brought to him. 'You see these fetters,' he said. 'That's how we fools are robbed. They must weigh all of six and a half pounds. As a matter of fact I've got a bracelet of quite ten. . . .' To show he wasn't lying he had the scales brought in.

The display of gold among private citizens, in the form of jewellery and plate, was the natural counterpart of imperial magnificence on an even more sumptuous scale; and this, combined with the constant outflow of gold coinage to buy luxuries from the East, must have made it a matter of some importance both to seek new supplies and also to exploit existing ones to the utmost. Of the new sources in the early imperial age great hopes were placed on Britain. Caesar knew, at the time of his armed reconnaissance in the fifties B.C., that the Britons used gold currency in the form of coinage—a surprising adaptation of the Celtic gold coinage .   Plate 23e of northern Gaul, and a phenomenon which, even before Claudius' full-scale invasion of A.D. 43, the emperors undoubtedly turned to advantage by way of unofficial tribute from friendly kings in the south. Caesar's reports were presumably one reason for the public pressure vainly put upon Augustus to annex the island himself, not least in the poems of Horace. A century later the historian Tacitus could write of Britain that 'it yields gold and silver as the prize of victory'. And so it certainly did, though it is unlikely that the quantity of British gold could ever compare, even relatively, with that of the silver from the mines of Derbyshire and the Mendips. The gold of Britain came almost wholly from Wales (that of Lanarkshire, Perthshire and Sutherlandshire which was being washed in Elizabethan times was probably never drawn upon now), and was

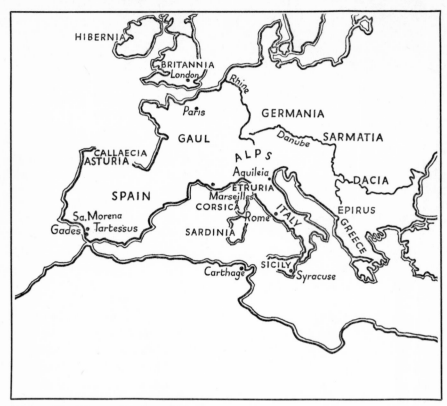

Map 4 The Western Provinces of Rome

centred in Carmarthen near Dolaucothy, where fairly deep shafts were sloped down into the veins of auriferous pyrites and a long canal was devised to bring water from the River Cothi to a settling tank in which the gold could be separated from the crushed rock. How long this mine lasted under Roman methods of extraction cannot be said: possibly its life was short, though Welsh gold existed in a quantity which, as late as 1863, made it possible to extract over 300 lb. in one year from around Dolgelly.

The necessity to exploit new sources was clearly realized by Nero, whose level of expenditure, and indeed of imperial extravagance, especially in the rebuilding of Rome after the great fire of A.D. 64, made it vitally important to replenish the treasury by any means possible. Tacitus told a story designed to illustrate both the necessity and also the credulity of an

35   Roman medallion of Valens (A.D. 364–378)
found at Szilágy Sómlyó, Rumania

37   Roman vase, inscribed with
details of weight: 1st century A.D.

36   Roman bar stamped by the
mint of Sirmium: later 4th century A.D.

a

b

c

d

e

38 Coins of the earlier and later Middle Ages:
a London, b Paris, c Florence, d Venice, e Damascus (?). Scale $\frac{3}{2}$

emperor whose memory he loathed. A certain Bassus, a Carthaginian by birth, and unstable in his mind, had a dream after which he sailed to Rome in A.D. 65 and sought an audience of Nero.

> He had discovered on his land a cave of immense depth, containing a vast quantity of gold, not in the form of coin but in the shapeless and ponderous masses of ancient days. . . . Dido, after fleeing from Tyre and founding Carthage, had concealed these riches. . . . Nero, without sufficiently examining the credibility of the author of the story, . . . encouraged the report and sent men to bring the spoil, as if it were already won. They had triremes assigned to them, and crews specially selected for speed. Nothing else at that time was the subject of so much credulous gossip.

Alas: when the expedition arrived, and ground had been dug up, now in this direction and now in that, without avail, Bassus protested that never before had a dream misled him.

But Nero's behaviour in economic matters was not always fit for the acidulated pen of a Tacitus. His Ethiopian expedition, sent 'to investigate the source of the Nile', as Seneca put it, may have looked ultimately to the rich gold which Ethiopia had long been known to possess and produce. He was fortunate in the discovery of a new Dalmatian mine yielding 50 lb. a day. His use of the Hyrcanians, a tribe situated east of Parthia and south of the Caspian Sea, may have been not more a means of containing Parthian aggression westwards than a means of securing, if he could, an easier route not only for the gold of Bactria but also for the silks of China. His interest in the Black Sea district, coupled perhaps with a projected expedition to the Caucasus, may suggest an eagerness to increase the imports of gold from these indisputably rich areas: the eastern end of the Black Sea coast was still producing gold in quantity. Quite apart, however, from such sources as these—some imaginary, some new, and some perhaps exploited afresh—there was still abundant gold elsewhere. It was coming from Arabia (a treatise on the navigation of the Red Sea was written at this time); it was coming from the southern centre of Gaul; and above all it was coming from Spain, in quantities so large that Spanish gold must be regarded as one of the strongest financial supports of the Roman Empire. If the immense spoil taken by Augustus from a conquered Egypt after the battle of Actium in 31 B.C. enabled him to set the Empire firmly on its feet it was certainly the gold of Spain that contributed most thereafter in keeping its finances steady.

This gold came from an area in the north-west of Spain to which, under the Republic, Rome had not penetrated. One of Augustus' earliest steps after gaining power in 31 B.C. was to conquer that area; and, *Map 4*

93

whatever other reasons may also have prompted this conquest, it is certain that the wish to exploit the gold was prominent. For the mining operations which were afterwards carried out there show beyond doubt that, although the yield of Spanish gold from the southern districts had in earlier times been very rich, these newly worked goldfields in the north-west bore comparison with the richest goldfields of any previous civilization. Their output, according to Pliny, averaged about 20,000 Roman pounds of gold a year; and his detailed account of imperial gold-mining, based most probably on information from mining engineers in Spain, shows with what care and resolution the Spanish mines were systematically worked. His account deserves full quotation.

In the world of today gold is found in three ways. . . . First, in the sediment of rivers, like the Spanish Tagus . . . , purer than any other gold and polished by attrition in the running stream. Otherwise it is dug out by sinking shafts, or gained by the destruction of mountains. Let me explain both methods. Those who seek gold first of all remove the surface earth which has indicated gold. Underneath is a deposit of sand: this is washed, and an estimate of yield is formed from the gold precipitate. Sometimes, by uncommon good luck, gold is found immediately in the topsoil. . . . The name 'canalicium' (or, according to others, 'canaliense') is given to gold mined from shafts. It appears shot through the marble gravels [i.e. quartz] . . . embracing the marble particles. The veins wander this way and that in channels along the sides of the shafts—hence the name 'channel gold'. The earthy roof of these shafts is held up by wooden props. When they have dug out the ore they crush it and wash it and burn it and reduce it to powder. The refuse which is thrown out of the furnace—they call it 'scoria'—in the case of gold is crushed and heated again: the furnaces themselves are made from . . . a white earth like potter's clay, for this is the only sub-stance that can bear the blast of the fire and the incandescence of the gold.

The third method of mining may seem to surpass the achievements of the Giants. For by the light of lanterns mountains are hollowed out by galleries driven deeply into them. Lamps are also used to measure the length of the miners' shifts, for many of them do not see daylight in months together. Mines of this kind they call 'arrugiae'. Fissures can suddenly open up and crush the miners [i.e. with roof-falls] . . . and so arches are left at frequent intervals to hold the mountains up. In these mines—and in the shaft-mines too—flint is met with, and the miners break it up by using first fire and then vinegar: more often, because the galleries thus become full of suffocating steam and smoke, they break it with iron rams of 150 lb. weight. The pieces are carried out, night and day, on their shoulders in the darkness along a human chain: only the last in the chain see daylight. When all is ready they cut the 'keystones' of the arches, beginning with the innermost. The earth on top subsides, and gives a signal, and a solitary look-out on a peak of the hill observes it. With shouts and gestures he orders the mine to be evacuated, and he himself speeds down as well. The mountain then breaks and falls apart with a roar that the mind can hardly conceive, and with an equally incredible blast of air.

But even then, as Pliny went on to say, there was no certainty of finding gold-ore in the debris; and, if it were present, enormously difficult work still lay ahead. Water had to be brought, in strong streams and substantial volume, and often from far-distant sources, to wash the fallen material: reservoirs to contain it had to be built, so that the force with which it fell on to the ore could be controlled; and, after the washing, the water had to be carefully canalized as it flowed away, so that the gold should not be lost. Sluice-boxes were therefore constructed in the drainage trenches; and these boxes were filled with a shrub like rosemary, which trapped the gold, while the rocky residuum flowed down into the nearest available stream below the level of the operations, thence to find its way ultimately to the sea, which, as Pliny recorded, was already being driven out by the accumulation of silt. The 'rosemary' was periodically collected and dried and burned, and the ash was washed finally on a bed of turf which caught the gold.

Apart from the washing of gold from such rivers as the Tajo and Douro, the technique of which was as old as human tradition, the other and major operations described by Pliny were apparently of a scale and a complexity which exceeded anything before their time. The Romans were notoriously good engineers, and in Spain they could enjoy an advantage denied to the mines in Egypt about which Diodorus wrote—namely, a very good and powerful supply of water. This, of course, brought hazards of its own, since faulting in the levels that were being excavated must often have resulted in more or less serious flooding, against which (as archaeological remains show) the water-wheel and the Archimedian screw—each worked, of course, by human labour—were cumbrously employed. But it was also a great benefit, alike in the washing of crushed ore and in the removal of the washed residuum, and it enabled the Roman engineers to undertake the mining of Spanish gold on a colossal scale.

In one single shaft-mined area in Asturias, for example, it is estimated that some 30,000,000–40,000,000 tons of rock were treated: in another, in Galicia, estimates put the weight of quartz removed for crushing from a single large shaft at around 5,000,000 tons. Even more impressive, perhaps, was the scale of the operations which, for Pliny, 'surpassed the achievements of the Giants'. For these were designed to extract gold from high-level alluvial terraces of great antiquity, dating from those remote millennia when great floods and vast rivers covered the earth and excoriated its growing mountains. In these the material to be broken up was relatively soft, and elsewhere Pliny's detailed account makes it plain that water was

95

conducted to the site of these 'collapsed mountains' in such a way that it could play on the debris at selected points from a great height—anything from 400 to 800 feet, to judge from the present aspect of typical sites. As a result of the power which nature so generously provided, the Romans were thus able to treat enormous areas of old alluvial terraces for gold extraction. Even if a modern estimate of 500,000,000 tons may be thought too high the total, in the long period during which Spanish gold-mining continued, must nevertheless have been astonishingly large, and it becomes easier to understand Pliny's reference to coastal silting at the mouth of rivers which were nothing more or less than drainage channels for mining effluent.

The mines of north-west Spain were not the only source of Spanish gold, for the Sierra Morena (named after Sextus Marius, from whom the Emperor Tiberius expropriated his prolific industry there) also produced it in quantity; and in many parts of Spain it could easily be washed from rivers with equipment varying from the most primitive pan to a specially designed 'rocker' with a ribbed or pebbled bottom to catch the heavy particles as they settled. But the north-west was, without question, the principal source, and it was there that the mining techniques which were first acutely developed in Egypt were brought to a new stage of excellence. Prospecting, as always in the absence of instruments to make test-bores, remained a matter for the skilled eye. In matters, however, of drainage, propping, the firing and splitting of quartz, and the water-powered disintegration of previously undermined reefs the Romans made swift advance, and the rate of gold extraction appears to have been high, with little wastage. Their sedulous application met with a rich reward. The gold of Spain continued to be mined, in greater or lesser quantities, until the gold of America was discovered. Mined as the Romans mined it, Spanish gold probably furnished the richest single item of mineral income within the wide limits of the Empire; and it was natural that the control and supervision of gold-mines (no less than of silver and iron, of which fairly full administrative details survive) should have been kept jealously as the personal concern of the emperors.

A large and regular influx of gold to the treasury was, indeed, the only means by which, in a bimetallic world well supplied with silver, the relative prices of the two metals could be kept in fairly stable adjustment in terms of a currency which comprised great quantities of both gold aurei and silver denarii. It is difficult, today, to make even a rough estimate of the gold put into imperial circulation in the form of coin, for

CS BALTHASSAR + SCS MELCHIOR + SCS CASPAR

40　The three Magi; part of lower mosaic frieze in nave,
St Apollinare Nuovo, Ravenna: 6th century A.D.

41   The Pantocrator; dome mosaic, St Mary Pammakaristos, Constantinople: early 14th century

the gold coins of one age, if they are good in quality, will always tend to be melted down in another which may seem likely to debase its own gold coins. And the gold coinage of the Roman Empire was, with occasional exceptions, of remarkable purity: changes in gold‑silver ratios were handled either by varying the quantity of gold coined, or by debasement (and it was, in time, progressive) of the silver. Thus the gold coins of Augustus were as nearly fine as contemporary technology could make them, containing only about 2 or 3 per cent of alloy, and the majority of subsequent emperors down to the third century strove to keep to a standard which, if not always quite so high, was seldom very much lower.

Production of a gold coinage of such purity in bulk must plainly have eaten up supplies of gold bullion at a swift and steady pace. Yet more was undoubtedly immobilized in articles of jewellery and splendour manu‑ **Plate 37** factured for purchase within the Empire itself. Such treasures as that of the Boscoreale villa at Pompeii, with its hoard of gold coins and its massive silver plate, show the scale on which a magnate could live. There were guilds of goldsmiths at Rome under the Empire, and goldsmiths naturally existed in all large centres of population. Technically their work—judged by the Roman imperial jewellery that has survived—was of good quality, and derived from the previous Hellenistic traditions: the majority of these goldsmiths, indeed, were of Greek or Syrian origin. But for this same reason the stylistic quality of their work was usually not high, as they were producing, for a rich, usually uncritical and often even vulgar clientele in Rome and other great cities, gold‑work in which a traditionally Hellenistic style could too often be debased by an access of coarse fussiness or overloading or both.

Thus the splendid and often lovely gold coinage which the emperors poured out from Augustus onwards provides in a sense the best reflection of their wealth in gold, and especially in Spanish gold. This coinage is often superb in its technique, for the soft, sensitive yet luminous quality of gold lent itself with a special beauty to the Roman artists' particular skill in portraiture. This is to be seen in numberless examples of a long series extending over centuries; but if isolated pieces were to be quoted one might look to the delicate yet god‑like head of Augustus himself—this, **Plate 34a** certainly, by a Greek artist; to the short‑lived soldier‑emperor Galba—the **Plate 34b** very type of the hard‑bitten patrician; to Postumus, usurper in Gaul, **Plate 34c** gleaming and almost rubicund; or to the house of Constantine the Great, represented in an altogether new version of imperial remoteness and **Plate 34d** grandeur. There might be public guilds of goldsmiths, and indeed goldsmiths might even work privately for millionaire patrons; but the stream of imperial gold money was probably the clearest, as it was perhaps also the finest, reflection of the Empire's wealth in gold. It was for this reason, surely, as much as for any other, that the punitive laws against counterfeiting were devised under the Empire, with a severity which did not diminish as supplies of gold became increasingly difficult to obtain.

New sources, of course, were tapped from time to time; and, if the Augustan gold booty from Egypt and the organization of the Spanish mines by Augustus and his successors can claim to be two of the paramount factors hitherto in the establishment of Roman imperial gold supply, Trajan's conquest of Dacia provides a third. The richness and productivity of the whole Carpathian area of the North Balkans from very early times was noted in a previous chapter. So far Rome, while extending her control along the southern bank of the Danube down to the Black Sea, had been unable (or rather, had thought it imprudent—in the light of her army strength) to indulge in any extended campaigning, let alone annexation, north of the Danube. But Dacian tribes had demonstrated more and more their willingness to harry Roman possessions south of it: for this alone they merited inevitable attack and conquest. Thus, in the early years of the second century A.D., Trajan turned upon them, and in so doing secured (as he had no doubt hoped he would) a fresh gold source of legendary fame. The immediate dividends were to be seen in his capture of a vast royal treasure. Figures given by Johannes Lydus put this at 5,000,000 Roman pounds of gold and 10,000,000 Roman pounds of silver. Perhaps they are wildly exaggerated—perhaps even, as has been suggested, the true figures have been mistakenly multiplied by ten. But if they have the total is still impressive and enormous: 500,000 Roman pounds of gold would at this time have been enough to produce 2,250,000 gold coins, quite apart from the similar service rendered by 1,000,000 Roman pounds of silver in furnishing over 90,000,000 denarii. This, however, was not all, for by his Dacian conquest Trajan gained control of a large complex of very rich mines which, if not so productive as those of Spain, had at least yielded enough in the shape of the royal treasure to make them well worth the systematic organization which Rome could impose on them in the future.

The conquest of Dacia and the subsequent influx of Dacian gold after A.D. 106 may indeed have given an almost unwelcome shock to the Roman economy. There is evidence that between A.D. 97 and 127 the price of gold dropped by 3 per cent. It has been argued that the evidence for this drop—a comparatively sharp one in an age when the price of gold so obviously tended to be fixed by the emperors' mining monopolies —has in fact been misconstrued by omitting the cost elements of work-manship and distribution. On balance, however, it would seem that the absolute value of gold did decline and that if its value in terms of silver was to be maintained at the now normal ratio of $1 : 12\frac{1}{2}$–13, some manipulation of the silver would be necessary in consequence. In fact the alloy content of silver coins under Trajan tended to rise, doubtless because it was found necessary to increase the amount of silver in circulation to a figure which, independently of the royal booty, could guarantee the normal gold-silver ratio in this way. Roman economy, like that of the Greeks before, was irregular, opportunist and undoctrinaire. New factors were faced as they came; and the flood of gold which poured suddenly from Dacia had to be absorbed by methods suddenly devised to suit that situation in isolation.

Various causes contributed to an increasing strain on the Roman economy in the third and fourth centuries after Christ. The taste for luxury resulted in the constant immobilization of gold in the form of decoration, plate and jewellery, and also in the steady drain of gold over the frontiers, not only to the east now but also to the north, presumably for furs and amber. A cycle of political or strategic crises encouraged further immobilization by means of hoarding. And meanwhile no new sources of gold were found that compared with those that had blessed and relieved the earlier days of the Empire. Indeed, the power of Parthia, which had always been a grim threat, increased to the point at which a Roman emperor could be captured in person with his army, and it is to be supposed that less and less gold could reach Rome from the miscellaneous eastern sources which had fed her before. The general situation is clearly mirrored in the coinage of the third century. Prices were rising, and one means of counterbalancing this plainly lay in a further debasement of silver coinage, which was increasingly resorted to; and this in turn affected the quantity and quality of the gold in circulation. The gold clearly showed the strain; at times its volume was small and its purity very low, and it could scarcely claim to be the metal on the universality of which other metal values depended.

Then suddenly, under Constantine the Great in the first half of the fourth century, the situation changed, and gold coinage began to be issued in quantities that in the second half of the century rose to an extremely high volume. The source of this gold is hard to define. Nothing is known of the exploitation of any new mining areas, or of the specially profitable secondary working of old ones. In the case of Constantine the explanation may possibly lie in the protection which he gave officially to the Christian Church, from which he is said to have accepted baptism before his death although he had been content to recognize a miraculous battle vision many years earlier. He may well have taken advantage of the visible decay of the old paganism to impound the treasures in precious metal that had been stored, immemorially, in numberless pagan temples. For his successors the explanation is altogether simpler, since it is known that the imperial government insisted increasingly on the payment of taxes and other dues in the form of gold.

A later writer was to compare this system with the terrors of the Last Judgement itself; and certainly the rigours and the severity were great. The trading classes had to pay a quinquennial levy in gold and silver (in the case of one eastern city this could amount to 140 Roman pounds of gold); a proportion of the land-tax was levied in gold; 'voluntary' offerings of congratulation, celebrating imperial accessions and anniversaries, were in fact forced levies payable in gold, as when Valentinian II, in A.D. 384, was voted 1600 pounds. By such methods as this the emperors of the late fourth and early fifth centuries A.D. contrived to maintain their stocks of gold. It was imperative that they should do so, for not only was military loyalty in the upper ranks of the army dependent on the payment of salaries in gold but—much more serious—gold was the only means of buying off the active and immediate hostility of the powerful nations and tribes that were pressing inexorably at a dozen points around the frontiers, awaiting the opportunity of bursting in upon a moribund empire. The principle of such subsidies had been recognized long ago in the first century A.D. by Domitian, in conciliating those Dacians whom Trajan later conquered; but the drain on Roman gold through subsidies in the late Empire was much greater and much more serious, for it could end only with the final collapse of the Roman Empire, and that collapse was brought inevitably nearer by the loss of such important areas as Dacia itself, which had done so much in its time to sustain the costs of imperial administration.

It is impossible to guess the quantity of gold drained off in the period of the late Empire, between about A.D. 350 and 450, in the form of subsidies to conciliate the barbarian nations just across the frontiers. Some of it may have gone in the form of gold bars, officially stamped, like those which have survived from the Balkan mint of Sirmium in the late fourth century. Much may well have been paid out in gold coinage, easily counted, easily divided, and easily melted down. Yet more took

Plate 36

the form of magnificent gold medallions bearing the imperial portrait —a subsidy payment in fact but, on the surface at least, an honorific presentation from the emperor of Rome to his 'friends' outside the frontiers. Medallions of this kind have been found, in groups, in just those areas where they might be expected: apart from four such groups found within the imperial boundaries the others belong either to its very fringes, as at Velp (near Arnhem) and Morenhoven (near Bonn), or—much more significantly—to external districts: Ó-Szöny in Hungary, Borča in Jugoslavia, Szilágy-Sómlyó in Rumania, and (even farther afield) three find-spots recorded in recent years in Poland all testify to the diffusion of Roman gold in this way among people from whom Rome was buying time. The device was effective until the middle of the fifth century A.D., when the frontiers burst, the tribes poured in from Central Europe, and the western half of the Roman Empire collapsed, leaving its tradition to be continued in the eastern half still securely centred on Constantinople.

Plate 35

With this collapse, it must be supposed, very great quantities of gold now passed from the ownership of citizens of the Empire to the invaders from Central Europe. Men might at first hoard their own privately owned gold coins, and communities might conceal their communal treasures of gold. But the economic hardship that comes swiftly on the heels of interruption in administration, communication and commerce cannot be resisted indefinitely; and it would not have been long before such gold came out of hiding, to be traded off discreetly for whatever advantages it would bring, And even now, after five centuries in which Rome had been spending her gold abroad in ample quantities, the amount existing within the confines of the Empire must have been very large. Estimates of gold production within those confines in those five centuries naturally vary widely; the immense riches coming from Spain have to be offset against a sharp decline in the yield of both Egypt and Asia Minor. But it must not be forgotten that Rome herself had inherited a major part of the world's gold stocks already in existence when she consolidated her huge empire: the amount of gold mined under Roman control in the first five centuries of the Christian era, however great, was only an accession to what had been mined and made up in the previous four millennia B.C. Nor should it be forgotten that, with all the emphasis laid—and rightly laid—upon the major sources of Roman gold such as Spain and Dacia, there were small prospectors and miners and alluvial washers in a thousand different areas, all swelling the total to some extent even if the proceeds were not invariably caught by the wide net of imperial administration.

Thus, even if Roman-controlled output of gold perhaps did not exceed that of the Graeco-Persian period (and it might even have fallen short of it), the addition of Roman to pre-Roman stocks must have resulted in a most formidable accumulation, which the steady drain of gold to east and north, while it certainly diminished the amount in Roman hands, could not for a long time reduce to a really dangerous level.

The age of Rome had been, increasingly, an age of luxury, based on secure strategy, provinces rich for exploitation, reciprocal trading on a world-wide basis, and an ample supply of slave-labour. Horace, at the very beginning of the Empire, had seen clearly under Augustus which way things would go.

> Gold, gold can pass the tyrant's sentinel,
> Can shiver rocks with more resistless blow
> Than is the thunder's. Argos' prophet fell,
>   He and his house laid low,
> And all for gain. The man of Macedon
> Cleft gates of cities, rival kings o'erthrew
> By force of gifts: their cunning snares have won
>   Rude captains and their crew.
> As riches grow, care follows: men repine
> And thirst for more.

The world extension of gold coinage, from Horace's day onwards, had put a new form of Roman wealth into the widest public possession; and now, after 500 years, that great accumulated store of wealth was to change hands.

Chapter VI

EBB AND FLOW
IN THE DARK AND MIDDLE AGES

At the moment of the collapse of the Roman Empire in the West gold had been used for over 4000 years to balance economies and to measure and store wealth. It had been sought with growing eagerness in numberless places: elaborately mined, or washed in the simplest fashion, it had been recognized over an immense area—stretching certainly from India to Britain, and from South Russia to Ethiopia—as a metal to be prized not only for its relative scarcity but also for its ease of working and its intrinsic beauty.

During this long period of time world stocks had steadily accumulated to a massive figure. There had been fluctuations in production: the high peak of Egyptian output was probably not matched by anything equally conspicuous until the Roman organization of the Spanish mines, and, just as the output of Egypt steadily declined towards Graeco-Roman times, so too other areas—western Asia Minor and Macedon, for example—declined to ultimate exhaustion. But the stocks accumulated: even allowing for hoarding, and the occasional loss of hoards, there was, in a literal sense, more and more gold in the world.

Its form might be constantly changing, of course. A Roman gold coin could well contain gold from Eastern or Egyptian treasures, or from earlier Greek gold coins, or even from earlier Roman gold coins or Roman jewellery, just as the gold in a modern ring may possess an infinitely mixed pedigree. But this was due simply to the virtual imperishability of gold. Short of throwing it into the sea, or hiding it in total inaccessibility, men could scarcely get rid of the gold which the world held. With the decline of one power and the growth of another it was always on the move, its economic centre of gravity varying from time to time. Such transitions, however, had not normally been very abrupt; and it is doubtful if the use and availability of gold had ever previously been subjected to the shocks and interruptions of uncertainty, fear and sheer loss of technical culture which beset the Western Empire of Rome from the fifth century onwards.

It is difficult for the keenest imagination to conceive the speed and chaos which marked the barbarian invasions of Europe at this time. Ever since historical record began there had been movement and pressure from the Asiatic east. The earliest Graeco-Persian times witnessed great waves of tribal migration pushing down the Caucasus into Asia Minor. Rome, on a dozen occasions, was faced with the mounting danger of tribes in South-eastern and Central Europe (Sarmati, Iazyges, Alani, Marcomanni and more northerly German peoples) who, always impelled from the steppes by some new impulse generated by remoter Asiatic hordes, strained to burst across the Rhine and Danube frontiers. Already there had been serious incursions. At the end of the fourth century the Visigoths had ravaged Greece and, under Alaric, passed from Greece to Italy, with-drawing from there to Gaul and then to Spain only when Rome was pillaged and Alaric himself dead. Gaul itself, in the early fifth century, had been invaded also by the Alani, Suevi and Burgundi. The Burgundi settled easily in the Rhône valley—the Roman policy of subsidy and 'friendship' brought a curious dividend in the ease with which they adopted a romanized existence there; to meet the others the Emperor Honorius had to buy the help of the Visigoths themselves, at the price of Aquitania. Spain finally absorbed the Alani, Suevi and Vandals, the last of whom crossed into Roman Africa. In northern Gaul the pressure came from the Merovingian Franks, who, though they successfully supported Rome against yet another (and far more terrible) menace from Attila and the Huns, ended up in control of all Gaul save Burgundy, until even Burgundy fell to them later. Thus the three greatest provincial areas of the Roman west, Gaul, Spain and Africa, were lost: Britain had been given up earlier; Italy had already served as a corridor for invaders, and the Balkan provinces north-west of Greece proper were yet another gateway along which fresh migrations were to travel into the ferment of Central Europe, where the arrows drawn upon the ethnologist's map form, at this time, a pattern of the most fluid and restless change.

The effects of this catastrophic sequence upon the production and behaviour of gold in what had been Roman Europe were simple and sharp. With the collapse of Roman civil and military administration the mines were left without skilled labour, transport, or a centralized market. There was now no organized labour corps to dig the ore and refine the gold. There was no system of long-distance transport, under safe custody, to take the heavy and costly consignments of bullion from the provinces to Rome. The ability of Rome, as a central market, to absorb and then distribute supplies of newly won gold had disappeared. It must be supposed that the mining of gold in Europe, as it had been practised under the Roman Empire, came virtually to an end. Certainly there is no reliable evidence of its steady continuation anywhere: shafts and galleries were probably abandoned to rising flood-waters, or left to the initiative of free-lance miners working dangerously for what they could get. The output of gold, naturally, is not likely to have ceased entirely in any major area. Even if the intruders knew nothing of deep mining, or found the pits ruined and flooded, they could still scratch about on a thousand slag-heaps; and apart from this there was always gold to be got by washing from the rivers. If nearly 800 lb. could be extracted from the rivers of Spain in a single year in the nineteenth century of our own era the yield throughout the fifth century need not have been negligible. Then, again, there was loot; to this could be added the volume of gold coinage actually in circulation, besides what the invaders themselves possessed on their arrival. The fact that Roman legislation in the fourth century had penalized those who traded gold privately to barbarians across the frontiers suggests (though it cannot prove) that some quantity had already got into barbarian hands, apart from what was paid over by way of subsidy.

In general, the picture which seems to emerge is that, although the previous Roman-controlled flow of gold had effectively stopped, the invaders possessed some quantity of it. For, easily taking over the habit of gold currency, they started coinages of their own in gold with very little delay, and by doing so (and producing gold coins of quite good quality) they almost certainly would have succeeded in setting free much gold currency which, until then, had been hoarded away out of fear and lack of confidence. The Visigoths in Spain and the Burgundians in France both coined in gold towards the end of the fifth century A.D., and in fair quantity. From the early sixth century onwards the Merovingian Franks coined even more. Mints for gold were set up in many places: some were operated by civic authorities, some by the churches, and some by the kings themselves—including Theodebert I (534–47), who summoned up courage enough to banish from his coins the almost sacredly traditional portrait and name of the Byzantine emperors, ruling far off at Constanti-nople, in favour of his own. It is interesting to note that the mature distribution of the Merovingian mints of the sixth century showed special coining activity northward from Marseilles, up the Rhône valley to Chalons-sur-Saône and thence to Paris, the Lower Rhine and the English Channel. In a period of ruptured communications and regroupings the immemorially old route from the Mediterranean to northern France was still active, and it is likely enough that considerable quantities of Byzantine gold coinage travelled through Gaul along this route, having been first carried to Italy and thence to Marseilles.

It is right to emphasize this continuation of gold currency in the West after the Roman collapse, for it is a clear index of both the availability and also the use of gold at that time. The new movement of gold momentarily touched even Britain, which, cut off from Roman administration since about A.D. 425 and systematically weakened by successive waves of Jutish and Saxon invasion, appears to have sunk into an economic plight which the glittering legend of Arthurian chivalry may redeem but cannot conceal. Late in the sixth century gold began to enter Britain. When Ethelbert of Kent married the Princess Bertha, daughter of Charibert I who reigned at Paris from 561 to 567, the Christian bride set up the little shrine at St Martin at Canterbury, where the gold coins and medallions subsequently found include one with the portrait and name of her private chaplain and confessor, Bishop Leudard. London

Plate 38a itself was coining gold soon after A.D. 600, probably from an ecclesiastical mint; and the famous Crondall hoard of Anglo-Saxon gold coins shows that by about 650 gold coinage in England was coming from a number of different mints. The coinage of Kent was perhaps the most profuse; there the quantity of gold coined may have been for a time quite large.

Here again, therefore, coinage serves as a very useful guide to the frequency of gold in circulation and the directions which it took in commerce. Without such a guide the evidence would be scanty indeed. Abandoned mines give no archaeological evidence. Literary references are very few and unhelpful. And the jewellery which has survived is (considering the wide area of Europe that is involved) very small in quantity. Nevertheless, it is from the jewellery that remaining details of the picture of gold in the West must be drawn. Its motifs and its general treatment are very often unroman; but its level of technical skill, at any rate down to about A.D. 700, is such as to suggest that the delicate working of gold, an art handed down age by age from ancient Egypt to a decadent Rome, was admired and prized by the new 'barbarian' kings. Indeed, the fact that so great a distinction exists between the high technical skill of gold jewellery and the frequently debased techniques of much of the work in bronze suggests almost that the possession of gold ornaments must have been something in the nature of a prerogative of kings and nobles, whose wealth, treasured in this special form, was worked up into objects of frequently great beauty by the best surviving skill of the day. There is an obvious contrast between the scale of the work undertaken at this time and that of the Graeco-Roman era. Then the possession of many a small object of delicately wrought gold—ear-rings especially, together of course with bracelets and neck-chains and small pendants—lay within the reach of large numbers of fairly wealthy owners. Now the range of ownership appears to be restricted to a few, whose possessions in gold were not only substantial in actual size but also of frequently remarkable magnificence in relation to other metal-work of the time.

Among the earliest objects are those of the 'treasure of Childeric', the effective founder of the Merovingian dynasty in Gaul, who was buried in A.D. 481 at Tournai in a tomb, afterwards quite forgotten, which a labourer found by accident in 1653. Childeric's regalia was buried with him—the influence of Christianity was not yet always strong enough to persuade men that they could more easily pass through a needle's eye than take their earthly wealth to the next world; and, together with a sword, bracelet, buckles, etc., there were 300 golden bees (part of Childeric's personal store of gold converted into decoration for his robe of State) and a signet-ring of gold. Every object in this treasure was inlaid with garnet or red glass in the cloisonné manner, by which the base of a gold object is covered with a pattern of small cells formed by thin, up-standing party walls to enclose the inlaid stones. The cloisonné setting of garnets and other semi-precious stones was a feature that characterized much of the jewellery produced in the West between A.D. 500 and 700. The technique, of course, had come originally from Egypt and the East in much more ancient times, and had been employed by countless generations of goldsmiths ever since, right down to those who fashioned the cloisonné work found in the fourth-century 'Petrossa treasure' of the Balkans. But it now rose to a remarkable peak of splendour and beauty. And there were, naturally, special arguments in its favour: a jewel or ornament with cloisonné inlay combined economy of gold with brilliance of effect. This is well seen in early Anglo-Saxon cloisonné work, which perhaps owed its greatness to the desire of invading kings and chieftains to take advantage, in such royal metal as they could come by, of the traditional skill of sub-Roman jewellers. The sumptuous circular brooches from Sarre and Kingston gleam with dark richness: these were the possessions of great and noble figures in their time, just as the jewellery in the ship-burial found in 1939 at Sutton Hoo had evidently been made for kingly state and pleasure. In the latter there were, all told, over 4000 individually cut garnets, each polished flat to a level at which it would lie perfectly flush with the tops of the surrounding 'cloison' walls; and it has been estimated professionally that (garnet being brittle) this feat alone, apart from the

Plate 43

Plate 47

task of forming the gold base and gold 'cloisons' for each object, must have taken substantially more than 4000 working days.

These, then, were the golden jewels of kings, fashioned, by means of inherited Graeco-Roman skill, with complete assurance. Garnet and glass inlay might be a means of economy in gold; but the effect was rich and luminous and graceful, and later jewellers, as in the nineteenth century, were to realize in their turn the immense elegance with which garnets and gold can be combined. Elsewhere than in northern France and Britain the need to economize in gold was not, perhaps, so pressing; and in Spain, to judge from the great 'treasure of Guarrazar' found in 1858 near Toledo, gold may have been used in fair quantity for the adornment of the Visigothic kings, for this treasure included eleven crowns of pure gold, variously set with precious and semi-precious stones. These crowns appear to have been royal dedications, for the names of two kings—Swinthila (621–31) and Recceswinth (649–72)—hung from their massive gold circlets in the form of dangling golden letters inlaid with cloisonné work (the circlets themselves were adorned with many pearls and sapphires) and underneath the crown of Recceswinth there hung also a great gold cross, $4\frac{1}{2}$ inches long and $2\frac{1}{2}$ inches wide, again set with the largest of pearls and sapphires. No doubt jewellery made in Spain could, even now, make more use of gold than was possible for the remoter Frankish and Anglo-Saxon courts: the gold of Spain could not disappear in a moment. And presumably it was the sea-routes of the Mediterranean that could bring to the Visigothic kings in Spain the more precious Eastern gems, via Constantinople and Italy, which farther north in Gaul and Britain had to be replaced by garnets and glass.

The Christian character of the Guarrazar treasure is a reminder of the extent to which patronage in the making of gold jewellery or ornament had passed from the ordinary rich citizen of the Graeco-Roman world into the hands of the new kings of Western Europe, by whom the Church was fostered. Many a priest of that age was trained in some handicraft, and many became artists of the highest skill, whose talent, when it did not adorn abbey or monastery, was at the service of the royal power. Thus Eligius—St Eloi of France—served the Merovingian dynasty both as cleric and goldsmith in the early seventh century, after receiving his training in metal-work from the great Abbo of Limoges; and later on many a cathedral or abbey, such as Ely and St Albans in England, was to be the centre of a goldsmiths' school. Cause and effect are easily to be seen. Gold in general was very scarce. Such as there was would, normally, find its way

Plate 38b

into royal possession. Some would be used, as Childeric used it, for personal regalia (the quantity of which would increase as Christian teaching increasingly argued against its burial, reign by reign). But some, again, would be held as a royal reserve; and the making of golden objects for dedication within the sanctity of a church satisfied the problem of safe-keeping no less than the desire to honour God and gain repute as a champion of the Christian faith. A good deal of work in gold was therefore carried out in the tranquillity of the cloister, the occasional remoteness of which may perhaps explain why the style of jewellery could sometimes be very conservative in an age when so many new influences were sweeping Europe. For example, the imposing gold and cloisonné-garnet pectoral cross of St Cuthbert, buried with him at Durham in A.D. 687, is a technically poor echo of the infinitely finer Anglo-Saxon cloisonné work of a century or more before—if, indeed, it is not itself an inferior older piece taken over, and perhaps repaired, for Cuthbert's later use.

From about 500 to 700, therefore, there are good reasons for supposing that, although the supply of newly mined gold in Western Europe fell away almost to vanishing point, there was sufficient gold in general possession to allow the continuation of gold currencies in France and Spain, to encourage the brief revival of similar gold currency in Britain, and to give scope for the still quite varied and often highly skilled activities of jewellers and goldsmiths. Gold for these purposes would have been secured from existing stocks of currency in the West, from the melting down of older treasure of different sorts, from the continued washing of western rivers (especially in Spain, France and the western Alps), and also, without doubt, from the importation of some quantity at least of gold from the eastern Mediterranean, whether in the form of Byzantine coins or as bullion direct from Egypt or (via Syria) Arabia. But there were already signs that the gold supply, in any case seriously diminished, could not keep pace in Western Europe with the expanding economies of the new powers now consolidated there. For although one school of historical thought holds that the West in this period still enjoyed a comparative wealth of gold, Western currency gives a very different picture.

Already rising prices—and probably the scarcity of gold as well—had resulted in the reduction of the standard unit of gold coinage to a weight only one third of what it had been under the Roman Empire. And when it is seen, towards A.D. 700, that the Merovingian coinage of France declines from gold into silver (a process exactly repeated in the short-lived gold currency of Britain) the answer must be, simply, that there was not enough gold available generally either to furnish or to guarantee an economy based on gold coins. The few reliable records that exist of monetary transactions after the middle of the sixth century make it quite clear that large monetary payments in gold became rarer. It is true that, even after A.D. 700, a little gold was still coined in the West. The Lombard kings were minting some gold in Italy, and gold could still be coined for exceptional purposes elsewhere, for example, in Britain. Offa, King of Mercia (757–96) struck a little gold in the form of Arab dinars, and gold coins, now unique, also exist of Archbishop Wigmund of York (837–54), King Edward the Elder (900–25), Ethelred II (979–1016) and Edward the Confessor (1042–66). But these were the special productions necessary either to pay the 'Rome-scot' to the Holy See or for presentation to lesser dignitaries, and there is strong significance in their immense rarity: even the dominions of Charlemagne himself, after he had assumed the crown of the Holy Roman Empire, appear to have acquired a gold currency much less extensive than would have been expected of so powerful a territorial unit. The supply of gold in the West had reached a point of scarcity at which gold currency in the true sense became impossible and even jewellery became very rare; and this Western lack of gold was in fact to continue more or less acutely for five centuries from c. A.D. 700.

There was a very good and simple reason why, from this date, gold in the West should decline to a trickle. The Byzantine Empire in the East, unshaken by the collapse of the Roman half of the world, had embarked on a period of commercial prosperity (if not always combined with territorial power) as a result of which Constantinople rapidly became the centre to which gold was normally attracted by every device at her disposal. To a very great extent the story of Rome in relation to gold is repeated in that of Constantinople. A large and constant importation of luxuries had to be paid for in gold. Constantinople might, indeed, pride herself on her own luxury industries. Her textiles—cotton, linen and (above all) silk—were world-famous: silk was at first imported raw, and made up at Constantinople, but the demand for it grew so quickly that home production of silkworms was established, the main silk factory being situated actually within the emperor's palace. And besides textiles there was Byzantine metal-work, again of great renown, together with a mass of other industries. But the articles of luxury made at Constantinople often stayed at Constantinople: the best was reserved, in particular, for the imperial court and the enrichment of a growing number of increasingly magnificent churches, and could not be used as exports to balance the cost of all the imports, whether of luxury or necessity, that were brought in: Chinese silk, Indian ivory and jewels and spices, Persian carpets and Russian furs. These, and a long list of other imports as well, could be paid for only in gold.

It was natural, therefore, that the maintenance of a large and pure gold currency should be the basis of Byzantine stability; and the gold coined either at Constantinople itself, or (early on) at such major subsidiary mints as Antioch and Alexandria, was famous for its extraordinarily high purity from the time of the collapse of Rome in the fifth century right down to the eleventh. The many costly imports during this period suggest that Byzantine gold must to some extent have been obtained on very favourable terms from areas where its price was comparatively cheap. Two such areas could be exploited. The first could be tapped easily and directly, for Constantinople was well placed to receive whatever could be attracted from the perennially great resources of the Caucasus (via Colchis and Trebizond) and Central Asia (via the steppes down to Crimea); thus, for goods or services, as when Byzantine craftsmen were employed to build and fortify a Khazar town on the Sea of Azov, gold from the Urals could be released in return, while the gold of the Caucasus was open to entrepreneurs from Trebizond itself. The second area lay in Africa, and consisted of Nubia, Ethiopia and the Zambezi district. Here the trade in gold lay in the hands of Egyptians, who brought it northward either overland, down the Nile valley, or—in the case of gold from the Zambezi—by sea in Abyssinian ships. The gold of Africa, being brought from more remote sources, was naturally the more precarious supply of the two, and could indeed be cut off if Abyssinia was threatened or overrun by hostile peoples. And even in the north the menace of nomad invasion from the steppes was never far removed.

Nevertheless, even though much of the African gold probably never got much farther than Egypt and Syria—centres, at this time, of notable luxury and the greatest manufacturing activity—the Byzantine Empire was certainly assured of very large supplies by one means or another, as is shown by her long record of great prosperity and the paramount fineness of her gold coinage, so much of which was minted only to disappear for ever into Persian or Arab possession in the Levant hinterland. Cosmas Indicopleustes, a merchant writing in the sixth century A.D., attributed that prosperity to Christianity and a good coinage; and the gold for that coinage was steadily obtained. Sometimes it was swollen by booty, as when a large part of the Persian royal treasure fell into the hands of Heraclius (610–41). In the period of iconoclasm in the eighth and ninth centuries large quantities of gold were removed from churches and appropriated as State treasure. A system of taxation no less rigorous than that of the late Roman Empire was designed to extract all possible gold from the possession of private citizens. The reserves might vary and even fluctuate seriously, as when African sources were interrupted or a heavy series of annual subsidy payments (e.g. some 1000 lb. annually in the ninth century) had to be made to Persia. But the plain fact remains that, even after the Arabs had overrun Egypt in the middle of the seventh century, Byzantine gold coinage continued equally pure, however much its volume might tend to alter. Indeed, it is likely that the Arabs, enriched by Syrian and Egyptian gold booty, and thus bringing it westward in their swift passage along the north coast of Africa into Spain, actively benefited Byzantium, for the gold thus introduced into Western Europe enabled Western courts to trade it back to Constantinople for the Byzantine luxuries which they required.

Nor does the evidence of the currency stand alone. It is confirmed by the knowledge of the immense wealth in gold which could be accumulated by the Byzantine emperors themselves and even by their subjects; and the richness and profusion of the work of Byzantine goldsmiths tells the same story. The Emperor Anastasius at his death in A.D. 518 left a personal treasure of 320,000 lb. of gold. Theodora, when she handed over power to Michael III in 856, possessed 109,000 lb. Basil II, as late as the tenth century, could feel secure with a reserve of 200,000 lb. in his strong room. When, to figures such as these, there are added private holdings of gold often in the region of 2000–3000 lb., together with the great stocks of gold held as church treasure, it is clear enough both that the Byzantine Empire was rich in gold and also that this very richness—the convection of all possible gold to Constantinople as an element in her trading structure— was itself a cause of the gold famine which spread over Western Europe after about 700. The very fact that the Byzantine emperors of the sixth and seventh centuries minted light-weight gold coins which, to judge from their find-spots, flowed out from Constantinople to northern Italy, and thence over the Alps and down the Rhine valley to Friesland, suggests that although the need for trade with central and northern Europe was recognized there was no intention of liberating more gold in Europe than was strictly necessary for Byzantine convenience. This was no more than a means by which the profits of Western trade could be increased without

42 The Alfred jewel, found at Athelney, Somerset: 9th century A.D.
43 The Sarre brooch, found at Sarre, Kent: 7th century A.D.

44 The German Imperial Crown: 10th century A.D.

special cost to Constantinople; and it might normally be expected that a good proportion of the light-weight gold currency traded to the West would in any case return home in due course.

It was, nevertheless, inevitable that a consumer economy so luxuriously unbalanced as that of Byzantium should sooner or later fall into difficulties with the supply of gold; and the wonder is that Byzantine gold lasted as long as it did. Heavy imports, a remarkable scale of internal luxury, frequent and costly wars, and subsidies to foreign powers seemed for a considerable time to cause no very serious damage. But the elements of ultimate collapse were building up formidably, and serious trouble was becoming evident in the tenth century and was officially reflected in the eleventh, when the standard gold coin of the Byzantine Empire—the 'bezant' which had until then carried all before it because of its splendid purity—was suddenly alloyed up to an amount of 25 per cent. And by now there could be no recovery of the vast quantities of gold which Constantinople had been lavishly spending out for five centuries, for these had in large part fallen into the hands of those whose migratory current was flowing in a strong westerly stream along the Mediterranean. The Arab conquest of the Middle and Near East wholly dislocated the structure on which much of the previous Byzantine prosperity had been based. Moreover, the Arabs in their westward sweep quickly absorbed great accumulations of gold, some of which in other circumstances would normally have been traded back to Constantinople. Persia had employed a silver currency, and the wealth of gold which the Byzantine mint of Antioch had for so long poured into Persia through the channels of trade or subsidy had accumulated into a great gold reserve, which fell into Arab possession. In Syria, likewise, they could appropriate the great stores of gold, whether coined or in the form of luxury articles, which assiduous traders and middle-men had built up over centuries. The same applied to Egypt, where in addition there were other prizes to excite Arab cupidity. Ancient Pharaonic treasure was systematically sought out from hiding-places that still remained inviolate (one ninth-century find of such gold amounted to nearly 9000 lb.), and besides this there was immense Islamic activity in the fresh exploitation of Egyptian, Nubian and Ethiopian gold-bearing areas, not so much in the reopening of old mines as in the easier search for rich alluvial deposits.

The Arab conquest of Persia and Syria in the seventh century A.D. was immediately reflected in the establishment of a gold coinage, of great purity (about 97 per cent) and ultimately great profusion, which quickly

Plate 34e

Map 5   The medieval focus of gold

attained the status of a major international medium, ultimately rivalling and even exceeding that of Byzantium in its range and penetration. For the Arab invaders the possession of large stocks of captured gold offered either the transition to instant habits of personal luxury or the opportunity of taking from the Byzantine Empire whatever could be taken of her widespread commercial contacts. They chose the latter course, and in so doing set themselves up as a trading race of an activity and a success that was comparable only with that of the Phoenicians and Syrians, who had now for so many centuries monopolized the commercial movements along the whole southern expanse of the Mediterranean as far as the

Atlantic. At the end of the seventh century the first Arab gold coins appeared under the Caliph Abd el-Melik at Damascus, the immensely rich capital of the Ummayad dynasty: at first they imitated contemporary Byzantine types, but almost at once changed to the form in which Arabic dinars were to be famous for hundreds of years to come, not only in the Levant and Africa, but in Europe as well, with all pictorial ornament religiously excluded in favour of quotations from the Koran. The character of the Islamic coinage was not affected by the overthrow of the Ummayads by the Abbasids: indeed, the main result was that the Ummayads then spread farther westward, taking with them both gold and the habit of gold currency, until they finally crossed into Spain and set themselves up in Andalusia, where they minted gold profusely from the early tenth century onwards.

Plate 38e

By this time, however, the immense output of Arab gold coinage itself demanded the provision of gold supplies greater than could be secured either from taking over Byzantine commerce or from receiving Byzantine subsidies, or by the use of the accumulated treasure of Persia and Syria and Egypt, or even by the fresh exploitation of the gold-bearing areas of Arabia, Nubia and Ethiopia. And, although the precise chronological steps by which the necessary new sources were opened up are difficult to trace, there can be no doubt where they were. More than a thousand years earlier Herodotus had known enough about Carthaginian contacts with the African coast outside the Straits of Gibraltar to be able to describe the trade in gold which had helped to build up the power of Carthage, then and later, to such a formidable extent. Cosmas Indicopleustes, in the sixth century after Christ, had similarly been well aware of the West African wealth in gold; and it must be supposed that this had been commonplace knowledge throughout a long period of history in which the exploitation of West African gold had only been neglected because the Roman and Byzantine empires, which never in any case had the military strength to penetrate and hold more than the Mediterranean fringe of North Africa, had found ample supplies of gold nearer to hand.

But now North Africa was in the hands of a new nation, essentially mobile and essentially commercial, streaming westward, exploiting all possible means of trade, and setting up new towns which, in contrast to the primarily administrative and military character of the many Graeco-Roman foundations that studded the coast, were mainly large market centres in origin. The dates tell their own story: Tunis at the end of the seventh century, Mahdia in the middle of the eighth, Tlemcen and Fez in the

Map 5

middle of the ninth, and Marrakesh—far beyond and south of the Straits of Gibraltar—in the eleventh. Apart from Tunis these, as will be seen, were all inland towns (though Algiers, as a second large Arab port, originated in the tenth century); and this fact becomes significant when it is considered together with Arab activity much farther south, seen in the planting of new commercial centres which, like Gadames 500 miles south of Tunis and Timbuktu 1000 miles south of Marrakesh, and lying in the uppermost arc of the River Niger, pointed to a focus in the rich gold-bearing area of Nigeria and the Gold Coast.

The distances were fearsome: from Timbuktu to Gadames there lay a stretch of 1500 miles of Sahara desert. But the difficulties can easily be exaggerated, and the rigours of crossing the Sahara, for a modern European who is unaccustomed to burning, dry heat and uncertain of the reactions of his motor transport, may well be greater than they were for a nomad people equipped with the most perfect of all means of desert crossing, namely, the camel. For it was, in short, the efficiency of camel caravans that enabled this great traverse to be made; and there is no reason to think, in the light of later records, that the rewards were not disproportionate to the efforts made. Timbuktu from the eighth century became active as a collecting centre for the gold that was washed from the topmost reaches of the Niger and Senegal rivers. It was a 'city of gold', to which were brought such quantities (together with slaves and ivory and spices) that a long caravan-route across the Sahara, itself a prelude to the ultimate costs of refining and minting, was apparently well worth the trouble and initial outlay.

It is probable, indeed, that refining presented no great problem. The gold that crossed the Sahara from Nigeria to Marrakesh and Gadames, and found its way thence to Tangier and Algiers and Tripoli and Tunis for shipment north to Spain or east to Syria, was in the form of 'gold-dust'. In other words it consisted of finely ground particles of river gold which, after being washed either from the water itself or from the alluvial terraces near the rivers, was simply packed tight, and not smelted into solid masses. Such alluvial gold is usually of high purity; and, since the yield of Nigeria appears to have been very large, it is not surprising that it was sought by different sections of the Islamic world in obvious rivalry. If camels could traverse the Sahara northward with cargoes of gold they could also go eastward to the Sudan, so bringing to Egypt the gold necessary for maintaining the voluminous currency of the Fatimid dynasty, which ruled there from the tenth century. Dongola, above the third Nile cataract, had

45   Coronation crown of Richard, Earl of Cornwall, as King of the Romans: 13th century

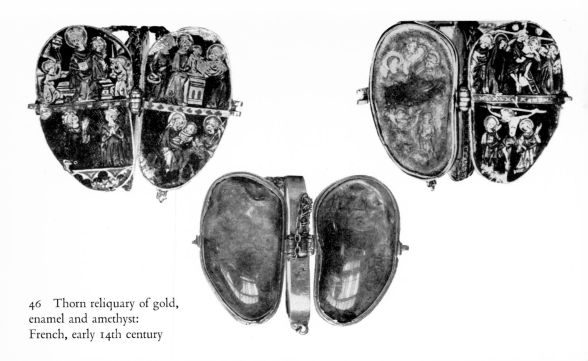

46 Thorn reliquary of gold, enamel and amethyst: French, early 14th century

47 Anglo-Saxon purse mount from the Sutton Hoo Treasure, Suffolk: 7th century A.D.

been in Arab hands from the middle of the seventh century A.D. as a strategic collection-point for all the desert routes radiating west and south through the Sudan.

Thus the sharp decline in the purity of the Byzantine gold coinage in the eleventh century occurred at a time when the Arabs had firmly established their positions and their commercial contacts from Persia to Spain, and southward to the gold of both the Nubian-Ethiopian area and also of West Africa. The gold which they inherited, in coin or uncoined treasure, had enabled the Arabs themselves to mint abundant gold from the seventh century onwards. Continuation of Arab gold currencies depended on the continued availability of fresh gold sources; and the geographical progress of Arab consolidation in Africa suggests what those sources were. What is certain is that these currencies were extended and expanded until the late Middle Ages. In Spain, naturally, the southern occupation of the Ummayad rulers and their successors accounted for the presence of very large quantities of Arab gold: no doubt the imports of African gold were to some extent swelled by the addition of more from Spain itself. Arab gold coins became common in Sicily and southern Italy. They penetrated all the confines of the eastern Mediterranean. Because the revival of gold coinage in the now firmly delineated States of Western Europe dates—suddenly in many different places—from the thirteenth century some historians have concluded that the enabling factor is to be seen in the injection of Arab gold into Western Europe before that date. Only so (they would argue) would the famous lead given by Florence in 1252 have been followed by France in 1254, England (at first abortively) in 1257, Sicily and Naples in 1278, and Venice in 1284.

Both the facts and also the theory built upon them have attracted much speculation and controversy, not least because Arab gold coins, though they were commonly current in Spain and parts of Italy, are found only rarely in France and England. And other factors have been pointed out, of which the most important is that the Crusades, from the twelfth century onwards, must certainly have been responsible for bringing considerable quantities of gold coin and treasure from the Levant to Western Europe. This is obviously beyond dispute; but the coincidence between the full flush of Arab gold coinage on the one hand and the institution of a number of European gold currencies on the other is nevertheless very striking. For it is not as if the new gold currencies of Europe were all thin, or stillborn, as that of England at first was. Florence and Venice in particular minted gold in extraordinarily large quantities—so large, in fact,

Plate 38c, d that their respective florins and ducats quickly gained the status of an international exchange medium. It might be argued that the gold of which they were made could have come from newly discovered or newly exploited sources in Europe itself: gold was being washed, for example, from the Rhine valley, the Black Forest, Silesia, Thuringia and Bohemia in the thirteenth century. It is very doubtful, however, if the yield from such sources could possibly have provided the material for coinages on such a scale. The period of maximum European productivity in gold was still to come, in the course of the fourteenth and fifteenth centuries. In the thirteenth, so far as can be discerned, the bulk of the world's fluid supplies of gold was controlled or distributed by the Islamic powers of the Levant and North Africa. Its distribution was carried out in the course of commerce with Europe—a commerce which was so fruitful that the nascent powers of Europe were not slow to analyse its basic security: a Florentine map of the mid-fourteenth century could say, of the African Guinea coast, 'here gold is collected'; and Venetian caravans in the fifteenth could essay the southward trek from Tunis that the Arabs had so often performed. The very fact that Arab gold coins could come, in commerce, into the possession of young, strongly national States such as Florence and Venice is itself an argument for their not being found in northern Italy, for such States would almost certainly enact, as a matter of course, that imported Arab gold should be melted down and recoined into the florins and ducats designed specifically to attract trade to northern Italy.

The new gold currencies, typified most brilliantly by those of Florence and Venice, could only succeed within a context of expanding economies and expanding production: it is worth remembering that Henry III's experimental English gold coinage failed at a time when Florence, also with gold coinage, was full of active and prosperous wool factories. Expanding economies, in their turn, produced the need for yet more gold. This was to come, in the fourteenth century, from various sources in Europe itself in addition to what could be imported from ubiquitous Arab merchants or a decaying Byzantium: the process of washing for gold gave way increasingly to mining, which, though it was no more efficient scientifically than that of the Romans (and indeed it may have been less), at any rate greatly hastened and increased the flow of gold. From the digging of shallow pits miners progressed to the digging of shafts, the lower limits of which were ultimately controlled by the perpetual threat of flooding, against which, in the absence of mechanical power, there were only those safeguards of elaborate drainage trenches and cumbrous water-wheels and screws which the Romans themselves had used. Primitive though the technique continued to be, however, the European yield of gold quickly became large, if only because of the multiplicity of active mining sites along the auriferous belt from the Rhine to the Carpathians.

Not all were essentially rich. Silesia, Bohemia, Thuringia and the eastern Alps may not have produced, in the whole of the fourteenth century, more than 50,000 lb. of gold between them, though Reichenstein, the city of rich stone, could ultimately rise to a processing figure of 26,000 tons of ore a year. Some areas, however, were much richer, and Hungary at this time was the paramount producer of gold: its output, which rose steadily from the thirteenth to the sixteenth century, has been estimated at between 2000 and 5000 lb. annually. Hungarian gold has been claimed as the cause of the further multiplication of European gold currencies in the fourteenth century, including the now well-established issues of England (from 1344) and France, and has been reckoned as forming about half of Europe's own yield of gold at this time. Gold currency, modelled closely on that of Florence, began in Hungary in 1324-5: a century and a half later the coinage of one year at Kremnitz could consume 90 lb. of gold in the form of 12,000 coins; and at the same time African gold merchants could style themselves 'Hungarians'.

By about 1500, therefore, Europe was again stocked with apparently good supplies of gold. The hatred felt by Christendom for Islam, and the resultant uncertainty of commercial contacts between West and East, had tended to allow the stagnation of a major source of gold coming from Africa via Syria and Egypt. The decline and final destruction of the Byzantine Empire in 1453 had given to the Turks the surviving remnants of Byzantine treasure. But, to judge from the profusion and universality of European gold coinage, such deprivations were not serious. Europe by now was a very considerable gold producer: her output had been rising for two centuries, and, if the gold-silver ratios had tended on occasion to show curious instability, fluctuating in the thirteenth and fourteenth centuries between 1:10 and nearly 1:14, this was due jointly to an initial hunger for gold followed in turn by a rise in the price of silver as silver became more sought after. Apart from the gold of Europe there was that of Africa, and West Africa in particular. France had shown interest in the Gold Coast as early as the fourteenth century. In the fifteenth Portugal determined to secure a maritime monopoly of the area: in 1415 she captured Ceuta in Morocco, and from 1450 onwards she steadily extended her power, setting up fortress-marts like Fort Elmina from which such products as textiles could be traded against gold⁄dust. By 1488 Diaz had rounded the Cape of Good Hope; by 1498 Vasco da Gama had reached Calicut in India; and the gold of West Africa, which had previously enriched Lisbon and enabled John II to call himself Lord of Guinea, could now begin to flow on the sea⁄route eastward. It was to be replaced, in Europe, from sources of undreamed⁄of richness in the new continent which Columbus had discovered just five years earlier.

The transition over the major part of Europe from the acute poverty in gold evident in the centuries after A.D. 500 to the relative abundance of the fourteenth and fifteenth centuries was a long and often difficult process. At one end of the period the European economy saw gold virtually disappear from currency, its use being restricted narrowly for the adornment of kings, and by them of their chosen shrines. By the other end of this millennium gold currencies were abundant in Europe, and gold itself was available for possession by any man with the means to buy it: once again, as in Persia and Greece and Rome, the provision of gold currency had put gold into the hands of the ordinary citizen. It might be necessary from time to time to conserve supplies prudently, as when Hungary in 1325 put an embargo on gold exports and Edward III, in England, established coast⁄guards to keep watch against illegal export. But this was a matter not so much of general as of momentary scarcity: the balance of trade and of payment in gold must inevitably tend to come more and more into the hands of central governments as the pattern of trade crystallized within the context of international friendships and enmities. And in fact the corrective is supplied by the whole picture that emerges, by the end of the fourteenth century, of the activity of goldsmiths. Jean de Garlande, in writing of Paris, about 1200, described the gold⁄smiths at work 'sur le grand pont', each with his furnace and his work⁄table, making all the different kinds of jewellery that fashion and taste demanded—cups of gold and silver; bracelets, clasps and brooches; and jewel⁄settings. Just over fifty years later the Paris guilds of goldsmiths were regulated; by the end of the thirteenth century more than 120 smiths were at work there. In England the goldsmiths of London were incor⁄porated by royal charter in 1327. And by the middle of the fourteenth century there were, in Florence, over forty goldsmiths' shops on the Ponte Vecchio alone—shops which, as time went on, were ordered by law to be open to the street on all days except festivals, so that the methods of the smiths could come under constant public scrutiny.

The initially great rarity of gold in the dark age of Europe, and its increase down to about 1500, are intimately connected with the history both of alchemy and also of jewels and jewellery in this period. Alchemy in the Graeco-Roman period appears to have been the expression not so much of technical experiment as of a growing philosophical mysticism. There might have been, and indeed usually was, a strong and universal desire to find the precious formula by which the transmutation of baser metals to gold could be achieved; but the essential principles of metallic structure and composition were so imperfectly understood that there was always a strong temptation to view transmutation in terms either of moral virtue and vice or of astrological influences upon which an arbitrary pattern could be imposed by the credulous. Progress from this baffled stage of esoteric thought was marked by the rise of a new school of alchemical effort in the Islamic cultures of the eighth and following centuries, and the first in this line was the great Jabir ibn Hayyan (known also under his westernized name of Geber), who emerged as alchemist at the court of Harun al-Rashid in Baghdad in the late eighth century.

Jabir himself was much concerned, like so many of his predecessors, with both the application and modification of the Aristotelian theory of matter and change; and his work in this connection did no more than to substitute one rearranged set of principles for another. Moreover, he held that the influence of the planets was a strong factor in the formation of metals. But he went beyond mere theorizing in his work on the chemical behaviour and classification of metals. His recipe for the preparation of nitric acid is the earliest known. He was familiar with processes for the making of steel and the rust-proofing of iron. And he worked on a number of processes involving the manufacture of dyes. To a large extent his record might seem to duplicate that of earlier workers in the same field, but the fact that his experiments and recipes were gathered into a corpus gave them an obvious importance for his successors.

The greatest of these was the Abu Ali ibn Sina, known to Europe as Avicenna, born near Bokhara in 980, and destined to become one of the most learned men of his age. Avicenna's earliest training was in medicine, and in this alone he achieved a position of lasting fame, not only because of his indefatigable work in isolating and classifying medical substances but also because of his theories of disease—including that of contagious diseases. In addition he was astronomer, mathematician and musician. He studied heat, gravity and motion as well; and it was inevitable that this brilliant practitioner and polymath should apply himself to the long disputed question of the composition of metals and the possibility of transmutation. But his study of metals, in which he well understood qualitative processes arising out of refinement by chemical action, left him in no doubt about transmutation, and although his rejection of transmutation did not fail to arouse scepticism or hostility in others, he was firm in his view that while metals could be imitated through colouring no change in their essential nature could be achieved.

Avicenna's refusal to allow the possibility of transmutation did not deter many successors from continuing to believe the opposite, and the growing miscellany of alchemical works by Islamic authors, once imported into Europe through Spain, naturally made a strong impact on medieval European philosophy—to use the term in its widest sense. The new learning was, of course, a gift to the unscrupulous, and balm to the credulous, in an age which was still so poor in gold. Nevertheless, such a man as Albertus Magnus was in agreement with Avicenna in rejecting the possibility of turning baser metals into gold. This great man, who was one of the foremost scholars of the thirteenth century, philosopher, theologian and natural scientist, held that alchemy could imitate but not change species. Indeed, as century followed century and chemical processes became more exact and also more complex, the picture that presented itself to men like Albertus Magnus was not that of a world in which transmutation could succeed, but one in which the interplay between an increasingly large range of recognized and purified substances became more subtle. It was only when the naturally scientific mind was too readily coloured by belief in magic and astrology to explain what observation would not explain that progress was halted: credulous minds would always believe the elaborate magic of a really learned man—for example, Roger Bacon, whose devotion to experiment, instruments, languages and the occult made him so notable a figure in thirteenthcentury England.

Alchemy in the Islamic world of the Middle Ages coincided with a great Islamic wealth of gold, the very abundance of which may have encouraged research into the making of yet more. In Europe the spread of alchemical doctrines fell at a time of gold poverty; and there was every reason to pursue them in the hope that they would make good an obviously crippling deficiency. The dream was to continue long after gold became abundant in Europe; and from the time of the fifteenthcentury Paracelsus onwards kings were increasingly anxious to avail themselves of skilled alchemists who, if they could not make gold, could anyhow turn out a metal so resembling gold in colour and finish that it might well pass for it in articles of domestic splendour. But true gold, heavy, lustrous, imperishable and superbly malleable, had to be secured in the traditionally hard ways, either by commerce or by mining.

While it was still scarce, and much of it reserved for medieval kings or churches, goldsmiths were forced by circumstances to make essential changes in the forms of personal jewellery. Throughout immense periods of the Graeco-Roman and earlier cultures the finest jewellery had often consisted either of pure gold, skilfully worked into the most complex shapes and adorned by added details of filigree or granulation, or of gold set off by precious or semi-precious stones or enamel in such a way that these were themselves an additional decoration. Lack of gold in Europe from about 500 to 1200 induced a contrast—a contrast between jewellery of gold and the 'jewels', essentially medieval in origin, in which gold was used (and sometimes quite sparingly) as a setting for stones of comparatively large size. A general interest in stones had, indeed, grown up in much earlier times: in the ancient world they had been prized for their rarity and their colours, elaborate theories about their astrological significance had been constructed, and their geological origins were studied—even to the point at which different stones could be regarded as being male and female, and capable of breeding. They were, in short, viewed in the magical context which alchemical theory always encouraged so easily, and they were credited with the possession of supernatural properties that made them universally popular as talismans—a word itself derived from the later Arab version of the Greek *apotelesma*, the effect of celestial bodies upon the universe.

Plate 44

Discourses upon the potency of stones and gems, whether medical or more purely magical, multiplied from the eleventh century onwards. Islamic influence, here again, was strong: the famous Jabir had written at length upon them, and his lead was followed by eminent Europeans such as Marbode, bishop of Rennes in the eleventh century, whose treatise in Latin verse is known to have existed in more than a hundred manuscript copies—the equivalent, in days before printing, of an extremely large edition. By the fifteenth century Europe as a whole had gained a familiarity with gems and stones, and had come to ascribe to them such an importance that the style and fashion of jewellery was intimately affected throughout all later centuries. Moreover, the combination of several different decorative traditions had resulted in the production of goldsmiths' work which, while usually increasing in delicate elaboration, at the same time placed a growing emphasis on the gay brilliance which is obtained by the association of bright colour with the steady glow and lustre of gold.

New influences, in particular, must have been exerted by the gold-work and jewellery of the later Byzantine period. For while the earlier work of Byzantium showed a conspicuous continuation of the Hellenistic and Roman love of solid gold jewellery, sometimes set with gems but often adorned by nothing more than the intricacy with which the gold itself was worked, in wire and filigree, the passage of time produced a profound change. This astonishing empire, in which the religious element (at least in Constantinople) was a primary factor in the thoughts of men and governments, and in which the systematic adornment of churches, not least with gold mosaic, went to lengths of extraordinary luxury and splendour, turned from the classical Graeco-Roman taste, often heavy and coarse in its later forms, to a new conception of gold in which it could be set off by ivory, by precious or semi-precious stones (much used in the decoration of crosses and reliquaries and the covers of liturgical books) or by enamel. It was, indeed, in enamelling that the later Byzantine jewellers excelled: their whites, blues, reds, violets and greens (produced by the addition to powdered glass of tin oxide, cobalt oxide, gold, manganese and copper respectively, the resultant composition then being made into paste and fused on to a metal base) were of superb clarity and brilliance. They excelled in actual technique as well, for besides cloisonné work (already noted in many earlier periods) they were masters of champlevé enamelling —in which the enamel was laid in depressions scooped out in the metal base—and finally (and perhaps most memorably) of 'basse-taille' work, where the enamel was painted very thinly over its metal base, producing on gold and silver an effect of most beautifully translucent colour.

Plates 40, 41 least

Plate 39 (Frontispiece)

The importation, however sparingly, of these later Byzantine enamelled masterpieces into Central Europe spread both the popularity of this decoration and also the desire to rival Byzantine skill. Though some time passed before it could be fully learned, it was learned well; and Western enamelling was to be the equal of Byzantine in combined richness and good taste. Ninth-century England produced a marvel of the goldsmiths' art in the 'Alfred jewel', found in 1693 during excavations near the island of Athelney in Somerset, where King Alfred was hiding from the Danes in 878. This little ornament—it is less than $2\frac{1}{2}$ inches long, and nowhere wider than $1\frac{1}{4}$ inches—is perhaps one of the most famous in the world: a figure bearing two sceptres, executed in cloisonné enamel (usually the earliest form everywhere), is covered by a thick piece of rock-crystal, itself set in a framework of filigree gold which contains the inscription ✠ AELFRED MEC HEHT GEWYRCAN, 'Alfred had me made'.

Plate 42

48 Jewel bequeathed to
New College, Oxford,
by its founder
William of Wykeham:
14th century

49 The Towneley brooch, French
or German: 10th–11th century

50 French ship pendant
of gold, crystal and enamel: c. 1600

51, 52 Vessels from the Treasure
of Los Quimbayas found near
Finlandia, Colombia: late pre-Spanish

Whatever the purpose of the jewel—the tip of a staff or the central jewel of a crown—two things are clear. The association with King Alfred seems too strong to dismiss, so that this is yet another example, in the very highest class, of the royal patronage of medieval goldsmiths and jewellers. And the techniques are what would be expected of a country poor in gold: the use of crystal and of coloured enamels enables gold to be restricted to the furnishing of an intricate open-work pattern. A country poor in gold was poor in precious stones as well: they are conspicuous by their absence from the 'Alfred jewel', which uses crystal instead as a gem.

From the hard, trim glitter of earlier Frankish and Saxon gold and cloisonné garnet to the Alfred jewel there is a significant transition. Varied colour, assisted by translucency, had come to reinforce the perennial beauty of gold; and this was in general the developing pattern of gold-smiths' work, large and small, until the end of the medieval period—a pattern increasingly diversified by the use of precious stones as their supply to western Europe increased. In the Towneley brooch, of eleventh-century **Plate 49** French or German work, a sumptuous combination is seen of pure gold, worked into elaborate forms, and enamel. The splendid contemporary brooch of the Empress Gisela found in the Mainz treasure exhibits the same techniques but in a form at once bolder and ligher. Thereafter the setting of precious stones and pearls in gold became more common. At times the effect was of utter profusion, more particularly in the case of classical cameos—always highly prized—for which a luxuriant gem-studded setting in gold was frequently devised. This popularity of cameos is illustrated most vividly, perhaps, by the lovely and elegant ritual crown worn in 1257 by Richard, Earl of Cornwall when he was crowned **Plate 45** King of the Romans in the cathedral at Aachen, where it is still pre-served—a solid but perfectly proportioned circlet (once surmounted by a crocketed arch) inset with numerous cameos, intaglios and cabochon (i.e. unfaceted) gems.

In the thirteenth and fourteenth centuries the point was reached at which gold, enamel and gems could be freely combined. The little thirteenth-century reliquary pendant in the British Museum, constructed by order of the King of Aragon to contain one of the precious Holy Thorns bought by St Louis from King Baldwin of Jerusalem, is in all senses a ravishingly perfect jewel: two very large cabochon amethysts are set in **Plate 46** gold, each hinged to the other, and the golden backing of each is most richly enamelled in glowing and translucent colours with scenes relating to Christ's Passion. The early fourteenth-century jewel left to New College, Oxford, by its founder, William of Wykeham, marks a further advance towards the immense range of small personal jewels, of the utmost beauty and delicacy, which were to delight the pious or wealthy of the next two centuries. William's jewel was in the form of a Lombardic letter M, framing the Virgin and the Angel of the Annunciation. Pearls together with cabochon rubies and emeralds encrust the limbs and arch of the M; white and green enamel pick out the lily and the Angel's wings in a composition that shows a graceful elegance and restrained splendour which it would be difficult to surpass.

Apart from the making of such exquisite pieces of small jewellery, in which enamel could produce a wonderfully rich and translucent effect in association with gold, and gold and crystal were to be so happily married, some goldsmiths carried out enamelled gold-work on a much larger scale in which the characteristic splendour of their work was devoted with outstanding effect to the adornment of churches. One of the most lovely examples of this is to be seen by those who make the short, winding and pleasant journey out of Vienna to Klosterneuburg. There, in what is now a small and peaceful country town, they can admire the genius of Nicholas of Verdun, whose altar was made for the fine church there in 1181. Hardly anything else by his hand is known: he was, presumably, an itinerant goldsmith who, like many others of his age, accepted commissions in many places, wherever he could get them. But he now needs no more than the 'Verdun altar' to commend him. It is an object of the most sumptuous conception and the most disciplined taste, consisting, in its present form, of a central panel above the altar-table, flanked by two great wings. All three sections are superbly decorated with gilding and enamel on a copper base. The gilding is massive in extent, and glows and blazes according as the light is dull or bright. The enamel contains nearly all colours, but the emphasis is on bright cerulean blue, a colour reserved for the fullest suggestion of holiness, just as gold suggests glory. There can be few examples of work where richness of effect, excellence of taste and complete technical mastery are as brilliantly displayed.

On a smaller scale there is the so-called 'Royal Gold Cup' made in the fourteenth century for the Duc de Berri. This passed into the possession of John, Duke of Bedford, and thus into the royal line of English kings, until James I made a present of it to the Spanish envoy, from whose land it ultimately returned to England (and the British Museum) at the end of the nineteenth century. Though considerably altered in form from its

Plate 48

Plate 50

Plate 54

original appearance, this cup is a superb example of enamelled gold, with scenes from the life of St Agnes painted over the gold (which is of the purest) in colours of the richest translucency.

But there were still occasions which called for large-scale work in gold alone, without gems or enamel to set it off more than sheer artistry alone could do; and the series of 'Golden Roses' bestowed by successive Popes upon those who served Christendom well provide a specially interesting and lovely section of medieval goldsmiths' skill. At times they were fashioned in considerable numbers: thus Giovanni Bartolo made eleven between 1365 and 1395, and Henry VIII himself, a little surprisingly, was to receive as many as three, one of which (as Stowe described it) was 'forged of fine gold and wrought with branch leaves and flowers resembling roses set in a pot of gold, which pot had three feet of an antique fashion of measure half a pint. . . . The tree was of height half an English yard, and in breadth a foot.' This Golden Rose of Henry's was comparatively large: a simpler and perhaps much more charming version (and designs were very various) is to be seen in that presented by Pius II to the city of Siena in 1458–9. This is all delicacy and scrupulous naturalism in lustrous gold; Plate 55 and the special fascination which such Golden Roses seem to exert (and they are still made and presented now) brings to mind the similar sense of wonder which, according to Prescott's narrative, the Spanish conquerors of Peru experienced when they found royal gardens laid out with golden flowers.

The reappearance of gold in Western Europe, and its growing frequency down to 1500, saw it turned to a thousand decorative uses quite apart from its vital place in European economy. It still played, as it had always played, a special part. Though, with abundant gold currencies, it was no longer the exclusive perquisite of kings and nobles and churches, it was kings and nobles and churches who saw to it that its unique qualities of combined decoration and value should be exploited. Gold remained the princely metal of State and the almost sacred metal of the church: the solid gold-leaf backgrounds of numberless pictures painted by the earlier Plate 57 masters testify at once to the splendour of their patrons and to that special quality of divine glory which, in a religious context, gold alone could suggest.

Chapter VII

EL DORADO—OLD STYLE:
SOUTH AMERICAN GOLD AND
EUROPEAN ECONOMY

THERE WAS NO BREAK between the Middle Ages and the modern world. If break there was, it was between the ancient civilizations and the modern world. And it was in fact less a break than a long process, slowly and obscurely enacted during the medieval centuries, in which the classical Graeco-Roman tradition might well have been submerged if the great flood of migratory movement had been either swifter or more closely unified.

As it was, the migrants themselves were affected by a tradition which they absorbed to a surprising extent; and, when the Renaissance in fourteenth-century Italy began to reintroduce the classical conceptions of political humanism and artistic naturalism, large parts of Europe were ready to accept and welcome, stage by stage, the brilliance and freedom of the new ideas. Their acceptance marked the end of medievalism and the beginning of modernism in a real sense—a spiritual, intellectual and artistic sense. But, as the mind ranges over the world's history from the early civilizations of Egypt and Mesopotamia down to the present day, one other great turning-point—this time geographical—stands out. The discovery of the American continent at the end of the fifteenth century could not claim to have brought the Middle Ages to an end, for they were already ended. Yet, simply because it joined so immensely large and rich an addition to the already known tracts of the earth's surface, this discovery marked an essentially new age. If it was not the end of medievalism it was certainly the means by which the new spirit of Renaissance Europe was to be exercised and enriched; and Europe, which had itself lain at the mercy of so many barbarian hordes during the dark centuries, was now in her own turn able to embark upon a programme of foreign conquest and colonization unparalleled in any earlier age. It was the beginning of a movement in which all the diverse inhabitants of a vast and unknown continental land-mass were to be systematically subdued and their resources assiduously exploited as the old civilization moved westward.

When Columbus crossed the Atlantic and found the West Indies in 1492 his object had been, in the prevailing European mood of speculation and experiment, to circumnavigate the world until he came to the Orient,

53 Quimbaya Culture objects from graves, Cauca Valley, Colombia. Late pre-Spanish

54   The Royal Gold Cup of France and England: 14th century

Map 6 Pre-Spanish and Spanish gold production in the Americas

a limit so far attained only by those who journeyed or sailed eastward
from Europe, against the rising sun. For 2000 years the Atlantic had
teased and provoked navigators. The farther they ventured the more
might be found; and while remotest Thule had steadily receded as men
reached the Canaries and the Azores, Britain, the Faroes and Iceland
(where Roman imperial coins have, incidentally, been found), mythological
Atlantis—the lost land of the great ocean—might still perhaps be thought
to stand for some further goal. Columbus, however, was attempting to
reach Japan and India. A desire of adventure for himself and of glori-
fication for his sovereign was combined, moreover, with determination
to seek new sources of wealth for Spain, including the gold and the gems
which long report associated with the Orient. The fact that Portugal had
already seized the advantage in opening up rich commercial contacts
with West Africa and its gold supplies doubtless acted as a particularly

129

keen spur. Lisbon was by now becoming an outstandingly important European centre for the collection and distribution (on Portuguese terms) of African gold; and if Spain could in any way diminish her advantage the rewards might be great in an age when gold was increasingly demanded all over Europe for coinage and articles of luxury. Columbus, *Map 6* dropping anchor in the West Indies, did not know that beyond the isthmus of Panama, still to be discovered, there lay yet another great ocean separating him from Japan, China and India. For the time being, however, that did not matter, for he was able at once to assure Spain of the natural wealth of the new lands he had found by shipping back gold, cotton, exotic birds and beasts and plants. And in his second voyage, in 1494, he made a settlement upon Hispaniola (the modern San Domingo) and founded the mining camp of San Tomaso in its goldfields. From then until 1502 Spanish power in the West Indies was steadily extended, and the quantities of gold sent back to Spain as steadily mounted.

But although Columbus had opened up so rich a source of gold to satisfy the natural cupidity of Spain there were areas of far greater wealth still to be discovered and exploited. Columbus himself set foot on the American mainland, in what is now Honduras, in 1502; and less than ten years later Grijalva, a lieutenant of Diego Velasquez, the Governor of Cuba, discovered Mexico. At this moment Spain came effectively into contact with one of the two great indigenous cultures of America which, as it seemed, might block her further progress. The Aztec civilization of Mexico, with its formidable religion, its architectural splendour, and its notable artistic and intellectual capacity, was by then flowering. The soil of Mexico was rich in metals: besides silver, lead, tin and copper there was a great deal of gold in active production, either found in placer deposits on the surface or washed from rivers, and then cast into bars or stored in the form of dust. The work of the Aztec goldsmiths was at this time highly skilled, and they were expert in the art of casting gold, by the 'cire perdue' process, into ornamental objects of elaborate form, using silver in combination with gold to secure a polychromatic effect which had been admired in the more ancient civilizations around the Aegean, as at Mycenae. The goldsmiths were numerous enough, in the larger urban centres, to be collected together in distinctive quarters of the towns: their efforts were concentrated on the making of luxury articles with which the royal palaces were sumptuously decorated. From a technical standpoint it seems that they had learned all that Asiatic and European goldsmiths had learned in the pre-medieval period, without however developing the art of enamelling. Gems they had in abundance for setting in gold, if they wished, together with many sorts of decorative semi-precious stones.

No account of Aztec work in gold can be more than the merest outline, for nearly all of it went into the Spanish melting-pot: the little that survives from chance discoveries made in later times is firm testimony to the thoroughness with which the Spaniards swept all manufactured gold into their own possession as a result of their swift conquest. At first it was not swift enough, and Velasquez replaced Grijalva by Hernando Cortes, who made a fresh landing on Mexican soil in 1519 on the site of what is now Vera Cruz. He was received with the usual gifts, including ornaments of wrought gold; and later there came gifts, from King Montezuma himself, which lose nothing in description by Prescott's rolling prose—

> shields, helmets, cuirasses, embossed with plates and ornaments of pure gold; collars and bracelets of the same metal, sandals, fans, *panaches* and crests of variegated feathers, intermingled with gold and silver thread, and sprinkled with pearls and precious stones; imitations of birds and animals in wrought and cast gold and silver, of exquisite workmanship. . . . But the things which excited the most admiration were two circular plates of gold and silver, as large as carriage wheels. . . . One, representing the sun, was richly carved with plants and animals . . . it was thirty palms in circumference and was valued at twenty thousand *pesos de oro*,

i.e. it weighed nearly 200 lb. And Cortes could detect promise of ample gold to come: he had previously handed over a Spanish helmet, on being told of the country's wealth in natural gold, with the invitation that this should be filled, and this was now returned to him, full to the brim with gold-dust.

The subsequent history is well known. Cortes destroyed his fleet to make withdrawal impossible, and, after a period of fluctuating success and peril, advanced on the city of Mexico, capturing Montezuma and, with him, an immense royal treasure.

> The gold alone was sufficient to make three great heaps. It consisted partly of native grains; part had been melted into bars; but the greatest proportion was in utensils, and various kinds of ornaments and curious toys, together with imitations of birds, insects, or flowers, executed with uncommon truth and delicacy. There were, also, quantities of collars, bracelets, wands, fans, and other trinkets, in which the gold and feather-work were richly powdered with pearls and precious stones. . . . The goldsmiths were sent for to take in pieces the larger and coarser ornaments, leaving untouched those of more delicate workmanship. Three days were consumed in this labour, when the heaps of gold were cast into ingots, and stamped with the royal arms.

To judge from the 'royal fifth' that was, as always in Spanish America, set aside personally for the King of Spain, the total quantity of gold now passing into Cortes' hands for melting down must have been between 1500 and 2000 lb., apart from the quantity of what was left intact, which may well have amounted to even more.

It is not surprising that examples of Mexican work in gold are now so rare that the discovery of a single tomb-group in modern times can be said to double the quantity that was known before. What survives today fairly enough reflects the general picture painted by the Spanish sources upon which Prescott's narrative was based. Mexican goldsmiths were expert in beating the metal out into broad plates and masks, adorned with gold wire which usually falls short of the fineness of true filigree; and their work in cast gold must also have been notable. To an eye trained in the styles of Europe and the Middle East their art perhaps appears to be more magnificent than exquisite: the impression that persists is that of an abundance of gold which is wrought with a skill of pattern rather than with minuteness of craft. But it is obviously impossible to generalize on the basis of what is now extant. The efficiency with which Mexico was stripped of its gold by the Spaniards has resulted in the extinction of evidence to a point which would have been equally true of ancient Egypt if the treasures of Tutankhamen had not been revealed.

Mexican gold was not, however, the most abundant that the Spaniards were to find in America, for as their explorations spread out from Central to South America the reports of natural wealth in gold were repeated and increased. From the West Indies their ships could range the coasts of northern Colombia, Venezuela and Guiana, in all of which rich supplies of alluvial gold were to be found. And with the establishment of their position at Panama they could begin the southward penetration of the west coast, beyond Colombia, that was to bring them enormous wealth in gold from Ecuador and Peru while confronting them, at the same time, with the task of subduing another and yet more powerful indigenous civilization. The great ridge of the Andes, still actively volcanic, continues until this day to be one of the world's richest mineral areas, providing gold, silver, copper, tin, lead and even platinum, in addition of course to many other metals which a technologically primitive culture neither desired nor knew how to refine. Of these metals, all found very freely, gold must have been worked in the Colombia-Ecuador-Peru area from early times. It abounded in easy placer deposits of great purity, and it could be washed, hardly less profitably, from the rivers. As was the case with early

55 The Golden Rose given to Siena by Pope Pius II, 1458–9

56   The Cellini Salt: 16th century

Egypt, the natural nuggets could easily be hammered cold, while, if the gold were in the form of dust, cold-hammering would again unite this into a solid yet softly workable mass. Such work in gold appears to have begun towards the middle of the first millennium B.C., and was possibly the dawn of metallurgy in the American continent as a whole. Archaeological finds of this period show that the technique of working gold was quickly learned, and that an age which first began to hammer gold into thin sheets for decoration almost at once acquired the art of repoussé work together with the ability to anneal, weld and solder, so that by about 500 B.C. such things as golden diadems, ear-rings, bracelets and plaques were not uncommon. The fact that some of these gold objects were painted suggests the inability to conceive or develop the art either of cloisonné inlay or enamelling.

For about a thousand years from 500 B.C. Peruvian workmanship in gold seems to have made no spectacular advance, and goldsmiths confined themselves to the techniques developed by their early predecessors. But from A.D. 500 fresh progress was made in a cultural period, lasting until about 1000, which coincided with the establishment and florescence of the stupendous site of Tiahuanaco—a site, 13,000 feet above sea-level, extending over a sixth of a square mile and constructed in a megalithic style so massive in scale and so fine in craftsmanship that a sense of speculation and mystery has always surrounded it. To this culture there succeeded, in turn, that which is associated with the Chimú people, under whose dominating influence along the northern coast of Peru many cities were built. The most notable of these was Chanchan (near the site of the present Trujillo)—a capital city 8 square miles in size, with its great walls and teeming buildings all made of large adobe bricks. It is not easy to form an estimate of gold-work in the Chimú period, for this lasted until soon before the penetration of the Spaniards into Peru, and much of it was quite certainly looted afterwards by the Spaniards. From what remains, however, it appears that it had some major characteristics in common with Mexican work of the same period. There was the same love of beating out thin gold into such things as vessels and masks, and there was the same proficiency—it falls short, perhaps, of the highest skill—in the use of gold wire for the elaboration of design. A grave of the Chimú period, found to the north of the modern Lima, has recently provided a number of splendid and opulent objects in this general style. Many of them are highly complex in construction, involving the soldering together of scores of small pieces of gold; and the effect of such technique is undoubtedly one of great magnificence.

Plates 51, 52, 53

Plates 59, 60

133

The Inca culture of Peru, emanating from the famous city of the Sun God at Cuzco, saw the dominance of a small militaristic group extended, finally, over the whole of the country and northward into Ecuador, the Inca Pachacuti being, in his time, a conqueror and imperial organizer of the highest ability and wisdom. It was this great empire, spread out along an immense coast-line, splendidly organized, rich in the accumulated gold of over 2000 years and still productive of abundant gold, which was to fall to Francisco Pizarro and his band of scarcely 200 men, who set out to conquer it in his third and final expedition of 1531. Seldom can disparity between civilizations have been more grotesquely displayed than it was between these two brilliant powers, of which one, with firearms and horses in the possession of a handful of men, could easily subdue the serried thousands of the other. But the Spaniards also relied on treachery of unsurpassed enormity in capturing the person of the Inca himself; and it was as a consequence of his capture that Pizarro was for the first time able to judge at all accurately the vast extent of Peruvian wealth in gold. Already, in his two previous expeditions from Panama in the fifteen-twenties, he had been offered the tempting variety of small gifts in gold that had been offered to Cortes in Mexico before him. But when the captive Atahuallpa, confined in his room at Caxamalca, told Pizarro that if he would set him free he would fill the room—it was not less than 22 by 17 by 9 feet—with gold as high as he could reach, the prize was plainly of another order altogether.

Prescott's memorable narrative, not less sombre than magnificent, describes how couriers were sent throughout the kingdom to collect the ransom gold. 'The returns came in slowly. They consisted, for the most part, of massive pieces of plate, some of which weighed two or three *arrobas*—a Spanish weight of twenty-five pounds. On some days, articles of the value of thirty or forty thousand *pesos de oro* were brought in, and, occasionally, of the value of fifty or even sixty thousand *pesos*.' The collection went slowly on, and meanwhile the Spaniards set about the systematic looting of the temples, palaces and rich houses of the Peruvians. Cuzco, the capital, in which stood the great temple of the Sun, provided the richest prize of all. They found it

literally covered with plates of gold. . . . The number of plates they tore from the temple was seven hundred; and though of no great thickness, probably, they are compared in size to the lid of a chest ten or twelve inches wide. A cornice of pure gold encircled the edifice, but so strongly set in stone that it fortunately defied the efforts of the spoilers.

The Cuzco spoil, like that from many other sources, went its way to Caxamalca to add to the Inca's ransom; but avarice got the better of patience and, before Atahuallpa's prison room could be filled to its stipulated limit, Pizarro decided that the gold must be divided.

> It was necessary to reduce the whole to ingots of a uniform standard, for the spoil was composed of an infinite variety of articles, in which the gold was of very different degrees of purity. These articles consisted of goblets, ewers, salvers, vases of every shape and size, . . . curious imitations of different plants and animals. Among the plants the most beautiful was the Indian corn, in which the golden ear was sheathed in its broad leaves of silver. . . . A fountain was also much admired, which sent up a sparkling jet of gold. . . . The business of melting down the plate was intrusted to the Indian goldsmiths, who were thus required to undo the work of their own hands. They toiled day and night, but such was the quantity to be recast that it consumed a full month.

The quantity of gold in this ransom was, in fact, not less than 13,000 lb., and there was as much again still to come from Cuzco—so much, in fact, that prices of ordinary commodities among the Spaniards themselves began to soar to impossible heights. 'Gold and silver seemed to be the only things in Cuzco that were not wealth.'

From Spain, delighted and dazzled as much by the richness of the spoil as by the ease of conquest, the Emperor Charles V now organized the production and transport of gold from the latest Spanish possessions in America with the same rigid control as had from the very first characterized the Spanish colonization of the West Indies and Mexico. The vital necessity of doing so is seen from the estimate of the amount of gold which was got from all the Spanish American territories combined (i.e. from Mexico down to Chile) in the 107 years from Columbus' landing down to 1600—nearly 750,000 lb. Of this total a proportion of not less than 10 per cent became royal property; but, apart from the motive of personal gain, the Spanish throne had to see to it that gold secured in the American colonies did not stay, secreted, in the colonies, and also that when it entered Spain it did so under proper governmental supervision, in order that Spain, now again Europe's richest supplier of gold, might rigorously control the price at which it was distributed. With Spanish imports of gold throughout this period running at an annual average of between 6000 and 7000 lb. Charles knew well that the joint prosperity of both Spain and Europe as a whole depended on the prompt arrival of the treasure fleets; and the story that he could be heard to cry with joy on hearing of their arrival is surely not wide of the mark. But it depended

135

equally on the internal organization of the newly and easily gained Spanish possessions, in which, as the colonists spread steadily inland from the coasts of both the Atlantic and the Pacific, gold was found in extraordinary abundance, especially to the south of the isthmus. In Colombia there were few districts where gold could not be profitably worked with the simplest effort: so rich, indeed, were its alluvial deposits that even in the middle of the nineteenth century, long after Spanish enterprise and urgency had skimmed off what might have seemed to be the cream, there was still employment for a labour force of 15,000 people in the industry. Though much less rich than Colombia, Venezuela and Guiana contained gold enough to make them well worth exploitation. Across on the western side Bolivia, while teeming with silver and tin, also had great deposits of alluvial gold; and this, as was the case with all the gold-bearing territories of the Pacific coast, was washed by swift torrents from the rocks of the towering Andes chain, where it was to be mined in an abundance that is vividly suggested by the story of a great mass of native (i.e. nugget) gold riven from a crag of Mount Illimani by a flash of lightning. Chile was scarcely less rich. Peru and Ecuador had perhaps already yielded a disproportionate amount of their gold in the form of manufactured treasure.

The administrative rigour with which Spain controlled the production of American gold implied increasingly a neglect both of the peoples she had conquered (who simply furnished an ample corps of cheap labour) and also—politically more important—of the Spanish colonists themselves, whose numbers year by year were swelled by a strong westward tide of emigration from their homeland. In the end this neglect was to cause the loss of what she had so daringly and unexpectedly gained. But in the meantime the policy of strict control and incessant exploitation paid a high dividend, and by the time the Portuguese colonizers of Brazil had begun, towards the end of the seventeenth century, to open up yet new sources of American gold (destined in time to be as prolific as any) Spain had for a hundred years been Europe's chief purveyor of a metal which more and more nations needed in larger and larger amounts as a result of their swiftly expanding economies.

Very strict records were kept of the precious metals which were shipped from America to Spain. American gold could be mined and collected privately by Spanish prospectors, but only on condition that this gold was delivered to local assay offices, widely distributed throughout the colonies, for refining, marking and subtraction of the royalty payment.

What was then destined for shipment to Spain—either for the crown or for the mercantile market—was brought together at one or another of a number of ports such as Vera Cruz in Mexico, Trujillo in Honduras, Nombre de Dios and Porto Belo in Panama, and Cartagena in Colombia, then known as New Granada. From these and other ports large convoys were made up for the crossing to Spain. As well as gold they carried much else: silver (in enormously increasing quantities), quicksilver (essential for the process of silver amalgamation), and spices and other luxuries. All shipments which included gold and silver had to dock in Spain at Seville: the Roman foundation on the Guadalquivir, down which had flowed, out of Spain, prodigious wealth in precious metal for shipment to the central and eastern Mediterranean in ancient times, was now itself the only legal point of reception for the not less prodigious wealth of Spanish America. Treasure unloaded at Seville was at once taken to the House of Trade, an office which regulated absolutely all commerce and travel between Spain and her colonies. There it was weighed and then either stored or coined (originally much of the gold from America was minted at Seville itself) or put on to the open market or sent to Spanish creditors in other countries.

The actual shipment figures are extraordinarily impressive. From 1503, when the first regular consignments of American precious metal began to arrive, the picture is one of twice-yearly Spanish convoys, systematically planned and regulated, sailing from America to Seville with abundant cargoes of gold, silver, gems and luxury commodities, eagerly awaited, scrupulously controlled, and distributed in a manner which could lead only to a vast increase in Spanish wealth and consequence. In the ten years from 1551 to 1560 nearly 100,000 lb. of gold were unloaded at Seville; and in the single year 1544 there were no fewer than 154 shipments of treasure, larger or smaller. These shipments varied in value, of course, from time to time. Between about 1503 and 1530 the figures for gold imports are immensely high: thereafter the quantity of silver is larger and larger, reflecting the profitable working of such mines as those at Potosí, and the totals of gold tend to shrink. But, whether of gold or silver, imports from America to Spain continued to be valued mainly for their metals. In 1594 gold and silver helped to make up 95 per cent of the value of cargoes from America, and in 1609 the figure was not much lower at 84 per cent.

Spanish imports of gold are set in very clear relief in the uniquely voluminous and interesting series of news-letters which were sent, from various commercial vantage points of Europe, to the House of Fugger. This astonishing family, with its business centre at Augsburg, its agents scattered around all major ports and capitals, and a wealthy income in any case secured by the control of mines of silver and copper in Central Europe, rose to a position where it might claim—as much as any of the great banking houses in Italy—to be a staple unit in the merchant-banking business of Europe. Into Augsburg there poured, from all parts of the Continent, the latest reports of shipping arrivals, losses of cargo, rates of interest, shortage of capital, war-scares, and indeed everything that might affect the international money market and bullion market. There the information was classified and analysed by those who, if they had desired anything so unwise, could have bankrupted kings and brought countries to famine. The letters which the Fuggers received are now stored in Vienna, and in their 30,000 pages the value of American treasure comes sharply to life. On 26 September 1583, for instance, it was reported from Madrid to the Fuggers

> that the fleet from Spanish India, praise be to God, arrived on the 13th of this month without misfortune. It carries a consignment of about fifteen millions [i.e. metal to the value of fifteen million gold ducats of $3\frac{1}{2}$ grammes]. People say that they unloaded and left a million in Havana because the ships were laden too heavily. It is a pretty sum, and will give new life to commerce.

The news on 16 September 1587 from Antwerp was that

> urgent letters from Spain say that the Marquis of Santa Cruz has arrived with the whole Peru fleet, altogether 117 ships. . . . It is said to be carrying fourteen millions in gold and silver, and more than three millions in merchandise—a great sum indeed.

From Venice the Fugger agent reported on 12 January 1590 that

> news comes from Lyons that letters from Lisbon report the arrival in Seville . . . of eight millions in gold. They expect more ships to arrive soon . . . with a further four millions. The reason why the first ships are late is that they sailed further north than usual to avoid the English ships waiting for them on their usual course.

The Spanish ships formed heavily armed convoys which, in fact, suffered comparatively small losses from raiders over the years. But piracy was obviously a constant danger on this long Atlantic traverse. The agent in London could report, in March 1569, that twenty-two Spanish and Portuguese ships, with a large cargo of spice, had been brought forcibly into Plymouth: there was also talk of the capture of many chests of gold destined originally for Antwerp, but now about to serve as material for the English queen's coinage. In March 1580 it was reported, again from London, that the French had intercepted gold, silver and pearls on their way from America. Perhaps Sir Francis Drake himself was to be the biggest bogy of all. Antwerp, for example, reported in July 1587 that according to letters from London Drake had just brought in to Plymouth 'the *San Philip*', belonging to the King of Spain himself and laden with 400,000 ducats of gold for the king's own use, 'as a new gold-mine has been discovered from which this gold has been obtained'. The Fuggers themselves had good reason to hope that the Spanish convoys would usually get through in safety, for though pirated gold would stimulate European economy wherever it was injected, the Spanish king was generally among their greatest creditors. A report from Rome in January 1597 recorded that Philip II had published an edict of intention to pay his debts to the various international bankers—payment being delayed, however, until their accounts were audited; and the House of Fugger appeared on the list with the second largest total. Philip was in difficulties: already in the previous year he had forbidden the export of gold or silver from Spain, and by the beginning of 1597 the merchant bankers were beginning to tighten the screws, hoping to recover something of the 6,000,000 he owed. Viewed as a whole, however, the long series of dangerous voyages by heavily laden ships appears to have resulted in small loss: even after Spanish maritime power had been diminished by the defeat of the Armada in 1588 the level of imports remained very high, and El Dorado (originally 'the gilded man', priest or king, who was said to bathe, encrusted with gold, in a sacred lake of South America) securely won its new sense of a land abounding in natural wealth.

Spanish enterprise in America naturally stimulated the ambitions and avarice of other countries; and Drake himself, whose intermittent booty from government-organized piracy in the Atlantic was not inconsiderable, came within a little of equally brilliant rewards during his famous voyage in the *Golden Hind* around the world in 1577 and after. He had sailed across the Atlantic, and passed through the Strait of Magellan and round Cape Horn, then turning northward up the Pacific coast of South America, destroying whatever Spanish vessels he could and collecting much booty, including a good deal of gold. By the time he had reached Central America the *Golden Hind* bore a cargo of 20 or 30 tons of precious metal looted in this way; and in searching for an anchorage farther north, where he could safely await a favourable season of winds for the homeward journey across the Pacific by way of the Orient, he appears to have put in just north of San Francisco, landing in what is now Marin County in California and claiming the territory in the name of his queen as New Albion. 'In this place Drake set up a greate post and nayled thereon a VI^d, which the contreye people woorshipped as if it had bin God, also he nayled uppon this post a plate of lead other [accounts say 'brass'] and scratched therein the Queen's name.' If it is not an elaborate fraud the plate of brass found in 1936 in Marin County is in fact Drake's own manifesto of annexation, in which on 17 June 1579 'in the name of Herr Majesty Queen Elizabeth of England and Herr Successors forever I take possession of this Kingdom . . . now named by me an to bee knowne unto all men as Nova Albion'. The accounts of his companions stated that 'there is no part of earth here to be taken up, wherein there is not a reasonable quantitie of gold and silver'; and in fact Drake, just north of San Francisco, was within 200 miles of one of the richest goldfields in the world. Thus, although the cargo with which he returned to a grateful queen was of immense value, he had missed (perhaps by missing the narrow entrance of the Golden Gate) a still richer prize. The gold of California was seen from time to time by Spaniards in the succeeding years—it was specifically mentioned, for example, in 1690—but for its major exploitation it had to await the discoveries of 1848.

The production of gold from all sources during the sixteenth century was on so large a scale that, combining with the quantities which Islamic enterprises had made available in the later Middle Ages, it mounted to a point at which monetary policy showed acute embarrassment. It has been said of the treasure from America that it raised prices, handicapped exports, created the sinews of war, fostered extravagance and weakened national man-power by encouraging emigration. The same goal, whether correctly interpreted in these terms or not, was being sought by other nations than Spain. In Europe the centres of production which had been opened up in the medieval period continued to work steadily, with a yield which, if it neither increased greatly nor bore comparison with the wealth of gold from America, nevertheless formed a notable total. The gold of West Africa was still abundant, and a powerful weapon in the hands of Portuguese colonizers. Farther afield there was a burning interest in the possibilities of new discoveries outside the orbit of the Mediterranean and the Atlantic. A letter from Venice to the Fugger headquarters in 1596 reported the discovery of an auriferous Chinese island, the exploitation of which was rendered difficult only by its poisonously unhealthy climate.

57 The Wilton Diptych (right panel): unknown master, French School: late 14th century

58 Reliquary of St Louis of Toulouse, decorated with 16th-century Venetian gold filigree work

And then there was Japan. Here there had been washing for gold from very early times; but in the sixteenth century production suddenly leapt ahead, with an estimated yield of some 10,000 lb. in the years from 1532 to 1554 contrasting with a spasmodic output measurable only in hundreds of pounds in earlier periods. This sudden change (which was reflected, characteristically, by the institution of a gold coinage at about the same time) seems to have been due most probably to the growth of mining proper as opposed to alluvial washing. Increased Japanese production was in any case an important new factor in the gold markets of the world of the time—so important, for example, that Portugal from 1540 onwards acquired considerable quantities of Japanese gold, especially from the mines of Sado, 'a treasure island made of nothing but gold and silver'.

With gold pouring into Spain from America and into Portugal from Africa and Japan, with Europe herself continuing her own lesser but still considerable output, and with banking centres like Lisbon, Seville, Antwerp, Vienna and Genoa acquiring great wealth from the handling of precious metals and the financing of the trade which they stimulated, it was not surprising that men like Drake had attempted, on behalf of England, to find and monopolize new sources of gold or that, under his queen, washing for gold should be undertaken in the Scottish remoteness of Lanarkshire or even farther north. For it was a fact, by now, that any European nation of consequence must be able to present a gold currency that was not only handsome but profuse. The gold coins of European kingdoms in the fifteenth and sixteenth centuries had shown a constant tendency to increase in size—under Henry IV in Spain huge gold pieces were coined up to something like $\frac{1}{2}$ lb. in weight. To some extent, of course, this reflected a cheapening in the price of gold as its total quantity in circulation increased. But it reflected also the general rise in price levels which was an obvious result of a cheaper gold price unaccompanied by expanded production of goods. For countries which could draw upon supplies of gold either under their own rigid control (like that of Spain and various States in mid-Europe) or closely monopolized (like that which Portugal could now secure from Africa, and was soon to get from Brazil), the economic problems of the times, though often difficult, need not be insuperable. For England they were much more difficult. There, too, prices were rising. So also, of course, was industrial output, and the wool trade in particular was a rich source of revenue, and earned much gold. But the gold was earned at rates which could well be manipulated in favour of those who controlled its sources of supply, and the effect upon

England was that gold rose steadily in value from the fourteenth to the sixteenth century. The problem was acute under Henry VIII in particular, and the gold used for the English coinage, which from the time of Edward III's first noble in 1344 had been virtually fine at 23 carats 3½ grains (24 carats=pure gold), now included metal of 22 carats (i.e. only 91·6 per cent fine).

The growing abundance of gold in Europe from 1500 onwards saw the art of the goldsmiths rise to a level at which it has not been excelled. Benvenuto Cellini's name is, without doubt, the most famous of a famous number; and by the time of his death in 1571 he had set an imperishably high standard in both conceptual artistry and also technique. His technique he had learned while apprenticed to the chief jeweller of the Medici family; his artistry, as his autobiography and specialist treatises show, was the product of a remarkable mind and spirit. Cellini's use of gold is most often associated with the sumptuous salt-cellar, a piece of superb extravagance, made for Francis I of France (who, said Cellini, cried out with astonishment when he saw it), and given in 1570 to the Archduke Ferdinand of Austria when his niece married Charles IX of France. But it was characteristic of the age that Cellini's skill should be lavished on churches as well as princes, and also on exquisitely small objects of personal jewellery such as clasps and brooches and badges. The combination of sheer virtuosity and love of the magnificent which marked the artistry of Cellini and his contemporaries is well seen in the vase attributed to him, and now in the British Museum—a beautiful vessel of antique Roman agate wonderfully adorned with gold at its foot and head. Lesser craftsmen might have wished to bedizen the lustrous surface of the agate more heavily with gold; but Cellini, if it was he, was content, by giving the vase a cunningly proportioned foot and head of elaborately wrought gold, to set off the beauty of the stone by the deliberate avoidance of overstatement.

Gold-work of the sixteenth and seventeenth centuries, indeed, developed along lines of new subtlety. There was still a love of cabochon gems and cameos, still a profusion of the most vivid enamelling. But greater attention was being paid to form; and while this could be achieved (and was perhaps ultimately urged) by a transition to faceted gems cut in regular shapes, it was shown most clearly in the intricate linear designs, in arabesques and scrolls and zigzags, by which expression could be given to Baroque feeling without sacrifice of lightness and elegance. Not that gold did not play its full part in the increasing splendours of the rising Baroque style. There was nothing, of a scale so large that the use of solid gold was

Plate 56

Plate 62

Plate 58

obviously precluded, that could not be richly gilded with fine and pure leaf-gold. In churches the use of gilding became more frequent, and the visual magnificence of royal and private palaces could be brought home to all observers by the lavish gilding of furniture and fittings. Chairs and tables, chests and mirrors and candelabra could all blaze with the message of wealth; and as if that were not enough there was the fashion for cloth splendidly woven with gold and silver thread: a news-letter to the House of Fugger from Cologne in 1581 described the preparations made for the Duc d'Alençon's reception by Queen Elizabeth, and said 'in Antwerp it is impossible to get enough gold and silver cloth'. And there was not a court of consequence in Europe which would not normally include a private goldsmith among its retinue.

Not unnaturally the great merchant bankers of the time, who were so deeply involved in the financial balancing of kingdom against kingdom, had to keep a wary eye upon the claims of those who professed to have solved the age-old problem of changing base metals into gold. A series of letters to the House of Fugger from Venice in 1589 shows the interest, not unmixed with apprehension, that bankers might feel in the art of the alchemist. A certain Antonio Bragadini was credited with the achievement of transmutation: his reputation had brought him great wealth and equal publicity, and he was said, literally, to be throwing gold about in shovelfuls —his recipe being the addition of a drop of liquid to quicksilver. He would not, of course, declare what the liquid was, and was soon reported to be turning out Venetian coins by the thousand on behalf of the State. A little later it was said of him that his process sufficed only for small quantities; and again a little later he passes out of the narrative. A threat to the role of the merchant bankers could now safely be disregarded by a family which, in the person of Sigismund Fugger, himself a skilled metallurgist, had doubtless made its own informed estimate of the limits to which alchemy could go without turning into the art of the charlatan. Nevertheless the hope of transmutation never died during this period. Charles II of England, with only £11 in the Exchequer at his accession, could well hope for results from his privately constructed laboratory. Christian IV of Denmark and the Emperor Ferdinand III were among the other seventeenth-century monarchs who employed alchemists to provide them, if they could, with man-made gold, and a golden metal was indeed produced, although (as with the similarly golden metal produced for Ferdinand's son Leopold I) it was evidently gold-like rather than gold, and with a very low specific gravity contrasting with the high figure of true gold.

Multiplication of gold supplies in the fifteenth and sixteenth centuries led to a position whereby the control of the price and movement of the metal began to slip finally from the grasp of kings into the hands of merchant bankers and goldsmiths in the larger centres of commerce. The process is well seen in England. There the goldsmiths had acted as bankers since the fourteenth century at least. By the end of the sixteenth their holdings had gained them secure power, and in the seventeenth—especially after the seizure by Charles I of the Tower mint and its bullion stocks—this power was increased when people came to prefer the entrusting of their cash to the goldsmiths rather than to any agency of the Crown. As a result of this profound change in social psychology the goldsmiths in fact gained the control of the bullion market (which previously the Crown had striven, through ministers and advisers, to direct) when Charles II relinquished it to them. The creation of the Bank of England in 1694 acted, at the same time, as a check upon the imprudent movement of bullion. For those movements could be very great: on the one hand, to quote but a single example, imports to England from India, payable in gold and silver, had risen enormously in the early seventeenth century (£30,000 worth of gold went East in 1626) while, on the other, English exports to the Continent could earn large quantities of gold from Europe. The stage had been reached where constant influx and efflux of gold was taking place. Foreign gold coin was coming in as English gold coin went out; and the necessity naturally arose for the purely mercantile refining of large amounts of gold, as distinct from that which the mint refined for the purposes of coinage. Hence arose, in 1684, the first of London's bullion firms, Mocatta and Goldsmid, which began then the business, now shared with a handful of others, of refining bullion (its very name means a melting-house) to standard levels of purity.

World production of gold in the sixteenth century has been variously estimated at between 1,500,000 and 2,000,000 lb., and that of the seventeenth at slightly more. Compared with eighteenth-century production (some two and a half times as much as either) the figures may seem small—perhaps less, in all, than 2 per cent of all the gold that has been won since 1493. Compared, however, with the medieval yield, they show a sudden and very sharp increase, to a point at which they may be level with the peak of long accumulating and closely controlled production under the Roman Empire. It was an increase which brought special problems of its own, notably in a general raising of prices (since the quantity of gold tended to outrun the production of goods that could be valued in gold) and also in an unstable relationship with silver. Silver from German sources was in adequate supply until the middle of the sixteenth century. From then onwards a flood of silver came from America to Spain, to be distributed thence to other parts of Europe; and gold-silver ratios showed constant uncertainty. In Spain, for instance, the ratio rose from nearly 1 : 10 at the end of the fifteenth century to over 1 : 15 in the middle of the sixteenth, and the figures for France are very close to those of Spain, with silver constantly cheapening in relation to gold. It was an age in which a great volume of newly discovered gold, followed by a great volume of newly discovered silver, produced an unbalance between the metals themselves and also between the metals and the goods which were valued in them. In the course of the next two centuries, from 1700 onwards, attempts were to be made to create greater stability in this respect. In the meantime gold had entirely recovered the position, long traditional in ancient civilizations, from which it had been dislodged by the disorder and running down of medieval economies. It had again become the universally prized metal, ubiquitous in currency, undiminished in the splendour of its uses, and universally sought both as a measure of value and also as a store of wealth.

Chapter VIII

EL DORADO—NEW STYLE:
THE NINETEENTH-CENTURY GOLD-RUSHES

Map 7

IF ALL THE NEW GOLD produced during the sixteenth and seventeenth centuries from all parts of the world amounted to less than 4 per cent of the total production between Columbus' discovery of America and the present day, the output of the eighteenth and nineteenth centuries accounted for something nearer 30 per cent. The increase was immense, and its impact on the economic history of the period was of the greatest importance and interest.

While viewing the span of nearly 6000 years during which gold has been systematically and eagerly sought it is impossible to avoid being struck by the differences of effect which have been caused in different epochs by sudden and intensified gold production. Ancient Egypt, in her own day, was easily the richest culture in the world, but her wealth, though it undoubtedly prolonged and embellished the life of that culture, did not (and perhaps could not) raise it to a point at which it might directly affect the subsequent history of the world. The same was true of Persia: here again the cultural yield of an epoch of notable gold prosperity was inconsiderable when set beside the astounding spiritual and intellectual achievements of the Greeks, always poor in gold. For Rome the picture is a little different: her rise to world predominance coincided with her relative poverty in gold, but the consolidation of her position, leading to the imposition of her skilfully flexible code of political and legal forms upon the whole extent of a colossal empire, could probably not have succeeded without the wealth in gold which by then she commanded, for it not only enabled her to secure the immense length of her frontiers for a very long time but also made it possible for a highly complex system of world trade to be build up to a point of real economic strength.

Much the same, though with a different emphasis, was true of the Byzantine Empire. With the Islamic States, on the other hand, the emphasis seems to have rested more on the possibilities of commercial imperialism which the possession of gold undoubtedly offered; and this was a point of view which appealed most instantly to those States of southern Europe which pioneered surprisingly large coinages in gold in and from the thirteenth century, at a time when so much of Europe was starved of gold. Henceforth the acquisition and distribution of gold, in a post-Renaissance context which had itself been created (in part at least) by large-scale resumption of Mediterranean and European trade, were assiduously applied to the furtherance of that trade. The only question at stake at the end of the seventeenth century was whether the volume of trade, and indeed the rate of industrial production, would keep pace with the greatly expanding volume of gold production. It was true that, while absolute monarchies continued, a substantial amount of gold would continue to be immobilized in the form of royal treasure and general decoration: historical record is full of details of the personal wealth in gold of kings and princes, by whom it was also distributed to churches and courtiers. But it was true also that the world's progress in technology was extremely slow and that, if gold was in fact a means of valuing commodities, distinct from such other intrinsically precious things as silver and gems, those commodities must grow in volume themselves.

There was no lack of man-power, but the man-power was, in a sense, wastefully employed for lack of mechanical power—a handicap which it is increasingly difficult to visualize in an age when mechanical power is so various and so universal and the machines themselves may include built-in 'brains'. Today one essential difference between backward and developed countries is that in the former the application of mechanical power does not match its potential output of manufactured goods. By the end of the seventeenth century most countries in Europe were producing fine goods in infinite variety, but they were all backward in the sense that, with populations tending to rise, they could not produce them in sufficient quantity to satisfy the supply-and-demand trade of a world which possessed an international medium of value in growing abundance. The most brilliant figures of Renaissance Italy had sought earnestly the means by which mechanical power could be devised and applied. But apart from the constant improvement of mere implements as such, Europe was still in bondage to the lever, the pulley and the screw. If the great influx of American treasure to Spain had been matched by a high degree of Spanish inventiveness, Spain might by the end of the seventeenth century have laid the foundations of some centuries of continuing dominance. But the inventiveness was to come, perhaps not altogether illogically, from a country which was then, as now, dependent for its gold on the ability to make and sell its goods; and the Industrial Revolution in eighteenth-century England was the beginning of a process by which European productivity swiftly regained a relationship with the growth in gold supplies. The development of her coal-fields in relation to her harbours and sea-routes, and the application of steam power both to manufacturing processes and also (hardly less important) to the drainage and working of the coal-mines themselves, introduced an epoch that was, in a sense, more sharply divided from its predecessors than any before it.

The gold for this period of industrial expansion did not any longer come mainly from Spanish-controlled sources: not even in this could Spain continue to wrest an advantage from the age. For by now Portuguese enterprise in colonizing Brazil was releasing supplies of a richness that, by the middle of the eighteenth century, fully matched the yield of Spanish America. Colonists in earlier times had discovered Brazilian gold in quantity, but it was not until the seventeenth century that the *Map 6* province of Minas Geraes, north of Rio de Janeiro, was systematically developed, together with a good many districts elsewhere. The gold was to be found in quartz veins, in anciently formed gravel terraces, and in alluvium. Around Ouro Preto, in Minas Geraes, it came most abundantly from quartz veins from the mountain ridges that intersected the whole area. Alluvial deposits were especially rich near the little River Rio das Velhas and the mountains that surround it, and the wealth from these resulted in the rapid growth and splendour of such cities as Villa Rica, which did not dwindle and decay until a profusion of alluvial gold, steadily deposited through untold thousands of years, had been assiduously washed out of the soil. Brazil has been credited with a production of some 33,000 lb. in the last decade of the seventeenth century. For the first twenty years of the eighteenth the figure rises to about 125,000 lb.; for the next two decades, up to 1740, to about 375,000 lb.; and the peak of production has been put between 1740 and 1760, with a total output of over 625,000 lb. Altogether the quantity of Brazilian gold obtained in the whole of the eighteenth century has been reckoned at over 1,750,000 lb.

Of this a large quantity, from the first, was by one means or another absorbed by England, where the number of Portuguese moidores in unofficial circulation, added to Spanish gold coins, ultimately resulted in its being a common necessity for merchants and traders to equip them-selves with little portable balances so designed that they would show the comparative value of English and foreign gold pieces. England, in fact, quickly became one of the foremost gold markets in Europe, and her position is implicit in the outcome of the many deliberations which took place in the early years of the eighteenth century regarding the currency relationship of gold and silver. John Locke, the philosopher, had come out in favour of silver monometallism at the close of the seventeenth.

59, 60 Breastplate and ear-ornaments from grave near Huarmey, Peru: late pre-Spanish

62 Vase of ancient agate with gold mounting attributed to Cellini (1500–1571)

61 Étui of grey striated agate
in gold mounts: ? English, 18th century

63 Box given to Mrs Siddons on her retirement
from the stage by George IV: English

Silver, he wrote, was the money of account and measure of trade all through the world, especially in England where, as he well knew, the pound of sterling silver had been the basis of the monetary system since Saxon days. He argued against bimetallism on the ground, so long familiar to monetary economists, that the relative values of gold and silver fluctuate. 'One metal, therefore, alone can be the money of account and contract . . . and the fittest for this use, of all other, is silver.' But in fact silver was flowing out of England, not least because its value in the East, where English trade was growing fast, was considerably higher than it was at home: over 200,000 lb. were exported in 1717 alone. At the same time gold was flowing in, leading to a notable increase in the amount coined, especially from 1709 onwards. In 1717 the mint price of gold per ounce troy was slightly lowered and fixed at £4 4s. 11½d. There was no obvious reason why this price should remain fixed, and indeed further variation was expected. But it did remain fixed—in fact until 1914—and by the middle of the eighteenth century, as has been said, it came to be recognized that gold had in England definitely supplanted silver as the standard of value at £4 4s. 11½d. per ounce troy. England, in short, had transferred from a silver to a gold standard, which, even if it was not adopted by Act of Parliament until 1816, was so secure as to be unquestioned.

To fix the price of gold at a certain figure, and to succeed in retaining that figure in an age which sees such greatly increased industrial output, implies that fresh supplies of gold will increase world stocks in a roughly parallel relationship. It was this approximate balancing that was achieved by the gold output of the eighteenth century, which was more than twice that of the seventeenth. Moreover—and the fact can never be overstated—gold was not perishable. Much, no doubt, might continue immobilized in treasure, sacred or royal, from age to age. And some was at all times lost to sight, perhaps temporarily, perhaps for hundreds of years, in hoards carefully hidden by those who died with the secret of the hiding-place. Considered as a whole, however, the sharply rising level of gold output in the eighteenth century must be viewed not absolutely but as an addition to stock inherited from previous centuries, represented most obviously by the sequence of over 400 years of generally profuse gold coinage. So far as any essentially very rare metal could be ubiquitous, or even common, gold achieved that distinction after 1700. It was the staple of international, if not of national, trade; and perhaps it may even have acquired something of the feeling of a commercial commodity for the first time, as distinct from that of a preciously decorative possession. For it

Plate 61
Plate 63

is remarkable how, from this time onwards, taste in jewellery required of goldsmiths in most European countries that they should emphasize stones rather than the gold in which they were set. Solid gold, if it was employed, must be chased or contrasted to secure an effect of lightness: silver gilt, tinged with a pale and luminous grace, became increasingly popular with the goldsmiths of Europe, among whom those of Augsburg were outstanding for the light elegance of their forms, mouldings, flutings and chasings. Enamelled gold greatly declined in vogue. Instead, the brooches and clasps and bracelets and necklaces in which much of the best inventiveness of eighteenth-century goldsmiths was to be seen blazed with cut jewels—sapphires, amethysts, rubies, topazes, and above all diamonds, together with the crystal and paste that were thought to be no mean substitute. Many of these gems came from the Eastern trade; many, again, came from Brazil, where the output of gold was matched by the splendour of its wealth in jewels.

The balancing of increased gold output against increased industrial output, performed mainly by supplies of Brazilian gold in the eighteenth century, became in the nineteenth the function of Russia, which for a short period enjoyed the distinction of being the world's richest source of gold. It is impossible to imagine that the washing of alluvial gold had ever entirely ceased in areas that were responsible for so much of the wealth that had entered the Persian, Greek and Byzantine civilizations. But the tracts of Asiatic Russia are so vast and so remote that no record of con-sistent enterprise survives before 1720, when Peter the Great, reacting quickly to reports he had received, encouraged the search for alluvial gold in the already long-famous valley of the Oxus. The first systematic production of Russian gold belonged, however, to the years after 1750 and took place in and around the Ural mountains north of Ekaterinburg. Here there were quartz veins to be mined in the mountains, but much more tempting were the beds of alluvium formed by the ageless action of the rivers flowing from those auriferous mountains.

The description of these alluvial beds in the mid-nineteenth century, when their fame was at its height, shows the whole random richness of an area over which had flowed rivers far larger than they were then. The beds varied in size, but were mostly elongated—spits of ground originally half-submerged in mid-stream: sometimes they were found high and dry, sometimes they were still near their parent rivers, overgrown by reeds and trees. They varied in thickness, too; and apart from this the gold might sometimes be found high up in the alluvium, even sticking to the roots of grass, and sometimes covered by a thick layer of mud, and indeed lying on the bedrock itself. The average depth of an alluvial bed was from $3\frac{1}{2}$ to 5 feet: for this reason true mining need seldom be attempted, when a normally active man could exploit the riches of these shallow beds with no more elaborate equipment than a shovel and a pan. And even a pan might be superfluous, for large nuggets were not uncommonly to be found just for the digging; and the finding of a single large nugget (as when a young girl discovered one just under the turf near Neviansk in 1813) could at once result in the exploitation of a whole new alluvial area.

Alluvial gold from the Urals was generally of high purity, and, together with what was secured from true mining in the quartz veins of the Urals, it made up the great bulk of Russian gold output down to the eighteen-thirties: for the years 1814 to 1839 the total yield has been put at over 175,000 lb., with an annual average of 5000 lb. or more. At this point, however, a decline set in, either because the alluvial gold had had its richest deposits removed or because attention was switched to new and very rich sources lying in the remote territory west of Lake Baikal in the valleys of the Altai mountains. For here too there were numberless alluvial sites, the combined yield of which quickly surpassed that of the Ural region: 40,000 lb. were obtained in the decade 1830 to 1840, and the annual average rose thereafter very sharply to 13,000 lb. and, even higher, to 17,000 lb. With this great productivity Russia had now outstripped Brazil for the distinction of being the world's largest producer of gold. Much more important, perhaps, was the fact that Russia, which had at times stood somewhat distant from the main streams of new gold being pumped into the world's commercial arteries in preceding centuries, now commanded a store of bargaining wealth with a reputation that was, temporarily, second to none.

Nevertheless, the world rate of production, viewed as a whole, was beginning to slacken in the first half of the nineteenth century. If the yield of the eighteenth century is taken as less than 4 per cent of all gold won from 1500 onwards, that of the period from 1800 to 1850 was probably not more than about 2 per cent, and this meant that for the first time since American gold had transformed the economy of Europe the quantity being produced showed no rise. The suddenness and plenitude with which this slackening was now to be arrested forms one of the most fascinating episodes in the history of gold in all ages. Innumerable finds of gold of immense richness had been made for over 5000 years before; but none could compare, either in the immediate profusion of the gold that

*Map 7 The World's main gold sources from c. 1800 onwards: 1 Yukon (from 1896); 2 South [
7 Rand (from 1886) and Orange Free State; 8 Urals; 9, 10 Altai; 11 Kolar; 12 Japan; 13 Phili[*

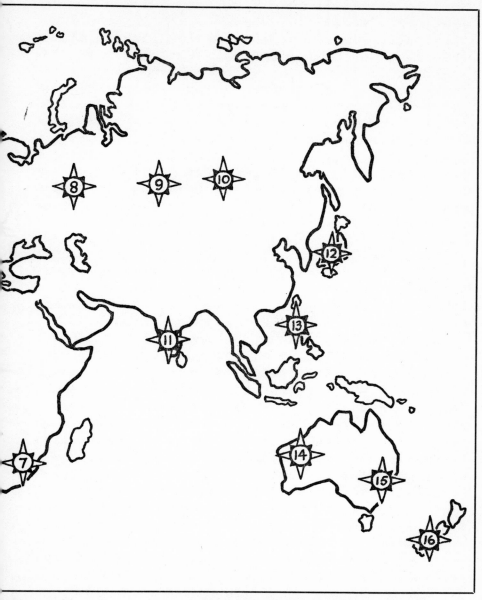

area; 4 California (from 1848/9); 5 Colorado; 6 Virginia, the Carolinas, Georgia, Alabama, etc.;
Australia (from 1892); 15 New South Wales and Victoria (from 1851); 16 New Zealand (from 1852)

was at once produced or in the social significance of the circumstances in which it was gained, with the Californian boom of 1848.

Gold had been found and exploited in the United States for some little time already in the States adjacent to the Appalachian mountains—Virginia, the Carolinas, Georgia, Alabama and Tennessee. The earliest discoveries may have been in North Carolina, and this was indeed to prove much the richest of the States at first concerned. It is said that the existence of gold there was realized by the finding of a nugget, 'of the shape and size of an ordinary domestic smoothing iron', which weighed 28 lb. Other and larger nuggets were to come, and in 1821 a mass of pure compacted gold of the weight of 48 lb. was found fixed in a crevice of rock, where the fragments of gold from a decomposing vein had silted up and solidified. These early discoveries, not only in North Carolina but also in Virginia and Georgia, where gold was quite freely if not abundantly found, were alluvial, according to the pattern of most original finds. Without adding significantly to the total quantity of gold being extracted in the rest of the world at this time they were nevertheless large enough to be welcomed: by 1850 they had amounted perhaps to some 50,000 lb. But they were discoveries which, after half a century of attention, seemed unlikely to lead to the finding of any dramatically rich deposits.

Until 1848 the history of California had been chequered. The influence first of the Jesuit missions, then the Franciscan and finally the Dominican, extended the outward form of Spanish colonial administration along the coastlands during the eighteenth century. Californian territory at that time was, in a sense, open to any influence that could penetrate it, and already the eyes of Russian traders were upon it. In 1820 Mexico revolted from Spanish domination; and two years later California acceded to Mexican rule. The power of the friars rapidly diminished: equally rapidly the territory began to absorb immigrants. Some of these were Mexicans; some were Americans from the States lying east of the great barrier of the Rockies; some came in the wake of commercial enterprise, as when the Hudson Bay Trading Company in 1836 set up a trading-post at Yerba Buena—the later San Francisco. There was, inevitably, some desultory searching for precious metals; but the yield was negligible, for immigrants kept closely to the coasts, since the interior of the country was known to be mountainous and hard to traverse. By about 1840 it is doubtful if the total number of people of European stock in all California exceeded 20,000.

Among those who arrived in the country in 1839, through the stranding of his vessel in the bay of Yerba Buena, was John Augustus Sutter, originally an emigrant from Switzerland. He penetrated inland some 140 miles to the site of the present city of Sacramento, where he set up a European outpost in what was essentially Indian territory. 'Sutter's Fort' was the first stopping-place for those who braved the fearsome overland journey by desert and mountain to enter California from the eastern States. And so many were doing this that in July 1848, after Colonel John Fremont had declared the independence of California from Mexico, the Stars and Stripes were raised in San Francisco, and Mexico ceded Upper California and New Mexico to the United States in return for a payment of $15,000,000.

It was an unfortunate bargain for Mexico. The existence of gold in California was already supported by mounting evidence. What the Mexicans evidently did not know was that six months before the cession of California gold had been discovered at Sutter's Fort in circumstances which suggested some abundance in that district. Sutter had erected a water-mill at the confluence of the American and Sacramento rivers: the winter torrents of 1848 had damaged the race-way of the mill, and in February Sutter employed three Americans to repair it. One of these three, James Marshall, saw glittering particles in the bed of the stream— one story, indeed, ascribes their discovery to his small daughter. The particles were as large as grains of wheat; and inspection showed at once that they were of gold, and of such quantity that Marshall at once collected a hatful. News of the discovery spread very rapidly, considering the remoteness of Sutter's Fort from San Francisco and of California from the rest of the United States. By March there was already a letter in *The American Journal of Science* stating that 'gold has been found recently on the Sacra-mento near Sutter's Fort . . . and is said to promise well'. Reports of rich finds became more and more persistent. In November the *New York Herald-Tribune* declared that the United States was 'on the brink of an Age of Gold'; and President Polk, who had presumably held up any public announcement of the discovery partly because he wished to avoid a groundless stampede and partly because the ink on the documents negotiated with Mexico was hardly dry, could no longer keep the news back.

It was the signal for a gold-rush of a kind never recorded in previous history. Earlier discoveries of abundantly rich gold deposits had played into the hands of principalities and powers, by which they were promptly monopolized or at least rigidly controlled. California showed a new phenomenon: this latest El Dorado belonged to anyone who could get there and stake a claim, and its gold passed into the direct possession of those who could find it. Already by the close of 1848 there were some 4000 men searching for it. But this was a trickle compared with the flood in 1849, when over 100,000 more arrived. They came from all over the world. From the United States untold numbers braved the formidable journey across the continent from the eastern seaboard—a journey which for some might mean 3000 miles of travelling by horse or in wagons or even on foot, and which involved for nearly all the rigorous crossing of hundreds of miles of desert followed by the savagery of the Rockies and the Sierras, snowbound and unmapped. Thousands more reached California by sea, battling against the winds around Cape Horn and arriving at San Francisco in vessels that were by then fit only to rot. They came from every continent, including Australia: many of those whom England had deported now set foot in San Francisco in the notorious 'Sydney town' which they made their own. About 40,000 men passed in 1849 through the place that, so recently, had been the trading village of Yerba Buena. Considered as a whole, the mass migration to California in 1849 was on a truly colossal scale.

But the rewards were known increasingly to justify the excitement which the earliest news had aroused. In the United States there was soon visual evidence. A small quantity of the newly found gold—about 16 lb.—had been sent almost immediately to Washington for examination and assay, and this had been minted into quarter-eagles bearing the mark CAL. And after 1849 the minting of the new gold was widely undertaken in California itself, where over a dozen private companies were turning out a semi-official currency in gold—some of it in tiny denominations of half- and quarter-dollars—to provide an exchange medium more satisfactory than packets of gold-dust of irregular weight, so that by 1851 an official assay office had to be opened at San Francisco, followed in the year after by the decision to establish an official mint. But, apart from their ability to see the richness of California in the flush of gold coins actually in circulation, men could hear by ample report how great that wealth was. It was known even in 1848 that an individual washer could get from ten to fifty dollars' worth of gold in a single day: a month's work at that rate of yield would make him prosperous, a year's work affluent; and in fact the yield might be far higher. Pick, shovel and pan were the only mining equipment he needed, for the gold was found in dust, grains and nuggets on the slaty beds of streams, from which indeed it could often be picked out by hand; and every stream, every gulch and ravine that led, dry or wet, into

64 Gold and amethyst necklace: English, mid-19th century

65　Prospectors crossing the Chilcoot Pass to the Yukon: 1895–6?

a stream, was systematically worked over. It was not long before attention spread to the foothills of the Sierras from which nature had scoured all this gold, and from 1851 these were no less profitably exploited: the wealth of placer gold lower down had provided the capital necessary for the more expensive equipment needed in the hills, where, as the miners of Rome had found in their own time, the conducting and disposal of huge volumes of water was among the most difficult of their engineering problems. Elaborate systems of sluicing and washing were instituted: in the twenty years after 1850 nearly 5000 miles of water-sluices were made, and millions of tons of rock and gravel were displaced and washed.

The yield of Californian gold before 1851 is a matter for conjecture. But from 1851 to 1855 it was running at a rate of about 175,000 lb. a year, with a peak around 200,000 lb. in 1853. In these five years California produced what it had taken ancient Rome half a century to win from North-west Spain and what, much more recently, it had taken half a century for the miners in Brazil to produce. Set against current production in other countries at this period (for example, in Russia), the gold of California poured out in a flood which set altogether new standards: in fact it amounted to about a half of what was being produced all over the world at the time. Equally important, the Californian gold-rush had introduced a new pattern of exploitation. No previous age, so far as is known, had seen individual enterprise applied on that vast scale to the working of a freshly discovered and very rich goldfield. Hitherto the control by kings and governments had been so strict and careful as to be almost absolute. But now men could come from the ends of the earth to stake their claims and try their luck: Europeans, South Africans, Australians and even Chinese could mingle their efforts with the still greater crowds of Americans; and whatever governmental measures might finally emerge in respect of mining licences, assay charges and the like, the plain fact was that the old system of winning gold by State organization and the heavy outlay of State capital had been abandoned in favour of a system whereby privately mined gold could be bought by the State if it wished to buy it. The political change of attitude was fundamental; so, too, was the financial change which followed with it, for it was only a short time before companies were formed to provide capital for the unified (and much more profitable) working of large homogeneous gold-bearing areas, where the existence of common facilities, common plant and centralized planning avoided much of the wastage that was inevitable with one-man claims.

Nevertheless, although company organization was to go ahead in most of the world's major production centres in the next half-century or so, this half-century continued in a most remarkable fashion to belong to the individual prospector. From the earliest times there had been, in gold-bearing lands, men whose keenness of eye was a match for the interest they showed in current reports of finds of gold. Their geological knowledge might be and generally was quite superficial. But they had learned in all ages that gold washed down by rivers is deposited in certain ways; and they came to know from what characteristic rock formations such gold could be scoured out. The world's accumulated knowledge of gold-mining was already great, even though it had not yet extended to deep mining in the sense in which it is undertaken today. California's gold-rush was of special importance in that it gave the opportunity of practical experience to such numbers. Many men, nearly penniless already, might be broken finally by a venture which did not in the end pay off; but the great majority not only made a good and swift profit on their venture but also learned the simpler techniques of gold-digging, and even to some extent of gold-mining, to a point at which they were immediately prepared to try them out elsewhere. The result of this sudden growth of experience, combined with the unfailing excitement of rich rewards, was that gold was henceforth more diligently sought in all parts of the world, and that when it was found it was immediately exploited in a way that reproduced all the features of the Californian rush of 1848–9. In the next fifty years the pattern of immense mining migration, suddenly conceived urban settlement, and shifting capital was to be repeated on a major scale in three areas of the globe, each of them far removed from the traditional centres of mining enterprise.

Australia was the first. Gold had been found there, in small quantities, since the eighteen-twenties; but the great gold-rush of 1851 was due to a man, E. H. Hargreaves, who had left Sydney to dig for Californian gold but now returned to Australia in the certainty that his own country reproduced some of the geological features of California. A week of prospecting showed him gold in a tributary of the Macquarie river in New South Wales; and within a further two weeks 1000 men were already at work, while prospecting was going on over a much larger area. Into the great port of Sydney there began to flock a crowd of immigrants: the Californian scene was repeated, and many who had previously gone from Europe to California now headed straight for New South Wales, which by 1852 produced nearly 45,000 lb. of gold and by 1862, incidentally, had doubled its population. But the seekers after gold who entered New South Wales naturally included many from neighbouring territory, and in the State of Victoria there was such deep concern at the exodus that a specially appointed Gold Discovery Committee in 1851 offered a reward of £200 to the person first discovering gold within 200 miles of Melbourne. The direct and almost immediate result of this was the finding of rich gold gravel, from which was developed the famous Ballarat goldfield—a further cause of intensive immigration to Australia: from England alone nearly 370,000 immigrants arrived by 1852, and three years later the total had risen to over 1,250,000. The rewards were rich, especially in Victoria, which in ten years produced nearly 1,750,000 lb. of gold (i.e. at a rate very closely comparable with that of California), including two famous nuggets weighing over 150 lb. apiece. From New South Wales and Victoria the search spread out: Queensland and New Zealand (the latter for a time to be a rich source) were producing gold by the eighteen-sixties, and the climax came with the discovery of the abundantly wealthy gold-fields at Kalgoorlie in Western Australia. By the first decade of the twentieth century, before a very sharp decline set in, Australian gold output was running at an annual rate of nearly 230,000 lb.

Meanwhile a profuse harvest of gold was being reaped elsewhere. In the United States, naturally, the brilliant success of operations in California stimulated eager—and often desperate—search in other areas. Sometimes the results were fortunate beyond belief. The wealth of the Comstock Lode in Nevada became legendary. It was only some 4 miles long; but within this short distance the rock contained a vein incredibly rich in both gold and silver—so rich, indeed, that from 1859 (when it was found) it was for twenty years America's primary source of gold. In other States, too, it seemed that men had only to look for gold to find it in profitable quantities. It was found in Colorado, which at once experienced a gold-rush of its own; it was discovered in Montana; it was found in the conglomerate beds of South Dakota, where the old Homestake mine remains to this day the most abundant current producer of United States gold. As in California, the locusts came and devoured: the gold deposits on or near the surface, in streams and rivers and old alluvial terraces, were swiftly and relentlessly worked out. Here and there there were mines—or stories of mines—that were said to equal the Comstock Lode in the richness of their deeper veins; and intermittent interest, combined with a sense of adventure, has tempted many an exploration of mountains lying so remote in the desert lands that failure to find gold has often been much less serious than failure, even in modern times, to take enough food and water on the expedition. But on the whole the sequence of rushes, now in this State and now in that, saw the gold quickly cleared. Small towns or villages might spring up for the time being, which local mining communities regarded as the beginnings of larger cities. With the gold worked out, however, their populations drifted away, leaving the Ghost Towns (as in Colorado) as eloquent and melancholy witnesses of the speed with which fortunes could be made in gold and lost in capital investment. There was, after all, always the lure of the immense profits that could—with luck—be made elsewhere.

In South Africa the great search was pursued with results which, as will be seen later, were to make the Transvaal and the Orange Free State incomparably the wealthiest gold-producing area in the world. The first discoveries followed the usual pattern. Gold was known to exist in the Transvaal not long after its early settlement, and it has been estimated that its odd deposits, irregularly washed, perhaps formed 1 per cent of the world's output before the eighteen-eighties. Prospectors were busy in the seventies along the quartz veins of the high, bare lands which lie to the north and north-west of the modern Johannesburg, and shafts were sunk and lateral drives put in. The two brothers Struben—their memories now dignified by a plaque in the Africana Museum at Johannesburg—discovered an area of quartz-vein that was rich in gold at Wilgespruit farm in 1884. Their discovery was reported to the Government; and the Government had, indeed, already shown a lively interest in the Transvaal's gold potential, for ten years earlier President Burgers had visited the Pilgrim's Rest area and bought two nuggets which later, with a third, he minted into the South African Republic's first gold coinage.

Then, in 1886, came the major find—the discovery of the world-famous Main Reef Group of slaty-grey pebble conglomerate, from which the colossal development of the Witwatersrand gold-mining industry has chiefly followed. Accounts of the find are confused by time and prejudice, though they have been elevated to the shining status of legend. What is certain is that an Australian gold-digger and stonemason named George Harrison, after prospecting for gold in the eastern Transvaal, was at that time employed by the widowed Anna Oosthuizen in building a house on Langlaagte farm on the southern Witwatersrand slopes. It is possible, perhaps, that some of the stone which he used for the building came itself from the Main Reef, for this, as the simple sequence of events proved on a Sunday in February 1886, outcropped on Widow Oosthuizen's farm.

George Walker, a prospector friend staying with Harrison, stumbled over that outcrop on a Sunday walk. Curious, he broke off samples, which he crushed and panned back at the farm. It was rich in gold.

The fact that the Transvaal Government afterwards recognized Harrison, and not Walker, as the discoverer of the Main Reef Group suggests that Harrison, the resident, had perhaps told Walker, the visitor, of his own theory of the existence on the farm of auriferous conglomerate. At the time it probably did not matter, for a new gold-rush was on, and, as the Reef was steadily traced from farm to farm, there was space in plenty for all the immediate local claims that might be registered, even though the land values of the farms at once rocketed. But it was clear that the rewards might be great, and it was not long before the Government from Pretoria, near by, began to apply a modest element of supervision and control that was, in time, to enable the first scratchings on the surface of the Main Reef to develop into the enormously complex system of deep mining which the inclination of that Reef (60° at the surface, curving to 30° at depth) and its subsidiaries demanded. As a result of this it soon became possible, amid all the hurly-burly of buying and selling claims and obtaining licences, to form syndicates. It was obvious that Witwatersrand mining was not the 'poor man's mining' of California and Australia. The sinking of shafts was difficult and costly, but only from shafts could the conglomerate ore be obtained in quantity. The crushing of the ore, equally, called for money, for it was unlikely that men would be content for very long with crushing-plant as simple and cumbrous as the 1100-lb. dolorite boulder which was rocked to and fro by hand until it found a museum home. A heavy influx of capital was called for; and because control was exerted the capital was attracted. Within a year or two of the Langlaagte find a whole string of mining companies was busy. If the yield by then from all the mines did not much exceed 1500 lb. of gold, at least it was clear, with every new shaft that was sunk, that the thin, precious band of grey, pebbly conglomerate was everywhere to be found.

The day of the poor man's mining was not, however, quite over: one more very rich goldfield was to be discovered, in which every man was still free to dig for himself, to get rich, to starve, or even—in this case—to freeze. In the Klondike area of the Yukon river in Alaska—as near to the North Pole as northern Scandinavia or northern Siberia—there had been reports of gold by the few hardy and venturesome travellers who cared to penetrate a wasteland where the ground was frozen from September to May. Systematic prospecting from 1896 revealed immensely rich deposits of alluvial gold, and another gold-rush immediately started. In 1895 there had been no human habitation at the confluence of the Yukon and Klondike rivers. By 1897 Dawson City had sprung up, the supply centre for an enormous goldfield to which, in the now familiar way, men were flocking from all over the world. Their problems here were not the problems of California or Australia or South Africa. For although gold could be washed from rivers and streams its greatest abundance lay in a bed of gravel, up to about 15 feet thick, that was covered by a great deposit (up to 30 feet) of black and boggy soil that for most of the year was deep-frozen. To uncover the auriferous gravel they had to enlist the help of the hot Klondike summer, when the sun would thaw out whatever 'muck' they could progressively remove, or even burn their way through the frozen layer. But once again the yield was extraordinarily high. An output of some 5000 lb. in 1899 leapt to 45,000 lb. in 1900; and even if the figure declined thereafter it still remained notable for some years. Those who had taken an early place in the queue to cross the Chilcoot Pass—in single file so tightly packed along a narrow, snowbound trail that those who returned had to use a different track—could make a fortune quickly if not quite easily.

Plate 65

America, Australia, South Africa, Alaska: four astonishingly prolific finds of major goldfields within half a century. And these were only the major finds. For all over the world, in every continent, in every island of any size, the search for gold and the production of gold was going on, stimulated by these four great finds and often carried out initially by those who had gained their own experience in the hard way as individual prospectors in the big 'rushes'. As a result of this incessant exploitation the world's stocks of gold leapt up to what can only be called a fantastic height. The yield in the sixteenth century may have accounted for about $1\frac{1}{2}$ per cent of all gold newly obtained from that time onwards. The seventeenth century may have produced fractionally more. The eighteenth century could probably claim nearly 4 per cent, and the first half of the nineteenth about 2 per cent. But the estimate of gold produced from 1850 to 1900—about 23,000,000 lb.—is over 20 per cent. These fifty years yielded over twice as much gold as the two and a half centuries after Columbus' discovery of America. The figure might even have been a little higher if research into the amalgamation and refinement of gold from crushed ore had been undertaken a little earlier. For until 1891 something like a third of the gold from crushed ore like that of the Witwatersrand mines was being wasted by imperfect chemical methods of separation, and was literally flowing away in sludge and slime. The McArthur-Forrest cyanide process then reduced the wastage to a mere 5 per cent or so.

This new process was, indeed, the answer to a whole new set of problems. Until 1850 the great proportion of gold obtained from the earth was washed gold. Even in the Californian, Australian and Klondike gold-rushes huge quantities of gold were accounted for by the simple and age-old method of washing. But in California itself the disintegration and washing of massive gravel terraces had quickly pointed the way to the need for the heavy hydraulic power that Roman miners had done their best to devise in Spain; and from hydraulic power for washing out the terraces to other forms of power, applied in particular to the crushing of ore, was a short step in a period when ample capital could be attracted by the expectation of such rich dividends. The general change in the methods of gold-mining from 1850 onwards, caused jointly by the lapsing of royal monopolies, by the influx of private capital, and by the development of machinery, is reflected in the figures. From about 1850 to 1875 some 90 per cent of newly produced gold was alluvial, the remaining 10 per cent being mined from quartz veins. By 1890 the proportion of alluvial gold had been cut to 45 per cent: the gold from quartz-vein mining had risen just above this to 47 per cent and, significantly, the gold from deep-lying conglomerate beds or 'bankets' (so called from their resemblance, weathered brown at the surface, to Dutch burnt-sugar and almond-studded sweets of that name) had begun to make its mark with 8 per cent. By 1904 the figures were, respectively, 18 per cent, 60 per cent and 22 per cent, and by 1929 they were to be 8 per cent, 39 per cent and 53 per cent.

The Industrial Revolution in the eighteenth century emerged during the full flow of Brazilian gold. Its development contributed enormously to the abundant production of gold in the later nineteenth. Interplay between the two factors—the world's growing wealth in gold and the world's growing industrial output—was constant and complex, and it must be left to the professional economist to say which of the two was primarily active upon the other, or whether the swelling stock of gold was no more than coincidence. What is certain is that this swelling stock rapidly brought the world face to face with new currency problems. In England gold coinage had been, from 1816, the sole standard of value and legal tender for any amount, based on an official gold price of £4 4s. 11½d. per fine ounce of 480 grains. The English gold standard was, in a sense, all the more powerful because London had rapidly become the most important gold market in the world. From all over the globe gold flowed to the London bullion market to be bought and sold: the original bullion firm of Mocatta and Goldsmid was joined by others, and refining plants were also established to deal with the great quantities of gold, of very varying fineness, that were brought to London. It was natural that the discoveries in Australia and South Africa should help in making London's dominance ultimately even stronger.

It was natural, too, that the glut of fresh gold obtained from 1850 onwards should tempt countries other than Great Britain to adopt gold as their sole standard of monetary value. The second half of the nineteenth century witnessed the great disputation: should one favour gold mono-metallism or silver monometallism or bimetallism? Should one even try to advance (as a few economic visionaries urged) towards a point where a truly international gold currency unit could be developed and accepted? Theories and arguments were bandied to and fro. Sometimes the idea of the gold standard was popular, as from 1850 to 1870 and again after 1895: sometimes it was unpopular, and the exponents of the silver standard recovered lost ground. They were, in any case, firmly entrenched in Central Europe, South America and the East. France and the United States were on bimetallic systems; England and Portugal were the champions of the gold standard. But the Paris conferences of 1867 made it plain that only gold could provide the basis of a workable system of interlocking national currencies; and slowly the gold standard became more widely adopted. Germany went over to gold after the Franco-Prussian war; Austria-Hungary was on gold from 1892, Russia from 1897, and the United States (after long hesitation) in 1900, when the dollar of $25\frac{4}{5}$ grains of gold 90 per cent fine became 'the standard unit of value; and all forms of money issued or coined by the United States shall be maintained at a parity of value with this standard'. Though still not universal, the gold standard dominated the world by 1900 and provided enormously important backing for the bank-notes which were by now issued in such quantity by so many countries. It had become that substance, above all, which furnished a medium of currency, whether for internal or external exchange, and guaranteed every subsidiary form of token currency.

Chapter IX

THE ENDLESS TREASURE
OF SOUTH AFRICA

G OLD IS BEING MINED TODAY in all the continents of the world. Although the production figures of about 1941 were a peak from which there has since been a small decline, due as much to rising costs and general economic dislocation as to any essential diminution in the amount of gold to be extracted, the amount of new gold obtained from the earth each year is running at a rate of just on 2,000,000 lb., worth about £350,000,000 sterling.

It is still coming from Central and South America, from West Africa, India and Japan. It comes from the Philippines and from New Guinea and Fiji. In very small quantities it comes even from Sweden. But the bulk of this massive annual quantity—a quantity, each year, which it would have taken Roman miners more than a hundred years to extract from their deposits in Spain—comes from five areas in particular. Australia supplies just under 5 per cent of the annual world total. From the United States there comes just over 6 per cent. Russian output is veiled behind the curtain that hides so much else, but is put around 7 per cent. Canada furnishes over 15 per cent, and her figure may rise substantially with the discovery and exploitation of new goldfields in the Quebec region. And, finally, South Africa claims the astonishing figure of nearly 50 per cent—a figure which has much to do with the fact that 80 per cent of the world's gold is now mined in countries of the British Commonwealth.

The richness of the South African yield is all the more a matter for wonder because it may well go on at that rate for a long time to come. If the world's appetite for gold remains unabated there is no reason why South Africa should not continue to satisfy it. For the discovery made on that Sunday morning walk in 1886 was the beginning of a vast process. Systematic and scientific prospecting has revealed the existence of layers of gold-bearing ore which have already been traced in a great arc, 300 miles long, from the original Transvaal mines down to the new mines which have only lately been opened in the Orange Free State, where the yield in some places seems likely to be abundant. It is known that along the line of this arc there run, at varying depths and varying inclinations, thin bands of grey pebble conglomerate more or less richly stored with particles of gold. Nothing could be less romantic to look at than these layers of dark, hard-packed rock. Sometimes they outcrop on the surface: sometimes they lie just beneath the surface, and, always inclined, they continue as deep as machinery can go and men can work—bands no more than 3 or 4 feet thick, in which the eye can usually detect no trace of gold whatever. The excitement of the gold-rushes in California and Australia and the Yukon lay in seeing the glitter: gold there shone in the beds of streams or in the banks and beds of gravel which earlier and often greater rivers had formed, and a man had only to use his eyes to know if he had struck it rich. South Africa was to be different. George Walker might pan his armful of crushed rock from the Langlaagte outcrop and see shining gold. But that particular outcrop was relatively rich in gold. The thin grey band, tilting and undulating below the surface, varies greatly in richness. Nearly all of it, however, contains gold, and the problem (as it was quickly realized) consisted in working it on a sufficiently wide and intensive scale to show a profit from deposits which are not always in themselves of great richness. In South Africa the romance of the prospector, whose keen eye is lighted with pleasure of seeing alluvial gold shining thick in his pan, is exchanged for romance of another kind, in which geologist and geophysicist, by the use of such instruments as the magnetometer and the gravimeter, quite apart from test bore-holes, trace and analyse the thin band which nearly everywhere gives gold even if the naked eye cannot detect a single particle of it.

Thus the prospector and his pan have left the mines of the Transvaal and Orange Free State to an immense and highly mechanized industry which, employing nearly 500,000 people, is one of the principal sources of income for the Union of South Africa as a result both of royalty payments (for the right of mining is vested in the Crown) and taxation of profits. Seventy years ago miners on the Witwatersrand were still sinking inclined shafts which followed surface outcrops as far down as relatively simple hoisting gear could manage. Today mining is conducted at any depth from near the surface to 10,000 feet; and the pursuit of the conglomerate layers is so intense that the amount of rock blasted and hoisted out of the mines every day would provide the material for a structure of the size of the Empire State Building in New York. The early miners of the eighteen-eighties could not foresee the necessities which the geological formations of the Witwatersrand would impose on them. This sloping reef, they might have thought, would sooner or later level off and possibly outcrop again after quite a short course underground. After all, the stresses and strains to which the earth's crust was subjected in its formative ages have been responsible for many undulations of strata where the differences of level do not exceed a few hundred feet. They did not know—and indeed they could not then know—that they were dealing with strata that had been tilted on so gigantic a scale that it would take half a century of carefully planned boring to follow them, below younger geological formations, along a 300-mile arc. As their levels sank steadily deeper they were, in fact, faced by a crisis only remedied by a massive influx of capital which made mechanical development, and thus deep mining, a practical possibility.

The geology of the Witwatersrand area combines a curious practical simplicity with certain very difficult practical problems. It has been well said that the gold-bearing bands of conglomerate ore can be visualized as pages in a book—each page from a few inches to a few feet thick in a book of rock 25,000 feet thick. The burial of the book, its tilting, its occasional crumpling, and (now and again) a faulting through its being torn or split, complete the picture. It might be supposed, with this simple picture in mind, that complex mechanical equipment left the mining companies with no greater problem than that of establishing territorial claims as near as possible to the hypothetical line of the outcrop (where the top edges of the 'book's' pages protrude, so to speak) and boring vertically downwards until they found the 'page' they wanted. But in actual fact their problem has always been much greater. For although the desired 'pages' can usually be found with something like precision the gold is not distributed evenly over them. One conglomerate band may be rich, with its gold occurring regularly, both laterally and in depth; the next, in comparison, may be much poorer, with no such concentrations. Moreover, quite apart from the existence of the principal reefs, there are smaller conglomerate bands branching laterally from them; and these in their turn may be either rich or poor in gold. This combination of widely spreading reefs or branch reefs on the one hand, and their uneven richness on the other, thus made it necessary almost from the first to map out the geological structure of the area by multiple borings, and that necessity still continues. But the average cost of sinking a bore-hole is now over £3 per foot: at a rate of £10,000 for a bore-hole of moderate depth some economy has to be shown, and it can only be shown if the experience gained by boring over the whole wide area, first in the Transvaal and now in the Orange Free State as well, is pooled in an attempt to reconstruct the factors causing the original deposition of the conglomerate reefs. In short, if the mining specialist can form the right theory to explain the deposits made 2000 million years ago he may in turn be able to predict geological variations in a given stratum of gold-bearing ore: from a correct premise, in fact, he will have been able to construct a reasonably accurate underground map of areas not yet explored.

The theories, however, vary. One thing only is certain. The reefs, which are normally from 3 to 4 feet thick but may be only inches thick in places, are the primary result of action by water, as is shown quite clearly by the well-rounded shape of the pebbles and small stones which are compacted in the grey stone matrix—itself the consequence of enormous pressure upon the finely pounded fragments of such pebbles. Two great questions now arise. Was the water that of sea or of river? And what was the original source of the gold that was to be so inexorably 'milled' by the power of water on pebbles that the eye cannot detect the particles?

On the first of these questions there is fundamental disagreement. One school of thought postulates a marine origin for the reefs. The process which it invites us, in imagination, to watch is one that preceded the development of any living creature, for there are no fossil remains whatever in the reefs. We are to picture, in the remotest of prehistory, a sea which beat upon a shore-line that stretched along the Witwatersrand. It was possibly a shore upon which the sea encroached steadily and massively, thus eroding and pounding deposits of gold which lay embedded in the path of its advance. More probably the sea received its gold by means of a great river which swept it down, already coarsely ground, to a point where the action of waves and pebbles, continuing savage and unabated over a measureless period, finally ground it to microscopically small particles. In either case the action of waves and currents—and perhaps also of tides, if tides existed—distributed the particles variously. In some places there was a heavy precipitation into a sea-bed compounded of grey sand and pebbles: in others, where the water flowed more swiftly and violently, there was less. There were, too, creeks and inlets along the shore-line, responsible for the forming of offshoots from the main mass of the beaten, pebbly, coastal deposit.

Supporters of the marine theory point, among other things, to the shape of the pebbles in the conglomerate ore—often with one flattish and one more rounded surface, suggesting the movement of what is spun round on its base by the ceaseless wash and swell of water rather than

66 Modern Johannesburg from behind its partial ring of sand dumps

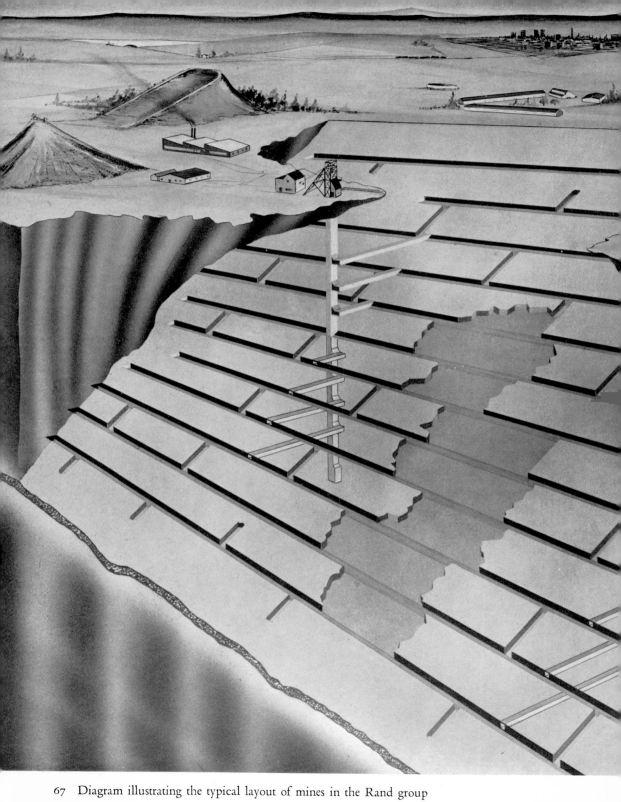

67 Diagram illustrating the typical layout of mines in the Rand group

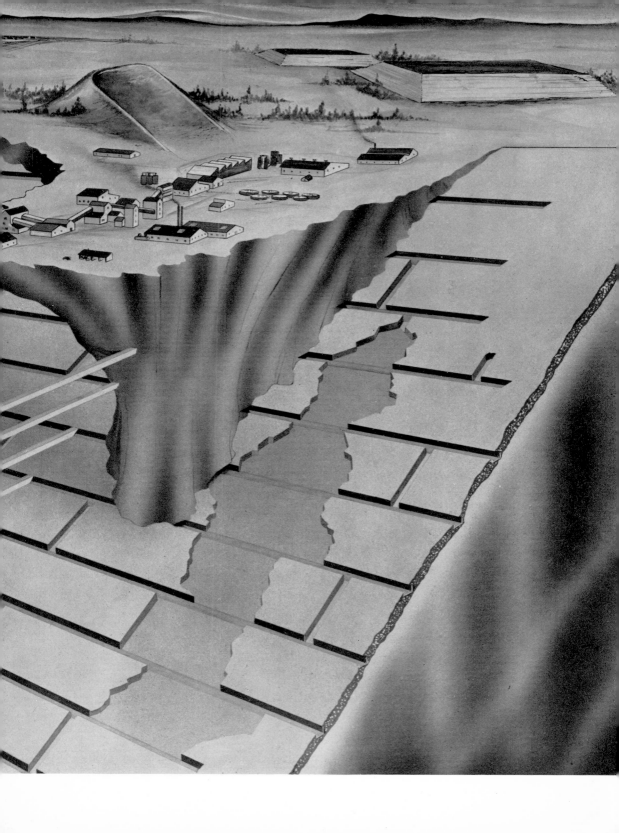

68   Five-pound piece of Queen Elizabeth II struck at the Royal Mint in 1953

69   Cigarette box of gold with platinum and diamonds by Jean Schlumberger of Tiffany: 1957

what is for ever rolled down in a river's flood. Nevertheless their views are rejected by the second school of thought, which asks us instead to conceive of a great river, springing perhaps even from a great glacier, in which rocky sediment was perpetually rolled down, crushing and grinding particles of gold scoured from some rich deposit through which it passed, and fanning out finally into a delta where pebbles and gold alike were deposited.

Each of these two theories is partially rejected by some of those who seek to answer the second of the two questions, namely, the original source of the gold. For the 'sea' theory and the 'river' theory both accept it as an axiom that the gold got into the conglomerate by water sedimentation after being crushed to great fineness by the tumbling and rolling of stones and pebbles in that water. After the sedimentary beds of mud, sand, pebble and stone were formed, impregnated with these minute particles of gold, they were themselves covered by fresh evolutionary changes in the earth's crust: under great heat and pressure changes took place in their structure, resulting in the presence of certain secondary minerals normally associated with high temperature. It is precisely the suggestion of these high-temperature factors in the conglomerate beds that has led some geologists to another view, which for the layman is only more difficult to believe in that it involves the conception of an earth crust so plasticized by heat that minerals could, so to speak, be fed from one layer upwards to another and permeate what lay above. For this, in simple terms, is the alternative picture that is presented by those who say that the sedimentary beds of conglomerate were gold-free when they were formed, and that the tiny particles were extruded by heat and pressure from the strata that lay below and absorbed by the still softer and more permeable beds of sediment above.

It is clear that, with fundamental disagreement obtaining on the primary causes of the geological formations, an accurate theoretical map of areas still untested cannot yet be drawn. Instead, decades of sample boring, together with all the experience gained by the actual following of the reefs into the ground, have combined to give something like a predictable pattern, though the differences in the geology of the Orange Free State mines have brought new problems of their own. In any case the opening of most mines will now involve operations at considerable depth. The days are long past when the conglomerate reefs could be attacked and extracted at surface or near-surface levels. A mine today will be a honeycomb grid of tunnelling probably not less than 3000 feet down, and so neatly planned and executed that in the superficial area covered by the combined surface claims of the mine the underlying reef is approachable from the very maximum number of positions.

From the surface of the ground no casual observer could possibly imagine either the depth or the complexity of this underground planning. It is true that the colossal extent of the 'slimes dams' and sand dumps around the older mines is eloquent testimony of the quantity of material extracted, ground and washed in past years: Johannesburg itself, a clearly rectangular modern city full of buildings that reach ever higher, is partly fringed by dumps of fantastic size and—in very many lights—curious beauty. But the upcast from quite young mines will appear small; and whether the eye travels along the high, bare and rolling ridges of open country at a distance from Johannesburg or views the flat and empty terrain of the new Free State mines, there is little, apart from the inevitable buildings that house the milling machinery, to suggest the scope of the work underground, or the almost formal perfection with which it is designed.

In order to reach the deep reefs vertical shafts are sunk. These are of large diameter, for they serve as the mine's 'high street', carrying not only the hundreds of men who pass in and out of the mine each day but also the great mass of ore which is extracted from below. The main vertical shaft of a mine intersects the sloping reef of ore at an angle which may make it necessary to prolong the shaft below the level at which the intersection occurs, for by throwing out horizontal cross-cuts from the main shaft, both above and below the point of intersection, it is thus possible to approach the reef simultaneously from a large number of positions. When these cross-cuts themselves intersect the reef the moment has come to open up the reef itself. Long horizontal 'drives', at right angles to the cross-cuts, are made by the removal of the actual ore; and these in their turn, since they are cut along an inclined plane, are themselves connected up by a grid-like pattern of shorter and subsidiary cuttings called raises and winzes according as their direction slopes upward or downward. The effect of this elaborate system of geometrical intersections is that the progressive removal of sections of the reef furnishes a means whereby tunnelling can be brought to bear on virtually the whole of the area of the reef covered by a mine's surface claims. Extraction of the ore from the reef is swift, for the reef itself is thin, and the strongest wooden props in a 'stoped out' area where removal has been completed will begin to compress and bend and disintegrate in a very short time under the relentless pressure from above.

Plate 66

Plate 67

Ability to reach the sloping face of the reef at various points, often widely separated, means that the modern mine in South Africa can decide on the areas which are most likely to give a good return on working. Initial costs of establishing a new mine today may be as much as £15,000,000 or more, of which a single shaft (and one is not enough) can account for £1,000,000. The recovery of this capital outlay in a reasonable period, together with the need to meet the subsequent cost of operating and still show a profit on the working, must naturally involve a keen distinction between sections of ore which are relatively rich and sections in which the gold will scarcely pay for itself. Effort will be concentrated on the former: the poorer sections will be left, perhaps to await a time when some general increase in the price of gold makes it worth while to extract them. Some of the richest sections of the conglomerate reef were those which were worked in the early days of Witwatersrand enterprise: more recently the new mines in the Orange Free State have come into contact with sections of outstanding wealth. Viewed as a whole over the last decade or so, the average yield of gold from this seemingly inexhaustible bed of South African ore has been running at a rate of about 5 pennyweights of gold for every ton of ore extracted. In other words, about 70 tons of ore have to be extracted, raised, crushed and refined in order to produce 1 lb. of gold. Below half that figure gold extraction would be uneconomic. The picture is very different from that of gold-mining in earlier periods when a twist of the pan would show a man what he had washed from river alluvium—large and visible particles of usually very pure gold. But at any rate there is no end to the gold of South Africa, which appears likely to satisfy a high proportion of the world's needs for a very long time to come. The glittering harvest of California could be quickly gathered and stored; but the conglomerate reefs—thin, pebble-grey, highly unromantic to the eye—stretch endlessly ahead and endlessly downward.

Moreover, it does not only yield gold. Large quantities of silver have for many years emerged as an important by-product—about 10 per cent by weight of the gold—and latterly the presence of uranium has added, in a literal sense, a tail-piece to the preliminary process of the refinement of gold ore at the mines themselves. The ultimate process of centralized refinement is characteristic of the strong pattern of general co-ordination which has emerged in the South African goldfields as a result of the concentration of so many interests upon a range of difficulties and problems which affects them all. There are now some sixty mining companies, active or in development. These are financed and controlled by seven major groups, representatives of which combine, in the Transvaal and Orange Free State Chamber of Mines, to pool technical experience, share in technical research, and develop common policy in matters affecting labour, mines welfare, taxation, the marketing of gold, and the like. The Chamber was founded in 1889, as soon as the future need for co-ordination was clearly seen, and one of its greatest benefits was to lie in the establishment of the great Germiston Refinery, which from 1921 has been at work, on a co-operative basis, dealing with the bullion bars sent in, partly refined, from the individual mines. These all weigh about 1000 troy ounces; but their purity may vary considerably, some having a greater proportion of silver or other alloy, others being relatively fine. They go through a process of extreme chemical complexity, in which the alloy is removed to a point where the Refinery's finished product is a bar of gold about the size of a normal brick. It weighs 400 troy ounces—in other words about 27½ lb.: its fineness is over 99 per cent; and, in its plain rectangular form, with the light playing upon the surface of the gold, soft in texture, glowing and lustrous, this bar—so small in size and so immensely heavy in weight—reveals in a curiously eloquent way everything that has always been felt about a metal that is at once so lovely in colour, so hard to get, and so perfect to work and shape.

Our bar of gold, the final product of the Rand Refinery, has been subject to more processing than any gold-miner could have foreseen before the late nineteenth century. It is the product of anything up to 1500 tons of ore, or even more. This ore has been hoisted to the surface from a depth usually varying between 3000 and 10,000 feet. Water has first washed it, and human hands have sorted the conglomerate from the waste rock. It has been crushed (to break up the pyrite grains which sometimes enclose the gold particles) and then ground into a fine slime in a huge tube-mill—a revolving cylinder filled with rock and water. The slime, now thickened, and with the water removed, has been passed into tanks to which a cyanide solution is added. The action of the cyanide upon the gold is to dissolve it, and the gold can only be attacked in this way if its particles—already of extremely small size in the ore—are further reduced and if the slime is constantly agitated so that each and every one of the particles can be touched by the cyanide solution. At this stage, then, the gold is itself in solution, and the slime which has thus far been its vehicle can be filtered off, to form the great and ever-spreading 'slimes dams' which surround every mine. The gold-bearing solution passes next to a point where zinc dust is added to it, causing the precipitation of the gold in concentrated form; and these gold concentrates are then smelted in the mine's own furnaces to produce the only partially fine 1000-ounce bullion bars.

These bullion bars, on delivery at the Rand Refinery, are melted so that an assay of their individual gold content can be made, in order to credit their parent mine with the correct value of the gold in their bullion. The molten metal is then poured into 400-ounce moulds, having by this time already lost many of its impurities, for fresh assay; and now the bullion is ready for the final process, in which, after it has been again melted, and borax has been added, and chlorine gas has been passed through it, it is poured into the 400-ounce bars in a state of almost total purity. So thorough is the planning of these ultimate stages of refinement that, while it is natural that all crucibles, general furnace-debris and floor-sweepings are in due course consigned to the furnace for recovery of any stray particles of gold, it is somewhat more of a surprise to find the whole system of furnace flues periodically treated for the recovery of gold which has reached them in the form of gas—a treatment which in fact recovers very useful quantities.

From the Rand Refinery the 400-ounce gold bars travel to any country that wishes to buy them. Their destination and their method of travel, and sometimes even their freedom to travel, are matters which engage the attention of the South African Reserve Bank, for gold is a primary source of South African national income and its movement on the markets of the world affect South Africa in a fundamental and intimate way. At present the bulk of South Africa's gold bars, which day in and day out are pulled prosaically along on trolleys after their final processing in the Refinery, is shipped to London for ultimate disposal on the London gold market. It has been bought, first, by the South African Treasury through the Reserve Bank; and the Treasury, in turn, sells it on the London gold market at prices ruling from day to day. The Reserve Bank informs the mining industry weekly of the average net price realized per ounce of gold on the London market, and can of course sell the gold elsewhere than in London if it is profitable to do so. In London the Bank of England acts as a selling agent for the South African Reserve Bank, just as the Federal Reserve Bank of New York acts in the United States.

If a disproportionate amount of space appears to have been given to the description of the gold-mines of South Africa and their modern development it is because South Africa alone can show the promotion of gold-mining to a point at which it becomes a major national industry. In ranging over all other countries in previous times we can find nothing to parallel this. Many an earlier epoch provided instances of the primary importance of gold, either viewed narrowly in relation to the royal budget or regarded as a wider economic factor. But there was no case in which the extraction and marketing of gold furnished a country with one of its primary industries and sources of revenue, and there was no case, either, in which there was such confident expectation that rich supplies of gold would be available for an indefinitely long time in the future. If South Africa can now provide half of the gold that the world asks for it can presumably continue to do so with negligible interruption or uncertainty. Poorer sections of reef are counterbalanced by the finding of newer and richer ones; and the potential supply seems to be, if not unlimited, at least not limited by any serious factors except one. That one factor is the factor of cost. At the end of the Second World War it cost £5 18s. 10d. to produce a troy ounce of gold from the established mines of the Witwatersrand. By 1957 the comparative figure was £9 12s. 6d. A large proportion of the labour employed in the South African mining industry is native labour; and but for this the cost of production would have been very much higher. There must be some theoretical point at which, with the official world price of gold still pegged at the figure of $35 per troy ounce fixed in 1934, the systematic working of only medium or low-grade ores would no longer be a practical possibility. And this in turn would raise, in a serious way, the question reserved for the next chapter, namely, whether the world's existing stocks of gold, enormously swollen though they are by the enterprise of the last century, are sufficient for the part which they are called upon to play.

For the moment, however, it is enough to pause and wonder at the phenomenon of South African productivity. It has taken place in a short period during which industrial development in most parts of the world has reached immense heights. In the same period there have been two of the most costly and (from a material point of view) unremunerative wars ever fought, together with all the social and political upheavals which are their natural consequences. Country after country has been impoverished if not bankrupted, its external investments often ruined or expropriated. It would have been surprising in the extreme if, in a world of tottering and precarious currency values, some attempt had not been made to isolate that thing above all upon which a secure monetary value could be placed.

And there is no doubt what that thing was, for the whole post-war system of international currency is in fact based on gold. As will be seen later, the new role of gold is very different from that which it played while the gold standard existed; but in some ways gold is much more important today as an international stabilizer of currency than it ever was in the days of the gold standard, with its primarily internal connotations. It is, indeed, difficult to imagine what the plight of the world might have been, viewed in the context of interrupted or oscillating production and consequently vulnerable currencies, if its stocks of gold—the firmest of reserves and the most solid of guarantees—had not been raised to the high figure for which South Africa is mainly responsible.

It is, in fact, true to say that although the last century as a whole and the last half-century in particular have seen such a phenomenal increase in the production of gold, raising the world's total accumulated stocks to an immensely high volume, there has at no time been anything but a shortage of it. For by no means all of it has taken the place which conventional thought automatically assigns it, namely, as the nationally held backing for national currencies. Very large quantities of gold have been absorbed in industry and the arts. About one-third of world output was so absorbed between 1835 and 1889: in the forty years after 1889, which included the First World War and saw the value of gold begin to rise very sharply, the proportion used in this way was still one-quarter; and real decline in the amount used by the industrial arts only became apparent after 1930, with further sharp rises in value and then another great war. And apart from these uses, which have supplied all the world with its jewellery and plate and ornament, together with the gold used in technical manufacturing processes, gold has been freely absorbed by the countries of the East, where, in default of any really widespread system of banks, town by town—a convenience which the Western world takes for granted—very considerable amounts have regularly been imported for private hoarding. About one-sixth of world output found its way to Eastern countries for such purposes in the hundred years up to 1929; and so great was the accumulation there that it became profitable to unload it in the years immediately following, when the value of gold was rising. As a result of these factors the proportion of world output in gold, over the last century or so, that has been devoted to currency or quasi-currency purposes is not more than about 75 per cent—and that in a period when production of commodities has vastly increased and world population, simultaneously, has shown a formidable increase. Without the grey conglomerate reefs of South

Africa—the endless, thin bands impregnated with minute particles of gold—both the total output in that century and also the proportions available for the arts, industry, Eastern hoarding and general currency purposes would have been markedly (and perhaps very uncomfortably) different.

Chapter X

THE GOLD MEASURE
IN MODERN CURRENCY

F OR MANY PARTS of the modern world it comes as a surprise
when the Press occasionally reports the minting of gold coins. For
example, it has recently been announced, in 1958, that the Royal Mint in
London has coined a considerable quantity of sovereigns bearing the
effigy and style of Queen Elizabeth II, and any member of the public,
if he is sufficiently interested in possessing specimens, is free to buy them
from numismatic dealers at a current price of about £4 5s. 0d. apiece.
Obviously the fact that a coin with the face value of twenty shillings is
actually worth over four times as much means that, for purposes of
internal currency, it is useless: no one is going to spend eighty-five shillings'
worth of gold on what need only cost him twenty shillings' worth of paper.
These sovereigns, of course, are no more, viewed in bulk, than small,
nationally marked ingots of gold for external trade. They may give rise to
academically interesting allegations of forgery if (as has recently happened)
they are imitated by private enterprise abroad. But, provided that the
imitations are themselves of full weight, standard purity and adequate
workmanship, they can do little except emphasize the historic part which
gold sovereigns have for so long played in world trade—and, by imitating,
they flatter.

Plate 68

Gold coinage, in nearly all parts of the world today, is just a means of
supplying gold for international dealing in quantities smaller than that of
gold bars. Supposing one were able to inspect the great national depositories
of gold, they would be found to be stocked partly with bar gold and partly
with gold coin. Unless estimates of Russian reserves are very faulty, about
seven tenths of the world's gold is now stored in the United States. Fort
Knox, in Kentucky, is of course the most famous of all depositories. It
not only contains a vast quantity of gold but its security system is notorious
for its strength and secrecy—this secrecy including the factor that the
number of guards is never divulged. There are other United States
depositories as well, spread out from New York to San Francisco; and it
is this phenomenon of huge amounts of gold locked away impregnably in
underground vaults in the United States that has so often prompted the
gibe that what has been so laboriously dug up in one part of the world
ends up in an artificially strong hole in another.

As a phenomenon, indeed, it is not very stirring, and it is natural that recent years should have seen more and more people asking if gold is any longer really useful, let alone necessary. In fact the question is quite an old one. Over seventy-five years ago John Ruskin could write that 'none but partially savage nations need, imperatively, gold for their currency'. Ruskin, understandably, was concentrating his thoughts upon the use of gold as an object of beauty in the hands of artists; but he was sufficiently touched by the theories of the time to doubt whether, in an age of established security, a country that had for centuries been based on a silver system, to which bank-notes could be anchored, needed to handle gold. And since his time the doubts have grown much stronger, culminating in the Keynesian doctrines of recent years. Let gold be used for ornament and jewellery. Let it be made into gold bars to be stored away as a national reserve of wealth. But it cannot any longer circulate as an element of a country's internal money system.

The relationship between these categories of use is really much more difficult to define than economic theory today will generally allow. As a metal, gold is still felt to be superbly beautiful; and this quality of beauty, combined with its ease of working, has never ceased to attract either the skill of the goldsmith or the desire of those who wish to see that skill applied. The purpose may be touched by utilitarianism, as when the Albert Memorial in London or a New York skyscraper present a gleaming, gilded roof that is both durable and untarnishable. More often it is purely decorative. 'Gold plate', i.e. silver gilt, has continued to be made in the finest tradition of taste and splendour by modern goldsmiths: the ecclesiastical gold plate made by Walter Stoye for presentation to King George V in 1929 and the many works of Omar Ramsden are successors to a long line that is unlikely ever to stop. Trophies are very often made of pure gold, such as the Wakefield trophy for the highest land speed, and a number of famous gold cups. In jewellery, while the use of gold has shown some decline from the quantity absorbed in the luxuriantly splendid creations of the nineteenth century, when necklaces and bracelets and ear-rings and diadems and brooches could be made *en suite*, glittering with jewels inset in gold, it is nevertheless still an essential. The amount of gold immobilized in finger-rings is immense; and if a man wishes to acquire a highly wrought Plate 69 gold jewel of the utmost skill and beauty for personal possession he can still do so, for there are luxury articles available to him, even today, in which the tradition of the magnificent colour and lustre of gold, set off by great elaboration of workmanship, is fully preserved.

As long as this property of beauty is felt to reside in gold there must, surely, be some feeling for it over and above that which is aroused by the mere quality of scarceness. When, therefore, the output of the world's gold-mines is formed into gold bars, their plain and practical shape cannot conceal the intrinsic beauty of the metal. Indeed, the sight of a pile of such bars, symmetrically arranged for effect with the light glancing off their bevelled edges, is scarcely less arresting than the appearance of a much smaller and more elaborate piece of jewellery or plate. It was very far from being unnatural that when gold was used as a material for coinage it should command admiration and respect, for everyone knew that this metal, so heavy and so bright, was also so scarce that its value at all times tended to rise. And thus, although modern doctrine holds that gold must be relegated, financially, to the status of reserve treasure, banished from circulation in the form of coinage and heavily guarded in vaults, it still remains true that countless thousands of people collect it, by one means or another, for purely private hoarding. Private hoards may consist of gold coin, assorted objects of gold, or even of gold bars. In Switzerland, for example, the private citizen or even the visitor can buy or sell gold in any form, and besides gold coin he can if he wishes buy a gold bar from a shop window. The total quantity of gold in private possession all over the world is immense. Recent estimates put it at over 11,000 tons, worth some £4,430,000,000; and of this quantity France is credited with an amount which, though precision is naturally impossible, may well be just over a quarter of the total, held by nearly all classes of the population.

The continuing scarceness of gold, and the continuing desire in very many parts of the world to possess it, are elements in a picture which modern economic doctrine has tried to remove from public attention; and it is a fact today that for millions of people gold is something which, though it once circulated in currency, is now no more than a luxury material for such things as jewellery. Thus defined, gold has returned to the status which it possessed in the ancient cultures of pre-coinage epochs, with the exception that, under government control, it now performs a vital function for the citizens of nearly every country in the balancing of their international trade. There are, of course, the strongest possible reasons why gold can no longer serve as a metal for internal currency. The essence of the gold standard, as it existed in Great Britain from 1717 to 1914 and was slowly adopted elsewhere, was that the external value of a national currency was rigidly tied to a fixed quantity of gold that also dictated the same value for that currency when used internally. In Britain, for example, a troy ounce of gold was valued at £4·24773, which meant in effect that this ounce of gold was itself money to the value of £4·24773, since it was convertible into 4·24773 units of £1 in the form of gold (or, if required, of paper that could be exchanged for gold). When the gold standard of one country worked in combination with that of another the result was stability in currency exchange, for if *A* divided an ounce of gold into 10 units, and *B* into 20, the currencies of *A* and *B* were obviously stable in the ratio of 1 : 2, and by this means exchange fluctuation, if not impossible, was at least limited. In consequence capital could be committed to international transactions, long-term as well as short-term, in the confidence that speculation in currency exchange would not occur; and trade and industry were able to plan ahead.

This system could continue as long as supplies of gold kept pace with the increasing world demand for it (and it has been seen how nineteenth-century supplies did in fact grow) and also as long as a country's internal and external prices remained in a fairly stable relationship. In Great Britain, as elsewhere, the gold standard was killed by the First World War, which started a long and acute process of inflation in which too much money was, in the familiar phrase, chasing too few goods in the home market. At any other time the gold standard might have supplied its own automatic corrective: inflation at home would have meant that gold, in itself, was a more profitable export than any goods, and a partial drain of gold abroad would thus normally have resulted in a contracted volume of money at home, making it necessary to reduce imports until a balance had again been reached by an intensification of cheaper exports. But in a deadly war events cannot be waited on, and, although Britain could at first recover a quantity of gold invested abroad, by 1915–16 she was spending it profusely in the purchase from the United States of the armaments which could bring no more tangible a dividend than victory. Her gold coinage ceased, never to return since: she was off the gold standard; and gold, instead of being money (jointly internal and external) as before, was now a commodity to be bought and sold externally only, at a price fixed by factors beyond her own control.

Collapse of the gold standard was followed by the era of credit currency. We accept a bank-note for the payment of £1, but in accepting it we receive in fact only the bank's promise to pay £1. We accept a cheque, similarly; but a cheque again is no more than its drawer's promise that his bank will pay us another bank's promises. The growth of 'money' in this sense—and of course it is not money at all, in any true sense, but an extension of credit—is one of the most remarkable features of economic life since 1914. Paper currencies, in themselves, need not be bad or unreliable. In the period of the gold standard notes were common; but these were covered to a very substantial extent by the existence in reserve of gold coin, which could be insisted on in preference to paper, and, even though the gold coin in reserve would not have been enough for everyone if they had all simultaneously demanded gold, there was enough on call to meet any average demand. But when paper currencies multiply far beyond any guaranteed backing the point of danger has been reached. The promises to pay pile up, and though there is almost always one more person, at the end of the line, ready to trust in them the circumstances can any time arise (as they arose in Germany in the nineteen-twenties) in which all confidence collapses. For this reason most paper currencies have been based, since the end of the gold standard, on reserves of gold held centrally and never issued as coin.

It is at this point that the view of gold as an unnecessary economic complication tends to rebound upon those who propound it. Paper currency is credit currency. Where does the credit lie? Not in the paper and the ink, but in the ability of the issuing country to give some tangible return for the paper when it is traded back, for it is, after all, a promise to pay. Redemption may take the form of goods or services, but if the country in question is politically unstable, or strategically vulnerable, or industrially slow and unenterprising, it may not be able to honour its paper with the goods or services required. At the present moment there are two factors which give a paper currency real validity. One—affecting both internal and external trade—is general confidence in the economy of the issuing country: we are content to trust pound and dollar alike (paper though they are) just so long as the evidence of our eyes and ears persuades us that the countries which issue them are on an even keel. The second applies principally, or at least primarily, to external dealings: the acceptance of a promise to pay from a country with an adequate reserve of gold is much to be preferred to one from a country where the reserves are weak.

Ultimately, therefore, countries behave like individual people, and wish to be sure that, with credit transactions always mounting, there is a liquid store of value in the background which can if necessary be tapped. For, just as the basis of many a private transaction is the unspoken question felt by one party about another, 'Has he got the money?', so in international dealings the question must be 'Has the other country got the value of what it promises to pay?' Until now there has been no suggestion that there is any mutually acceptable medium of value, on which an emergency call could be made, other than gold. However thriving a country's economy may be, however rich its natural resources, however secure or brilliant its general prospects, confidence in its ability to pay is fundamentally proportionate to the quantity of its treasure in gold. Gold, in fact, continues to be a commodity of a very curious kind. It can lie governmentally hoarded and idle, and at the same time perform a function which nothing else has yet been found to perform—that of creating confidence. Whether it is in the form of bars or coin it is, in the last resort, the only real, hard money: it is a medium of value difficult to get (and thus precious), easily divisible (and thus much more convenient than precious stones), and still in active production.

Whether production is adequate for the needs is another question. Just before the last war the world's stock of 'monetary' gold, i.e. gold held in national reserve, was equivalent in value to nearly half of the note issues in circulation. In other words those note issues, viewed as a whole, enjoyed what was nearly a 50 per cent backing in gold. Ten years later, in consequence of another great war, economic dislocation and general inflation, the world's monetary gold (although its absolute volume had since increased by a third) provided backing of only 20 per cent; and figures which were true of the world as a whole were also true, individually, of the United States as well, where vast holdings of gold had not kept pace with growth of credit currency. A long period of stability in the world might, it is true, reduce the immediate dangers of this shrunken coverage; but this is a cure which it would take something more than optimism to render plausible. There has been colossal expenditure on armaments, which, by producing no trade returns, consume value in a most literal sense. The population of the world is rising, and its productivity is increasing: there are more people to be paid for making more things to be sold. Obviously there will be, in consequence, more credit currency. But in the meantime the gold reserves lag behind, and although the output of the world's gold-mines is now steadying after a momentary post-war decline it seems unlikely that it will grow appreciably higher: certainly it cannot make up the deficit in values that has opened up between the gold reserves and the paper.

Failing the certainty, therefore, of fifty or a hundred years unstained by a new and not less bloody war, and given the certainty that credit currency will tend to increase, what can be done to close the widening gap between the gold reserves that still appear to command the confidence of all and the paper currencies that do not? Doctrinaire theory might argue that this widening gap is something that must be accepted and that, if the world persists in fighting ruinously costly wars, the essential non-productivity of war effort must inevitably be reflected in post-war inflation, with too few normal goods sought by too much currency, resulting in rising prices and the production of yet more currency. But gold itself falls within the category of normal goods. It is, as has been seen, a national product and a national export of the country which yearly produces a half of what the world yields: it is bought and sold like any other commodity. But, unlike most other commodities, the price at which it can be bought and sold is very strictly controlled by factors over which neither its producers nor its country of origin can claim control. A committee of half a dozen bullion brokers and bankers may meet in London every day to decide, in the light of supply and demand, what should be the price of gold in terms of pounds sterling. Yet as long as the world's principal consumer of gold—the United States—will pay no more for gold than $35 per troy ounce it is unlikely that the prices elsewhere will show more than marginal deviation.

The dollar price for gold was fixed in 1934 and has remained unchanged ever since. By contrast, the price of gold in terms of pounds sterling has shown a steady rise. In August 1939 it was £7 8s. 0d. per troy ounce; a month later it was £8 8s. 0d.; and by the end of the war it had become temporarily controlled at just over £8 12s. 0d. Then, in 1946, as a result of the Bretton Woods agreement a new system was established by which each country declared to the International Monetary Fund the number of its currency units which could be obtained for an ounce of gold, thus implying a degree of exchange stability between one currency and another. For the United States the figure was still $35; for the sterling area it was just over £8 13s. 8d. Room was left by the agreement for the future revision of figures, and revision came for the sterling area in 1949, when the pound was devalued and its relationship to an ounce of gold defined in the new figure of £12 10s. 0d. This was tantamount to a raising of the price of gold by the sterling area unaccompanied by any rise in its price in the dollar area.

As a not unnatural consequence the question has since come to be increasingly discussed whether a universal (as opposed to a unilateral) rise in the price of gold should not be effected by its revaluation in terms of dollars. In the last half-dozen years the value and volume of world trade has grown enormously. But the growth of the world's monetary gold reserve has fallen far behind, and it is clear that the annual yield of new gold is not given a valuation that enables it to express, even approximately, the value of the swelling volume of goods produced. Seeing that this is so, and that in the United States itself—the world's largest treasurer of gold— the gold reserves have fallen well below the previous level at which they guaranteed paper money, some economists now ask if a rise in the universal price of gold would not do two things simultaneously, namely, auto-matically increase the absolute reserves of all countries and decrease, relatively, the gap between their individual reserves and their volume of paper currency. Revaluation of gold would, of course, have a further important result in that it would enable the extraction of a good deal of additional gold to be undertaken from comparatively low-grade and currently uneconomic ore, thus stimulating the supply of what is still, apparently, in world-wide demand. If the production of gold could, in itself, be promoted to a level as much higher than the present level as the present level is higher than that of fifty years ago the world's gold deficit would be substantially remedied. But the extraction of gold, since it ceased to be controlled by rigid royal monopoly, became an affair of industry and commerce; and those who produce it, as a commodity for world consumption, cannot be expected to do so without their margin of profit, and certainly not at a loss.

It is possible that there might now be a greater general readiness to give gold a higher international value if the output of Russian gold and the policy behind its marketing were better known. As it is, Russian output is simply a matter of estimate; and the same is true of the figure of Russian gold reserves. Output is reckoned, provisionally, at about a sixth of what South Africa produces—less, that is to say, than the current yield of Canada and about the same as that of the United States. Reserves are impossible to judge, though the quantity of gold recently transferred from Russia to the West may suggest that they are considerable—as well they may be when the previous wealth of ore in the Ural and Altai regions is considered. Political divisions being what they are, it might be natural if reluctance met any proposal of which the effect would be to put a much higher value on hidden Russian reserves.

In the last resort, however, the only valuation that will, anywhere, be put upon gold is that which it will command as a precious commodity in supply and demand. For the fact is that it does still remain very precious. There is, of course, no reason why it should not have become so common as to lose its precious quality: at times between 1850 and 1900 many men must have wondered if this would indeed be the practical result of so many new and abundant discoveries. What they did not and were probably not entitled to foresee was that the gold from the new discoveries would act as a great stimulant in world production; and they could certainly not foresee that in an age rent and temporarily dislocated by global wars gold would come to be regarded as one of the only measures of real and lasting value. This, paradoxically, is a truth which the citizens of most countries do not easily realize. Gold, in the form of coinage—a personal means of measuring and exchanging value in their internal dealings—has long since been taken from them. But it has only been taken from them because its value has risen to a point at which it is vitally important, internationally, in external dealings, and because it is only by external dealings that the nations of the modern world can keep their standards of living, and so their internal currencies, on a reasonably steady level.

Bernard Shaw was not a sentimentalist, and his reflections on these questions were characteristically brusque and penetrating.

> The most important thing about money is to maintain its stability, so that a pound will buy as much a year hence or ten years hence or fifty years hence as today, and no more. With paper money this stability has to be maintained by the Government. With a gold currency it tends to maintain itself even when the natural supply of gold is increased by discoveries of new deposits, because of the curious fact that the demand for gold in the world is practically infinite. You have to choose (as a voter) between trusting to the natural stability of gold and the natural stability of the honesty and intelligence of the members of the Government. And, with due respect to these gentlemen, I advise you, as long as the Capitalist system lasts, to vote for gold.

Shaw's 'gold currency' is no longer a coinage of gold for a country's internal use. But it is in a very real sense the reserve of gold which each country, if it can, attempts to accumulate as a solid guarantee of its paper currency. As currency, gold still performs—though at a carefully controlled international level—the same function which it performed when Croesus originated the first true coinage of gold in Lydia twenty-five centuries ago. It does so because it is still the ultimately precious substance, the value of which (though it may occasionally fall very slightly and temporarily) normally always tends to rise. Gold as a measure of value has not been abandoned for any other rare and precious substance such as jewels. Loftily conceived substitutes like the 'man-hour' currency notes bred out of nineteenth-century political economy have made no impact upon it. It may be argued that, after twenty-five centuries of monetary usage, people should have developed enough confidence in each other and in human institutions as a whole to accept mere tokens as measures of exchange value. Country by country they have gone a long way towards this internally; but sheer common sense will quickly persuade them that, apart from their own willingness to work and produce, gold—and gold alone—must be in the background.

Thus, over the last 6000 years, gold has moved through human experience in a remarkably consistent pattern. It has nearly always been available to nearly everyone, but has always been notably rare in relation to demand. It has in every age been admired for its natural beauty—a feature which, in an odd manner, has qualified it as much for the coinage rubbed by greasy and avaricious hands as for the superb decoration and jewellery which goldsmiths have made out of it. Its refusal to disintegrate, to rust or to tarnish has resulted in its being regarded as something—and there are not many such things—that can be counted on to look the same and feel the same a century or five centuries ahead. This quality of near-eternity has naturally given it a reputation apart. Symbolically it has at all times stood for eternity—the light of the sun or the light of religious faith. Because it is both rare and beautiful it has been the metal peculiar to the glory of kings, whose patronage has evoked the highest skill of goldsmiths in the decoration of church, palace, or person. And, finally, a substance that is unchanging, rare, unmistakably true and so easily processed has provided the common man in every epoch—the present included—with the only measure of value which his fellows nearly everywhere would readily trust.

TABLE OF RELATIONSHIP BETWEEN
AVOIRDUPOIS AND TROY WEIGHT-SYSTEMS

Avoirdupois	*Troy*
1 lb.＝16 oz.＝7000 grains troy	1 lb.*＝12 oz.＝240 pennyweights＝5760 grains
1 oz.＝437.5 grains troy	1 oz.＝20 pennyweights＝480 grains
	1 pennyweight＝24 grains

* The Troy pound is now little more than a vestigial relic in English metrology. The Royal Commission of 1838 reported in 1841 that it was 'comparatively useless even in the few trades and professions in which troy weight is commonly used and to the great mass of the British population it is wholly unknown'. As a result the avoir-dupois pound of 7000 grains was legalized as the standard weight of reference by the Act of 1878.

SELECT BIBLIOGRAPHY

Different people will be interested in different aspects of the study of gold. In order to cater thoroughly for all interests it would be necessary, in compiling even a select list of books, to record many hundreds of titles. The list which follows attempts no such catholicity. It includes, however, many books and articles which, often with extensive bibliographies of their own, seem likely to provide a useful point of departure if wider study is desired in any part of the general field. If its weight is tilted strongly in favour of the period before 1850, this is in part because the profusion of modern books on the gold-rushes and the gold standard makes select listing very difficult and possibly unprofitable.

Adelson, H. L.	*Light Weight Solidi and Byzantine Trade during the Sixth and Seventh Centuries* (New York, 1957)
Agricola, G.	*De re metallica* (Basel, 1556)
Ashbee, C. R.	*The Treatises of Benvenuto Cellini on Goldsmithing and Sculpture* (London, 1898)

Bailey, K. C.   *The Elder Pliny's Chapters on Chemical Subjects* (London 1929–32).

Bloch, M.   'Le problème de l'or au moyen âge', *Annales* 1933.

Braudel, F.   'Monnaies et civilisations: de l'or du Soudan à l'argent d'Amerique', *Annales* 1946.

Breasted, J. H.   *A History of Egypt* (New York, 1905). *Ancient Records of Egypt* (Chicago, 1906–7).

Brooke, G. C.   *English Coins* (London, 1950).

Bruce-Mitford, R. L. S.   'The Sutton Hoo Ship-burial', *Proceed. Suffolk Inst. of Archaeology* 1949.

Burns, A. R.   *Money and Monetary Policy in Early Times* (London, 1927).

Burton, R. F.   *The Gold Mines of Midian* (London, 1878).

Busschau, W. J.   *The Measure of Gold* (Cape Town, 1949).

California Historical Soc.   *The Plate of Brass* (San Francisco, 1953).

Cambridge Ancient History

Cambridge Economic History

Carter, Howard   *The Tomb of Tut·ankh·Amen* (London, 1923–33).

Cary, M. and
   Warmington, E. H.   *The Ancient Explorers* (London, 1929).

Cellini, Benvenuto   *Vita*, trans. J. A. Symonds, ed. J. Pope-Hennessy (London, 1949).

Chaffers, W.   *Gilda Aurifabrorum* (London, 1899).

Charlesworth, M. P.   *Trade Routes and Commerce of the Roman Empire* (Cambridge, 1924).

Churchill, S. J. A. and
   Bunt, C. G. E.   *The Goldsmiths of Italy* (London, 1926).

Cipolla, C. M.   *Money, Prices and Civilization in the Mediterranean World, Fifth to Seventeenth Century* (Princeton, 1956).

Cochet, Abbé   *Le Tombeau de Childeric Ier* (Paris, 1859).

Dalton, O. M.   *The Treasure of the Oxus* (London, 1905).

Davies, O.   *Roman Mines in Europe* (Oxford, 1935).

Dye, J. S.   'American and Other Gold', in *Coin Encyclopaedia* (Philadelphia, 1883).

Evans, A. J.   *The Palace of Minos at Knossos* (London 1921–36).

Evans, Joan   *Magical Jewels of the Middle Ages and the Renaissance* (Oxford, 1922). *A History of Jewellery, 1100–1870* (London, 1953).

Engel, A., and Serrure, R.   *Traité de numismatique du moyen âge* (Paris, 1891–1905).

Feavearyear, A. E.   *The Pound Sterling* (London, 1932).

Frank, T., and others   *Economic Survey of Ancient Rome* (Baltimore, 1933–40).

Frazer, J. G.   *The Golden Bough* (London, 1925–30).

Fox, P.   *Tutankhamun's Treasure* (London, 1951).

Fugger News-Letters

Gadd, C. J.   *The History and Monuments of Ur* (London, 1929).

Grierson, P.   'The Debasement of the Bezant in the Eleventh Century', *Byzantinische Zeitschrift* 1954. 'The Myth of the Mancus', *Revue belge de phil. et d'hist.* 1954.

Hall, H. R.   *The Ancient History of the Near East* (London, 1950).

Holmyard, E. J.   *Alchemy* (Harmondsworth, 1957).

Homan, B.   'La circolazione delle monete d'oro in Ungheria dal X al XIV secolo', *Rivista italiana di numismatica* 1922.

Hudson, D. R.   'The Coinage Metals in Antiquity', *Metallurgia* 1944–5.

Humboldt, A. de   *Essai politique sur la Nouvelle Espagne* (Paris, 1811). *Asie Centrale* I (Paris, 1843).

Jacobsson, D.   *Fifty Golden Years of the Rand, 1886–1936* (London, 1936).

Jessup, R.   *Anglo-Saxon Jewellery* (London, 1950).

Jones, W. R.   *Minerals in Industry* (Harmondsworth, 1955).

Kirk, J. R.   *The Alfred and Minster Lovel Jewels* (Oxford, 1948).

Lombard, M.   'L'or musulman du VIIe au XIe siècle', *Annales* 1947. 'L'évolution urbaine pendant le haut moyen âge', *Annales* 1957.

Lopez, R. S.   'Il ritorno all' oro nell' Occidente', *Rivista storica italiana* 1953.

Maryon, H.   *Metalwork and Enamelling* (London, 1954). 'Metal Working in the Ancient World', *Amer. Journ. of Archaeology* 1949.

Mason, J. A.   *Ancient Civilizations of Peru* (Harmondsworth, 1957).

Mattingly, H.   *Roman Coins* (London, 1927).

Mickwitz, G.   'The Problem of Gold in the Ancient World', *Annales* 1934.

Minns, E. H.   *Scythians and Greeks* (Cambridge, 1913).

Pallottino, M.   *Etruskischer Kunst* (Zürich, 1955).

Partington, J. R.   *Origins and Development of Applied Chemistry* (London, 1935).

Pendlebury, J. D. S.   *The Archaeology of Crete* (London, 1939).

Percy, J.   *Metallurgy—Gold and Silver* (London, 1880).

Petrie, W. M. Flinders   *The Royal Tombs of the Earliest Dynasties* (London, 1901).

Pirenne, H.   *Mohammed and Charlemagne*, trans. B. Miall (London, 1940).

Pollen, J. H.   *Ancient and Modern Gold and Silversmiths' Work in the South Kensington Museum* (London, 1878).

Prescott, W. H.   *History of the Conquest of Mexico* (London, 1843).

Prescott, W. H. — *History of the Conquest of Peru* (London, 1907).

Prou, M. — *Les monnaies mérovingiennes* (Paris, 1892).

Quiring, H. — *Geschichte des Goldes: die goldenen Zeitalter in ihrer kulturellen und wirtschaftlichen Bedeutung* (Stuttgart, 1948).

Rickard, T. A. — *Man and Metals* (New York, 1932). *History of American Mining* (New York, 1932).

Ridgeway, W. — *The Origin of Metallic Currency and Weight Standards* (Cambridge, 1892).

Riis, P. J. — *An Introduction to Etruscan Art* (Copenhagen, 1953).

Robinson, E. S. G. — 'The Coins from the Ephesian Artemision reconsidered', *Journ. Hellenic Studies* 1951.

Röhrig, F. — *Der Verduner Altar* (Vienna, 1955).

Rostovtzeff, M. I. — *Iranians and Greeks in South Russia* (Oxford, 1922). *Social and Economic History of the Hellenistic World* (Oxford, 1941). *Social and Economic History of the Roman Empire* (Oxford, 1957).

Royal Institute of International Affairs — *The International Gold Problem* (London, 1932).

Schulten, A., and others — *Fontes Hispaniae Antiquae* (Barcelona and Berlin, 1922–47).

Schulten, A. — *Tartessos* (Hamburg, 1922).

Seltman, C. — *Greek Coins* (London, 1955).

Sidgwick, W. B. — 'The Gold Supply in Ancient Times', *Greece and Rome* 1936.

Singer, C., and others — *A History of Technology* (Oxford, 1954–8).

Smith, H. C. — *Jewellery* (London, 1908).

Soetbeer, A. — *Edelmetallproduktion und Wertverhältnis zwischen Gold und Silber seit der Entdeckung Amerikas bis zur Gegenwart* (Gotha, 1879).

Spooner, F. C. — *L'économie mondiale et les frappes monétaires en France, 1493–1680* (Paris, 1956).

Sutherland, C. H. V. — *Anglo-Saxon Gold Coinage in the Light of the Crondall Hoard* (London, 1948). *Art in Coinage* (London, 1955).

Thomson, D. — 'The Refining of Gold', *Journ. Chemical, Metallurgical and Mining Soc. of South Africa* 1948.

Thomson, J. O. — *History of Ancient Geography* (Cambridge, 1948).

Times, The — *Gold* (a reprint of the special number, 20 June 1933).

Toynbee, J. M. C. — *Roman Medallions* (New York, 1944).

Transvaal and Orange Free State Chamber of Mines — *Mining Survey*.

Vacano, von, O. W. — *Die Etrusker* (Stuttgart, 1955).

Vaillant, G. C. — *The Aztecs of Mexico* (Harmondsworth, 1956).

Werner, A.   *Augsburger Goldschmiede* (Augsburg, 1913).
West, L. C.   *Gold and Silver Coin Standards in the Roman Empire* (New York, 1941).
Wheeler, R. E. M.   *Rome beyond the Imperial Frontiers* (London, 1954).
Woolley, C. L.   *Ur Excavations.* II, *The Royal Cemetery* (London, 1934). *The Development of Sumerian Art* (London, 1935). *Excavations at Ur* (London, 1954).

Ancient sources used include:

Diodorus, Herodotus, Livy, Pliny the Elder, Strabo, Tacitus, Thucydides

LOCATIONS AND PHOTOGRAPHIC SOURCES

Courtesy of the Transvaal and O.F.S. Chamber of Mines, Pl. 1, 2, 66, 67; Courtesy of the Trustees of the British Museum, Pl. 3, 12, 15, 16, 17, 24, 25, 36, 37, 46, 47, 49, 53, 54, 62, 63; Cairo Museum, Pl. 4, 6, 7, 8, 14; Courtesy of the U.S. Information Service, Pl. 5; Cairo Museum (Courtesy of the Griffith Institute, Ashmolean Museum, Oxford), Pl. 9, 10, 11; Courtesy of the University Museum, Philadelphia, Pl. 13; National Museum, Athens, Pl. 18, 19, 20, 21; Courtesy of the Victoria and Albert Museum (Crown Copyright), Pl. 22, 27, 50, 64; Courtesy of the Ashmolean Museum, Oxford, Pl. 23, 31, 34, 38, 42, 43, 61, 68; Courtesy of the Glyptothek und Museum antiker Kleinkunst, Munich, Pl. 26; Courtesy of the Louvre and Archives Photographiques, Paris, Pl. 28; Courtesy of the Hermitage Museum, Leningrad, Pl. 29, 30, 32, 33; Courtesy of the Bundessamlung von Medaillen, Münzen und Geldzeichen, Vienna, Pl. 35; Museo Civico, Brescia, Pl. 39 (Frontispiece); Hofburg Vienna, Pl. 44; Courtesy of the Treasury, Aachen Cathedral, Pl. 45; Courtesy of New College, Oxford, Pl. 48; Courtesy of the Museo de América, Madrid, Pl. 51, 52; Museo dell'Opera del Duomo, Siena, Pl. 55; Kunsthistorisches Museum, Vienna, Pl. 56; Courtesy of the Trustees of the National Gallery, London, Pl. 57; Museo degli Argenti, Florence, Pl. 58; Courtesy of the National Gallery of Art, Washington, D.C. (Robert Woods Bliss Collection Loan), Pl. 59, 60; Courtesy of the Royal Canadian Mounted Police, Pl. 65; Courtesy of Tiffany and Co., New York, Pl. 69.

INDEX

192